**EMERGING
TRENDS IN SALES
THOUGHT
AND PRACTICE**

# EMERGING TRENDS IN SALES THOUGHT AND PRACTICE

edited by
Gerald J. Bauer, Mark S. Baunchalk,
Thomas N. Ingram, and Raymond W. LaForge

QUORUM BOOKS
Westport, Connecticut • London

**Library of Congress Cataloging-in-Publication Data**

Emerging trends in sales thought and practice / Gerald J. Bauer, [et al. . . . editors].
      p.  cm.
  Includes bibliographical references and index.
  ISBN 1–56720–036–2 (alk. paper)
  1. Selling.  I. Bauer, Gerald J.
HF5438.E568    1998
658.85—DC21       97–48619

British Library Cataloguing in Publication Data is available.

ISBN: 1–56720–036–2

First published in 1998

Quorum Books, 88 Post Road West, Westport, CT 06881
An imprint of Greenwood Publishing Group, Inc.

Printed in the United States of America

The paper used in this book complies with the
Permanent Paper Standard issued by the National
Information Standards Organization (Z39.48–1984).

10  9  8  7  6  5  4  3  2  1

# Contents

## PART III  FROM OLD TO NEW

## PART IV  THE FUTURE

# Preface

The genesis for this book was an ongoing discussion between sales executives and academicians that began in the mid-1980s. At the time, the academic community was concerned with several key issues related to research and teaching in the sales area. Sales research was a relatively new phenomenon, with rigorous studies having only begun in the late 1960s. By the mid-1980s, sales research was finally gaining acceptance as a legitimate area of inquiry within the academic community. However, little of this research had been disseminated to the business community. As a result, sales researchers were eager to share their findings and ideas with sales executives who might criticize, reject, or validate existing research. Also important, sales researchers were seeking new ideas for future studies, and opportunities to collaborate with sales executives.

Parallel to the growing interest in sales research, academicians were examining the course work in the sales area. This led to a commitment on the part of many leading sales academicians to integrate current practices of the most progressive sales organizations into course work. At the time, there was discussion about the perceived gap between what was happening in the field and what was being taught in the classroom.

During this same time period, sales managers were dealing with major changes as their organizations adjusted to an increasingly turbulent business environment. Sales managers, trainers, and consultants were looking for new frameworks to guide the development and implementation of sales strategy. Executives were showing a genuine interest in academic research as a possible source for new ideas.

These mutual interests set the stage for a series of programs jointly conducted by academicians and sales executives. The first of these programs was held prior to an American Marketing Association conference in Scottsdale, Arizona in 1990. This program was a major breakthrough in fostering meaningful dialogue between professors and executives. It was a thrill to watch the leading academic researchers furiously take notes while executives presented their thoughts, and vice versa. These joint programs grew in popularity as both communities learned from each other. Along the way, we came to realize that the gap between sales practice and the academic treatment of selling and sales management was not nearly as large as originally perceived. In fact, we came to the realization that the academic and business community was largely interested in the same issues. Further, we became totally convinced that there was a lot to be gained from a free exchange of our varying perspectives and approaches to managerial issues.

As these programs and discussions continued, it became clear that we should move a step further in presenting academic and managerial views. Instead of having separate presentations by academics and executives, why not have them make joint presentations? This format was followed on several occasions at major conferences, and was extremely well received. The concept for this book, of having academician–executive author teams write about emerging trends in sales thought and practice, was a natural extension of these joint presentations.

In pulling this project together, we hope to reach a wider audience of sales and marketing executives and academicians who share the basic idea that together we can improve sales practice, education, and research. It has been our pleasure to work with some of the brightest and most dedicated people from the business and academic communities on this project. We are grateful to all of the authors and their organizations for the contributions. Thanks also to the professionals at Quorum Books. It is our hope that this book will be a resource for researchers, executives, and students. More important, we hope it will stimulate additional exchanges of ideas that will improve sales thought and practice.

**EMERGING
TRENDS IN SALES
THOUGHT
AND PRACTICE**

Chapter 1 ────────────────────────────────

# Sales Organization Challenges and Trends

Gerald J. Bauer, Mark S. Baunchalk,
Thomas N. Ingram, and Raymond W. LaForge

Consider the following situation: The XYZ Company manufactures and markets various products to many different business customers around the world. The company employs a field sales force to sell all products to all customers within defined geographical territories. This approach produced reasonable sales and profit growth for many years. However, about five years ago, sales flattened and profits declined. What happened? Customers became more demanding and competition intensified. Many customers reduced their supplier base dramatically and XYZ lost customers. The remaining customers demanded more attention while competitive pressures kept a lid on prices. Thus, profit margins were squeezed. XYZ realized that its future growth required significant changes in sales operations.

This situation is typical for many sales organizations. Customers are changing buying practices. Many are working closely with a few suppliers to reduce the cost of doing business and to ensure higher quality standards. Competition for these customers is often on a global scale and has never been more intense. Companies such as XYZ are trying to give customers "more for less," but are also trying to increase profits by "doing more with less." Thus, the selling environment is increasingly turbulent and offers key challenges to sales organizations:

- How to sell to a diverse and demanding customer base?
- How to be successful in an intense competitive landscape?
- How to increase profits within this difficult selling environment?

Sales organizations are responding to these challenges in various ways. These responses often result in dramatic sales organization changes. For example, many automobile dealers are replacing the traditional high-pressured, price-negotiated deal between customers and commissioned salespeople with a more pleasurable, fixed-price experience with customer-oriented, salaried salespeople. Although specific sales organization practices differ, several general trends represent new developments in the sales area.

## BOOK PURPOSE AND APPROACH

The purpose of this book is to explore several new developments in sales thought and practice in a unique way. Author teams consisting of at least one academic and one sales executive were assembled. Each team independently identified an important new sales development. The selected topics were classified into similar categories and organized into the table of contents for the book.

The author teams met prior to a sales conference to clarify the topics and to discuss the basic scope and content of each chapter. Each author team then prepared a chapter addressing the topic. Each chapter integrates an academic and sales executive perspective toward the topic. The academic perspective focuses on presenting the latest thinking and research results, while the sales executive perspective emphasizes the "best practices" of one or more sales organizations. There was no predetermined chapter format. The objective was to let each author team determine the best way to present a topic. The result of this approach is a series of chapters addressing new developments in sales thought and practice in different ways.

## CHAPTER PURPOSE AND APPROACH

The purpose of this chapter is to set the stage for the remainder of the book. We will present five major sales trends that encompass the remaining book chapters. The key issues for each trend are discussed and supported by examples from sales operations at DuPont. The book chapters relevant to this trend are then identified. We discuss how the specific chapter examines the particular trend. Since many of the chapters address issues relevant to several trends, we classify each chapter according to its major focus.

## SALES ORGANIZATION TRENDS

Many sales organizations are moving in these directions (Ingram, LaForge, and Schwepker 1997, 7–15; Anderson 1996; Cravens 1995):

• From transactions to relationships
• From individuals to teams

- From sales volume to sales productivity
- From management to leadership
- From local to global

### From Transactions to Relationships

Successful firms are dismissing the hard-sell, short-term orientation of personal selling in favor of a customer-oriented, long-term selling model referred to as relationship selling. Transaction selling centers on the sales presentation, or "pitch," designed to secure an immediate sale. Little regard is given to the customer's true needs, particularly over the long run. By contrast, relationship selling focuses on developing and enhancing a mutually beneficial bond between buyer and seller. The focus changes from "making a sale" in the short run, to "getting and keeping the right customers" over the long term.

Although there is a clear trend toward more relationship selling, most firms serve a diverse customer mix. Some customers still prefer the transaction-oriented approach, while others desire different types of relationships. Thus, sales organizations are likely to employ multiple relationship approaches to meet the needs of different customers in a cost-effective manner.

DuPont has addressed this situation by developing a customer interface strategy for defined customer groups. This customer interface strategy delineates how DuPont plans to interact with the customer groups it serves. Strategic alternatives range from serving some customers with a transaction approach, to developing long-term strategic partnerships with others. Different types of customer relationships are also developed between these extremes. The customer interface strategy balances the needs of the customer with the costs associated with different types of relationships. DuPont is clearly engaged in more relationship selling, but employs different relationship strategies for different customer groups.

Two chapters examine the relationship selling trend. In Chapter 2, "Relationship Selling: New Challenges for Today's Salesperson," Michael J. Swenson and Greg D. Link examine relationship selling issues. They compare discrete transactions to relational exchanges and discuss the benefits and costs of relationship selling. Research results concerning the determinants of long-term relationships are presented, and the relationship practices of leading sales organizations are examined. In Chapter 3, "Relationship Selling: New Challenges for Today's Sales Manager," Kenneth R. Evans, David J. Good, and Theodore W. Hellman discuss the differences in sales management practices for transaction and relationship selling. The management changes required to move from transaction to relationship selling, and the difficulties of balancing transaction and relationship selling within a sales organization are highlighted. Examples from Procter & Gamble are used to illustrate the key points.

### From Individuals to Teams

The traditional stereotype of the successful salesperson has been that of the rugged individualist—the difficult-to-manage, but high-performing "maverick." Such salespeople are highly committed to their sales jobs, but lack commitment to their employers. This lone wolf is a dying breed, as today's successful salesperson is much more likely to be a team player.

The move to relationship selling is one reason that teamwork is needed within a sales organization. Few salespeople possess the knowledge and skills needed to develop long-term customer relationships by identifying and solving complex customer problems. Salespeople typically need help from others within the firm. Sometimes this teamwork is provided in an informal manner. In other situations, formal, cross-functional, or cross-business unit, teams are formed to meet the needs of specific customers. The role of the salesperson is to mobilize the resources required to develop and expand customer relationships.

Teamwork in selling is becoming more and more important at DuPont. National and global account programs represent formal selling teams that focus on specific customers. This approach allows DuPont to learn more about these customers and better serve their needs. Some large customers use products from different business units within DuPont. Cross-business unit teams are assembled to serve these customers. Formal sales teams are not necessary for many customers. However, DuPont salespeople work closely with others in the firm to execute the customer interface strategy for these customers.

Keith Chrzanowski and Thomas W. Leigh discuss different customer relationship strategies, but focus on the use of multifunctional teams in Chapter 4, "Customer Relationship Strategy and Customer-Focused Teams." The chapter emphasizes the importance of developing customer relationship strategies. Key issues are discussed within the changing healthcare industry with specific examples from the practices at Allegiance Healthcare. In Chapter 5, "Strategic Account Strategies," Lawrence B. Chonko and Herbert F. Burnap examine the partnering process with strategic accounts. The critical issues in developing and implementing strategic account strategies are presented. Donald W. Barclay, Judith M. S. Hatley, and J. Brock Smith address alliances between organizations to jointly sell to and manage relationships with customers. In Chapter 6, "Horizontal Selling Alliances," the authors discuss the issues and challenges of horizontal selling alliances and present the experiences at Royal Bank Financial Group as a detailed example.

### From Sales Volume to Productivity

Sales organizations have traditionally focused on sales volume. Meeting and exceeding sales volume goals has been the basis for evaluating and rewarding salespeople. Many sales organizations are finding that all sales and all customers are not equal. More firms are examining the profitability of specific sales and of serving individual customers. A common result of this process is the finding that a surprisingly large percentage of sales transactions and customer relationships are not profitable. Because of these findings, there is much more emphasis on improving profitability by increasing sales productivity. The emphasis on sales productivity expands the focus to the costs of generating sales and serving customers. Sales organizations are looking for ways to be more effective and efficient.

One approach is to not pursue unprofitable sales or customers. A more likely approach is to change selling practices so that specific sales and customers become profitable. Replacing all or some field selling activities with lower cost sales channels, such as telemarketing, direct mail, or interactive electronic marketing, is an increasingly popular way to increase sales productivity. Other approaches emphasize doing things differently or more efficiently. Often this includes employing new technologies to replace or improve existing operations.

Increasing sales productivity is a major focus at DuPont. Sometimes this results in reducing selling costs by replacing field selling efforts with less costly sales channels. For example, telemarketing is used to perform specific selling activities, or to completely replace field salespeople at smaller accounts. New technologies are also being increasingly used to transmit information and communicate with customers or within DuPont. Internet, Intranet, and Extranet technologies are employed in various ways to increase sales productivity.

Richard C. Bartlett, Sharon Morgan Tahaney, and Thomas R. Wotruba examine the use of new technologies in Chapter 7, "CyberSales Management and Direct Selling." The unique aspects of direct selling are presented and the opportunities and challenges provided by electronic technologies are discussed. A detailed presentation of Mary Kay's *In Touch* sales automation system and Internet site illustrate one approach for increasing sales productivity. Case studies of Amway and Shaklee present approaches used by two other direct selling firms.

### From Management to Leadership

In a stable environment, day-to-day supervision and routine management activities comprise the bulk of a sales manager's job. Such environments are the exception, and sales managers increasingly must be leaders capable of stimulating and directing significant changes. The sales manager as a leader must have traditional management attributes such as the ability to motivate others and strong interpersonal communications skills. In addition, leaders must be able to conceive of a strategic vision, articulate the vision, and get others committed to the vision, often in the absence of short-term incentives.

DuPont is changing the way it manages its sales forces. There are larger spans of control and more self-managed teams. Traditional sales managers are becoming more like sales leaders who can articulate a compelling vision and build self-esteem, emotional involvement, and a sense of excitement. They are expected to be able to develop the knowledge, skills, and abilities of their sales team. There is much less emphasis on controlling the day-to-day activities of salespeople, and much more emphasis on helping salespeople perform successfully.

The move to relationship selling approaches, various types of sales teams, and strategic leadership from sales managers requires changes in traditional sales management practices. Nowhere is this more important than in the performance evaluation process. In Chapter 8, "Sales Force Performance Management in a Changing Selling Environment," Greg W. Marshall and Esther J. Ferre review historical sales force performance evaluation approaches and suggest several changes needed in this new selling environment. Important questions to consider in developing an effective performance management approach in the new selling environment are provided.

### From Local to Global

A global perspective is needed in today's marketplace. Saturation of markets in countries with mature economies has led to increased sales activities in other parts of the world. Many sales organizations are operating in different international markets. Even firms that do not sell internationally need to think globally. Most companies face international competition, use international suppliers, serve multicultural customers in their domestic market, and/ or have multicultural employees. A global orientation is especially important to sales organizations in serving international, multicultural customers, and in managing a culturally diverse sales force.

DuPont operates around the world. In some cases, global joint ventures are formed, which would benefit both partners through an improved competitive position in international markets. There is an increasing emphasis on developing global strategies, but implementing them on a local basis. DuPont also competes against international competitors in the U.S. and foreign markets, and employs multicultural employees within its sales organization and throughout the company.

One of the keys to selling successfully in international markets is to adapt appropriately to cultural differences. In Chapter 9, "Global Sales Force Management: Comparing German and U.S. Practices," Sönke Albers, Manfred Krafft, and Wilhelm Bielert discuss some of the important cultural differences. Key sales management issues are presented, and a comparison of U.S. and German sales management practices examined.

### THE FUTURE

The new developments discussed in this book will certainly be important in the future. However, new trends are likely to emerge, or the existing trends will be executed in different ways. Sales organizations need to continuously monitor changes in the selling environment and emerging trends. Leading firms try to stay ahead of the curve, and proactively make changes to improve sales organization performance.

DuPont views the development of a world-class sales organization as an important component of its growth strategy for the future. The company is changing sales operations at many business units to sell effectively and productively in the future. Some of the changes include more targeted segmentation of customers, and more attention to the "best" customers. DuPont expects to employ more sales channels, especially telemarketing and electronic commerce, to serve different customer groups in a productive manner. Sales automation will increase, and customer databases will become more important. Salespeople will need to understand business processes, and have consulting capabilities to be able to develop and expand customer relationships in the future.

In Chapter 10, "Selling in the Future: Synthesis and Suggestions," Robert C. Conti and William L. Cron conclude the book with a gaze toward the future. The authors read all of the previous book chapters prior to writing their chapter. They present their view of selling in the future and refer to previous book chapters when appropriate. This chapter provides a synthesis of the book and some new ideas for sales organizations to consider.

## REFERENCES

Anderson, R. 1996. Personal Selling and Sales Management in the New Millennium. *Journal of Personal Selling and Sales Management* 16 (3): 17–32.

Cravens, D. W. 1995. The Changing Role of the Sales Force. *Marketing Management* 4 (2): 49–57.

Ingram, T. N., R. W. LaForge, and C. H. Schwepker, Jr. 1997. *Sales Management: Analysis and Decision Making*. Fort Worth, Tex.: Dryden Press.

# PART I

# From Transactions
# to Relationships

Chapter 2 ───────────────────────────────

# Relationship Selling: New Challenges for Today's Salesperson

### Michael J. Swenson and Greg D. Link

Because of the challenges of an increasingly competitive and cost conscious environment, sales organizations are reevaluating their approach to customers. With increasing frequency, sales practitioners are being advised to develop and maintain long-term relationships with customers. The academic literature suggests that the role of the salesperson is in transition toward that of a relationship manager rather than a seller (O'Neal 1989; Webster 1992). Wilson notes that buyer and seller relationships have become "an integral part of business-to-business operating strategies over the past ten years" (1995, 335). Ingram suggests that "in the current highly-competitive business environment, there is a strong movement toward relationship selling as contrasted with traditional, transaction-oriented selling" (1996, 5). Firms such as Xerox, Black & Decker, Motorola, Neiman-Marcus, General Electric, Ford, and others are looking to their suppliers to help them achieve a stronger competitive position (Emshwiller 1991). Dahlstrom, McNeilly, and Speh point out that "prolonged interfirm interaction is pervasive in industrial marketing" (1996, 110). Heide and John argue that "buyers and sellers are increasingly supplanting conventional 'arm's length' arrangements with 'alliances' involving closer ties" (1990, 24). All these scholars express the view that the nature of buyer–seller relationship has been undergoing some dramatic changes.

Developing and maintaining long-term relationships between buyers and sellers is not a novel concept, however (Stigler 1951). Citing a Middle Eastern proverb from ancient trade, Gronroos notes that "As a merchant, you'd better have a friend in every town" (1994, 18). Indeed, "Relationships between buyers and sellers have existed since humans began trading goods and services"

(Wilson 1995, 335). The renewed emphasis, however, is the result of customers becoming more demanding, and competitors becoming more intense.

## OBJECTIVE

The objective of this chapter is to examine and present the state of the knowledge concerning relationship selling. First we define the concept. Because selling practice shows confusion and mistakes between relationship selling and transaction selling, we suggest problem areas and issues where it seems judicious to emphasize one over the other. This discussion enables us to delineate the possible costs and benefits of relationship selling. We then review and evaluate the relevant academic work in this area. Next we present evidence of best practices by leading sales organizations. Then we attempt to synthesize the research and practice findings. We conclude with directions for researchers and practitioners.

## WHAT IS RELATIONSHIP SELLING?

A useful starting point for defining relationship selling is the core phenomenon for study in the marketing discipline—exchange (cf. Alderson 1965; Bagozzi 1975; Dwyer, Schurr, and Oh 1987; Hunt 1983; Kotler 1972). Over twenty years ago Bagozzi (1975) argued that marketing theory is concerned with two questions relating to exchange: (1) Why do people and organizations engage in exchange relationships? and (2) how are exchanges created, resolved, or avoided? More recently, researchers have developed frameworks for analyzing the relational content of exchange (Heide 1994; Macneil 1981). Webster (1992), for example, proposes a continuum of exchanges ranging from pure transactions to network organizations.

### Discrete Exchange

At one end of the continuum is discrete exchange, which excludes relational elements. In the microeconomic paradigm, this discrete exchange or pure transaction is characterized by the absence of differentiation, customer loyalty, trust, brand equity, service, credit, and commitment. Participation in the exchange is motivated only by the price mechanism of the marketplace. The pure transaction, then, is a one-time exchange between buyer and seller with no prior or subsequent interaction (Webster 1992). Macneil defines this form of exchange as "the separating of a transaction from all else between the participants at the same time and before and after . . . there is nothing else between the parties, never has been, and never will be" (1980, p.60). Dwyer, Schurr, and Oh provide an example of discrete exchange: "A one-time purchase of unbranded gasoline out-of-town at an independent station paid for with cash" (1987, 12).

## Relational Exchange

At the other end of the continuum is a long-term orientation with a high likelihood of future exchange (Ganesan 1994). Indeed, the "sale is not the end of the marketing process, but the beginning of a relationship in which buyer and seller become interdependent" (Webster 1994, 131). Doyle and Roth suggest that "the goal of relationship selling is to earn the position of preferred supplier by developing trust in key accounts over a period of time" (1992, 59). Macneil (1978, 1980) argues that relational exchange transpires over time; each transaction must be viewed in terms of its history and anticipated future. Table 2.1 presents Macneil's characterization of discrete and relational exchange on twelve dimensions.

Shapiro (1987) notes that "the relationship salesperson concentrates efforts on developing trust in highly selected accounts over an extended period of time." Jackson (1985) suggests that relationship selling is "oriented toward strong, lasting relationships with individual accounts." Morgan and Hunt (1994, 22) expand the scope of relationship marketing beyond solely customer relationships: "Relationship marketing refers to all marketing activities directed toward establishing, developing, and maintaining successful relational exchanges."

## Benefits

To the extent that relationship selling contributes to product differentiation and creates barriers to switching, it can provide a competitive advantage for the seller (Day and Wensley 1983; Jackson 1985). Building a long-term relationship with buyers provides more opportunities for the seller to sell new and additional solutions. The seller in long-term relationships may achieve higher profitability by reducing discretionary expense such as selling, general, and administrative costs (Kalwani and Narayandas 1995). In addition to financial awards, the relationship may provide the seller with access to new markets and increased competence to enhance innovation (Buchanan 1992; Heide 1994; Lyons, Krachenberg, and Henke 1990; Webster 1994).

Buyers benefit from being able to harness the strengths and skills of the seller to their advantage (Dwyer, Schurr, and Oh 1987). Specific benefits to buyers include improved quality and process performance, continuous cost reductions, enhanced support relationships, and contract predictability (Lyons, Krachenberg, and Henke 1990; Newman 1988; Trevelen 1987).

## Potential Problems

Insufficient understanding of a customer's orientation can lead to problems, such as attempting to form a long-term relationship with a customer when a short-term relationship is more appropriate (Jackson 1985). Conversely,

**Table 2.1**
**A Comparison of Discrete Transactions and Relational Exchange**

| Exchange Elements | Discrete Transactions | Relational Exchange |
|---|---|---|
| **Situational characteristics** | | |
| Timing of exchange (commencement, duration, and termination of exchange) | Distinct beginning, short duration, and sharp ending by performance | Commencement traces to previous agreements; exchange is longer in duration, reflecting an ongoing process |
| Number of parties (entities taking part in some aspect of the exchange process) | Two parties | Often multiple parties involved in the process |
| Obligations (three aspects: sources of content, sources of obligation, and specificity) | Content comes from offers and simple claims, obligations come from beliefs and customs (external enforcement), standardized obligations | Content and sources of obligations are promises made in the relation plus customs and laws; obligations are customized, detailed, and administered within the relation |
| Expectations for relations (especially concerned with conflicts of interest, the prospects of unity, and potential trouble) | Conflicts of interest (goals) and little unity are expected, but no future trouble is anticipated because cash payment upon instantaneous performance precludes future interdependence | Anticipated conflicts of interest and future trouble are counterbalanced by trust and efforts at unity |
| **Process characteristics** | | |
| Primary personal relations (social interaction and communication) | Minimal personal relationships; ritual-like communications predominate | Important personal, noneconomic satisfactions derived; both formal and informal communications are used |

pressure for short-term performance may result in a focus on immediate individual sales, despite customers' desire for long-term relationships.

## KEY FINDINGS FROM ACADEMIC RESEARCH

Much of the academic work in this area has focused on creating conceptual process models of relationship development, and identifying the salient determinants of long-term relationships.

### Process Models

Dwyer, Schurr, and Oh (1987) use exchange theory, marital theory, bargaining theory, and power theory to outline a process for developing buyer–

**Table 2.1** (*continued*)

| Exchange Elements | Discrete Transactions | Relational Exchange |
|---|---|---|
| Contractual solidarity (regulation of exchange behavior to ensure performance) | Governed by social norms, rules, etiquette, and prospects for self-gain | Increased emphasis on legal and self-regulation; psychological satisfactions cause internal adjustments |
| Transferability (the ability to transfer rights, obligations, and satisfactions to other parties | Complete transferability; it matters not who fulfills contractual obligation | Limited transferability; exchange is heavily dependent on the identity of the parties |
| Cooperation (especially joint efforts at performance and planning | No joint efforts | Joint efforts related to both performance and planning over time; adjustment over time is endemic |
| Planning (the process and mechanisms for coping with change and conflicts) | Primary focus on the substance of exchange; no future is anticipated | Significant focus on the process of exchange; detailed planning for the future exchange within new environments and to satisfy changing goals; tacit and explicit assumptions abound |
| Measurement and specificity (calculation and reckoning of exchange) | Little attention to measurement and specifications; performance is obvious | Significant attention to measuring, specifying, and quantifying all aspects of performance, including psychic and future benefits |
| Power (the ability to impose one's will on others) | Power may be exercised when promises are made until promises are executed | Increased interdependence increases the importance judicious application of power in the exchange |
| Division of benefits and burdens (the extent of sharing of benefits and burdens) | Sharp division of benefits and burdens into parceis; exclusive allocation to parties | Likely to include some sharing of benefits and burdens and adjustments to both shared and parceled benefits and burdens over time |

*Source*: Adapted from Macneil (1978, 1980); and Dwyer, Schurr, and Oh (1987).

seller relationships. The model highlights phase characteristics—awareness, exploration, expansion, and commitment—and the transitions between these phases that lead to ever expanding interdependency between buyer and seller.

Frazier, Spekman, and O'Neal (1988) focus on "just-in-time" exchange relationships between OEMs and suppliers of component parts and materials. They present four general stages in the relationship development process—interest stage, initiation–rejection stage, implementation stage, and review stage. Furthermore, the researchers provide an inventory of propositions relating to the various stages.

## Empirical Studies

The few empirical studies of buyer–seller relationships share many variables that make for a successful relationship.

- Biong and Selnes (1996) examined the effect salespeople have on the continuity of established buyer–seller relationships. They found that perceived salesperson performance has a direct effect on the buyer's motivation to continue the relationship. Furthermore, the salesperson affects the perceived reliability of the supplier and the perceived value of the supplier's services. The results of the study underscore the central role of the salesperson as a relationship manager (O'Neal 1989; Webster 1992).
- Ganesan (1994) developed a model of a retailer and vendor long-term relationship. Testing the model with 124 retail buyers and 52 vendor representatives, he found that trust and dependence play key roles in determining long-term orientation.
- Hallen, Johanson, and Seyed-Mohamed (1991) examined interfirm adaptation in business relationships. They found that adaptations are demonstrations of trust and commitment in the buyer–seller relationship.
- Using the normative theory of transaction costs, Heide and John (1990) developed a model of closeness in industrial buyer–supplier relationships and tested empirically the relationships between the dimensions of closeness and their antecedent conditions. Their findings show that close relationships emerge as responses to the need for safeguarding transaction-specific assets and to facilitate adaptation to uncertainty.
- Noordewier, John, and Nevin (1990) examined the relationship between the organization of the buyer–seller interface and performance in the acquisition of repetitively used items. Under conditions of uncertainty, performance in terms of acquisitions costs is enhanced when firms introduce more relational elements into the exchange.
- Crosby, Evans, and Cowles (1990) analyzed the nature, consequences, and antecedents of perceived relationship quality (i.e., trust and satisfaction) in the context of life insurance service. Their research revealed that relational sellers focus on cooperative intentions, mutual disclosure, and high contact intensity, which in turn affects customer's perception of relationship quality.
- Lagace, Dahlstrom, and Gassenheimer (1991) extended the research of Crosby, Evans, and Cowles (1990) by including ethical salesperson behavior. An examination of the relationship between pharmaceutical salespersons and physicians revealed that ethical behavior and expertise of the salesperson affect perceived trust of the salesperson and satisfaction with the exchange as noted by medical doctors.

## An Integrated Model

Building on the process model of Dwyer, Schurr, and Oh (1987), and extending the hybrid relationship work of Borys and Jemison (1989), Wilson (1995) took a first step in developing a model that integrates the relationship variables with the relationship development process. In the relationship development process each partner advances through five stages: (1) searching and selecting the relationship partner, (2) defining the purpose of the relationship, (3) setting the boundaries of the relationship, (4) creating value for each partner, and (5) maintaining the relationship.

The salient relationship variables "represents those variables that have both theoretical and empirical support" (Wilson 1995, 337). Although Wilson cautions that the list is not exhaustive, it provides a useful starting point. The list of variables, with definitions and relevant research, is presented in Table 2.2.

Figure 2.1 shows how Wilson (1995) combines the relationship variables and the relationship development process. During a particular stage, a relationship variable may become active or latent. As Wilson points out, "a latent construct is one in which the main issues have been settled to the manager's satisfaction." It becomes part of the operating environment.

## BEST PRACTICES AT LEADING SALES ORGANIZATIONS

As we contemplate the practitioner's perspective on relationship selling, we are struck by the sheer volume of writings on the subject and ponder what new thinking may be offered to the subject that might overcome the cynical "So what?" of our fellow practitioners. When we first wrote on the topic in the early 1990s, relationship selling was then on the leading edge, and by 1997, has become the acknowledged ideal in the field. Given that relationship selling is the accepted ideal as shown by the academic research, and by the practical application by companies like Saturn in the automobile industry, Ritz Carlton Hotels in the service industry, Nordstrom in the retail industry, Hewlett-Packard in the computer industry, and Northwestern Mutual in the insurance industry, what can be added? We suggest that the most practical value-added discussion may be how to consistently develop and maintain buyer–seller relationships and why they work. We say consistently, because randomly, sales relationships "click," and randomly they do not, creating frustration with practitioners, and encouraging more research and critical thinking on the part of academics. Many of the assumptions in sales training over the years have been flawed, based on the complexity of factors involved in making a sale or establishing a relationship. A salesperson may be taught a sales technique and apply it relentlessly and ultimately make a sale. The salesperson then attributes this success to the technique, which may or may not actually have contributed to the sale. In fact, we propose that many other potential sales may have been lost by the salesperson's relentless application of techniques and subsequent lack of empathy and authenticity. In the words of Maslow, "He that is good with a hammer tends to think everything is a nail."

Accordingly, in this section we focus on companies that practice relationship selling, as defined in the literature. These examples provide anecdotal evidence for how, when, and why relationship selling is useful, effective, and indeed, profitable.

**Table 2.2**
**Relationship Variables**

| Variable | Definition | Research |
|---|---|---|
| Commitment | An enduring desire to maintain a valued relationship (Moorman, Zaltman, and Deshpande 1992). | Anderson, Lodish, and Weitz (1987)<br>Anderson and Weitz (1990)<br>Dwyer, Schurr, and Oh (1987)<br>Hardwick and Ford (1986)<br>Jackson (1985)<br>Moorman, Zaltman, and Deshpande (1992) |
| Trust | The willingness to rely on an exchange partner in whom one has confidence (Moorman, Zaltman, and Deshpande (1992). | Anderson and Weitz (1990)<br>Crosby, Evans, and Cowles (1990)<br>Dwyer, Schurr, and Oh (1987)<br>Ganesan (1994)<br>Milliman and Fugate (1988)<br>Moorman, Zaltman, and Deshpande (1992)<br>Schurr and Ozanne (1985)<br>Swan, Trawick, Rink, and Roberts (1988)<br>Swan and Nolan (1985) |
| Cooperation | "Similar or complimentary coordinated actions taken by firms in inter-dependent relationships to achieve mutual outcomes or singular outcomes with expected reciprocation over time" (Anderson and Narus 1990, p.45) | Anderson and Narus (1990)<br>Morgan and Hunt (1994) |
| Mutual goals | "The degree to which partners share goals that can only be accomplished through joint action and the maintenance of the relationship" (Wilson 1995, p. 338) | Morgan and Hunt (1994)<br>Wilson, Soni, and O'Keeffe (1995) |
| Interdependence | The degree of the relationship partners' dependence on each other. | Anderson and Narus (1990)<br>Anderson and Weitz (1990)<br>Anderson, Lodish, and Weitz (1987)<br>Dwyer, Schurr, and Oh (1987)<br>Ganesan (1994)<br>Han, Wilson, and Dant (1993)<br>Heide and John (1988) |

## Trust

To simplify the process, we need to shift our focus from sales techniques to certain self-evident principles of relationships. One historically flawed sales assumption is that people buy from those they like. They don't. People buy from those they trust. To test this, simply look at your own experience. How

**Table 2.2** (*continued*)

| Variable | Definition | Research |
|---|---|---|
| Performance satisfaction | The degree to which the exchange meets the performance expectations of the partner (Wilson 1995). | Kalwani and Narayandas (1995) |
| Comparison of alternatives | The degree to which alternatives are available and the comparability of such alternatives. With few alternatives, the partner is less likely to leave the relationship. | Anderson and Narus (1990, 1984) |
| Adaptation | Altering a process or product to accommodate the relationship partner. | Hakansson (1982) <br> Hallen, Johanson, and Seyed- Mohamed (1991) <br> Hallen, Seyed-Mohamed, and Johanson (1988) |
| Nonretrievable investment | "The relation-specific commitment of resources that a partner invests in the relationship" (Wilson 1995, p. 339) | Jackson (1985) <br> Williamson (1985, 1975) |
| Shared technology | The degree to which each partner values the technology contributed by the other partner. | Vlosky and Wilson (1994) <br> Han and Wilson (1993) |
| Structural bonds | Forces that increase the barriers to terminating the relationship. | Han and Wilson (1993) |
| Social bonds | "The degree of mutual personal friendship and liking shared by the buyer and seller" (Wilson 1995, p. 339) | Wilson and Mummalaneni (1986) <br> Han and Wilson (1993) |

*Source*: D. T. Wilson, An Integrated Model of Buyer–Seller Relationships. *Journal of the Academy of Marketing Science* 23, no. 4 (Fall): 335. Copyright © 1995 by Sage Publications, Inc. Reprinted by permission of Sage Publications, Inc.

many overly friendly salespeople have you found you could trust? Trust is a fundamental business principle, as shown in the academic research. To build a customer base over time, a business must establish trust with its customers who must believe the business will meet or exceed their expectations. If customers' expectations are met or exceeded, the business grows. Conversely, if customers' expectations are violated, the business dies. Covey (1989) gives

**Figure 2.1**
**Integrating the Relationship Variables and the Relationship Development Process**

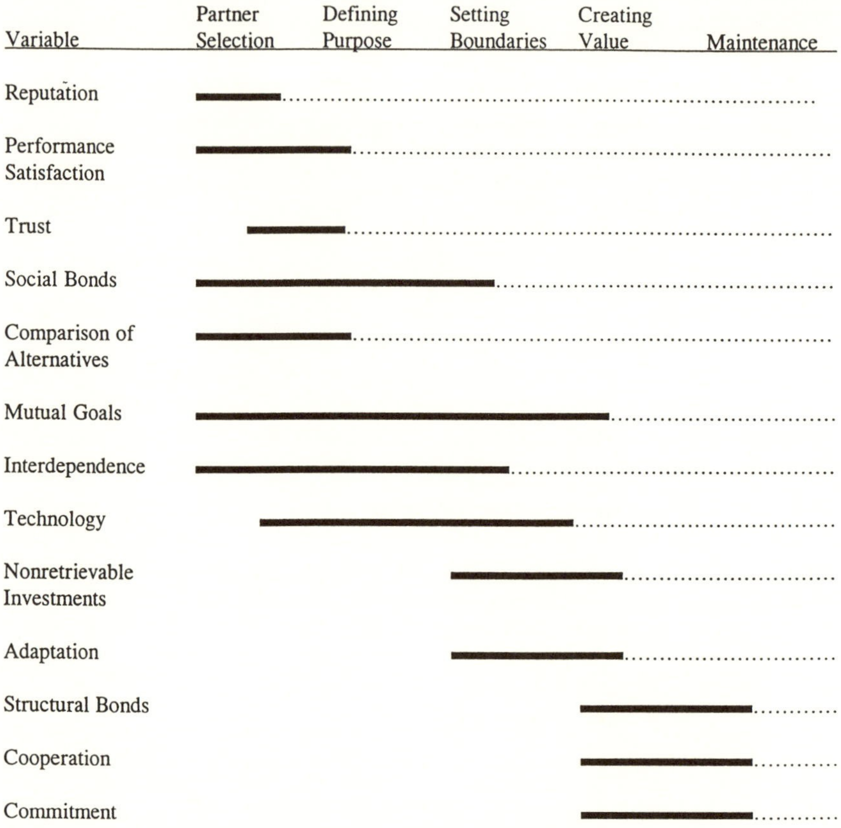

| Variable | Partner Selection | Defining Purpose | Setting Boundaries | Creating Value | Maintenance |
|---|---|---|---|---|---|
| Reputation | ████ | ········ | ········ | ········ | ········ |
| Performance Satisfaction | ████████ | ········ | ········ | ········ | ········ |
| Trust | ██ | ████ | ········ | ········ | ········ |
| Social Bonds | ████████ | ██████ | ████ | ········ | ········ |
| Comparison of Alternatives | ██████ | ██ | ········ | ········ | ········ |
| Mutual Goals | ████████ | ██████ | ██████ | ██ | ········ |
| Interdependence | ████████ | ██████ | ████ | ········ | ········ |
| Technology | ██ | ██████ | ██████ | ██ | ········ |
| Nonretrievable Investments | | | ████████ | ██ | ········ |
| Adaptation | | | ████████ | ██ | ········ |
| Structural Bonds | | | | ██████ | ████ ···· |
| Cooperation | | | | ██████ | ████ ···· |
| Commitment | | | | ██████ | ████ ···· |

Source: D. T. Wilson, An Integrated Model of Buyer–Seller Relationships. *Journal of the Academy of Marketing Science* 23, no. 4 (Fall): 345. Copyright © 1995 by Sage Publications, Inc. Reprinted by permission of Sage Publications, Inc.

this example: "I know of a restaurant that served a fantastic clam chowder and was packed with customers every day at lunchtime. Then the business was sold and the new owners focused on profit—they decided to water down the chowder. For about a month, with costs down and revenues constant, profits zoomed. But little by little, the customers began to disappear. Trust was gone, and the business dwindled to almost nothing. The new owners tried desperately to reclaim it, but they had neglected the customers, violated their trust, and lost the asset of customer loyalty." Salespeople, in a sense, are the CEOs of their own business, and their success in the long term is measured by the trust in their relationships with customers.

Trust is based on our personal trustworthiness. Our trustworthiness is a balance of our character and competence. Character has to do with our integrity, sincerity, honesty, and maturity—who we are. Competence has to do with ability, qualifications, and skills—what we can do. Both are necessary to establish trust. Customers expect both character and competence before they give their trust. As Bruce Nordstrom says, "We can hire nice people and teach them to sell but we can't hire salespeople and teach them to be nice." In other words, competence is easier to teach than character.

Covey Leadership Center uses the metaphor of the "emotional bank account" to describe how much trust has been built up in a relationship. Just like a financial bank account, you make deposits in and withdrawals from your trust account with others. Your account balance facilitates or hinders the exchange process. Effective salespeople work to maintain high emotional bank accounts with all their relationships, especially with their customers. They know if the account balance is high, customers allow them to make mistakes and the account balance will compensate for them. Conversely, ineffective salespeople suffer from the fact that a low account balance offers no margin for error, and even their well-intended efforts are perceived as manipulations. Effective salespeople regularly call for an account balance with key customers and use this feedback to proactively build their account balance. Ineffective salespeople, however, are afraid to ask about their balance for fear they are bankrupt. They superficially pretend that all is well, all the while not recognizing that their cosmetic flattery is a significant withdrawal, and that trust is nil.

## Performance Satisfaction

The essence of the quality movement is meeting or exceeding customers' expectations; and those expectations are largely established with the customers by salespeople. Sales and service are the front and back of the same hand, and salespeople must take responsibility for the total customer experience, whether they are the service person as well, or serving as a liaison and advocate for the customer for another person or department. Effective salespeople will pay the price to gain significant product and service knowledge so they can set appropriate expectations with customers.

Delighting customers by exceeding their expectations goes a long way toward building a trusting relationship. Nordstrom has a reputation for delighting customers, as described in *The Nordstrom Way* (Spector and McCarthy 1995). "A customer who was about to catch a flight at the Seattle–Tacoma Airport, inadvertently left her airline ticket at the counter of one of Nordstrom's women's apparel departments. Discovering the ticket, her Nordstrom sales associate immediately phoned the airline and asked the service representative if she could track down the customer at the airport and write her another ticket. No, she could not. So the Nordstrom salesperson jumped into a cab, rode out to the airport (at her own expense), located the customer, and delivered the ticket herself. (Nordstrom later reimbursed her for the cab fare)."

One of the more visible pioneers and best practice applications of relationship selling is Saturn. In 1992, the company challenged conventional wisdom in the automobile industry by introducing the no dicker sticker. Furthermore, Saturn salespeople seek to satisfy the customer by making sure every last detail meets his or her expectations. For example, a woman in Wyoming expressed interest in buying a new car. The closest dealership to her was in Salt Lake City. So, the Saturn salesperson in Salt Lake City flew to Wyoming, picked her up, and flew back to Salt Lake City to show her the car. She purchased a new Saturn. The company's sales results now speak for themselves. Revenue has increased every year since its inception, including a 23-percent jump last year (Cohen 1996).

Coca-Cola's salespeople in its fountain division do not just sell beverages, they help their customers' businesses grow. The company researches consumer behaviors in a variety of dining segments. Using this market information, salespeople serve as a restaurant's marketing partner. "They make recommendations not only about adding new products, but about promoting them on the menu, and on table tents and coasters," notes a senior sales executive (Brewer 1996). The result is that customers buy more drinks, which improves the restaurant's profits, and Coke continues to dominate the fountain business.

### Mutual Goals and Cooperation: Win–Win

The trust to establish and sustain a long-term customer relationship flows from the underlying motive of the salesperson. Much has been written about win–win relationships. It is a frame of mind and heart that seeks mutual benefit in all interactions and exchanges. It is the essence of relationship selling. With win–win, all parties obtain value from the relationship. Most people tend to think in terms of dichotomies—strong or weak, sale or no sale, win or lose. Win–win people see dichotomous thinking as fundamentally flawed. It is based on power and position rather than on principle. Win–win is the paradigm and principle that there is plenty for everybody—an abundance mentality that one party's success is not achieved at the expense of the other. It is a belief in a third alternative that is better than the position at hand.

Win–win negotiating has gained wide appeal in sales in recent years. We suggest that there is a powerful distinction of this principle that is not discussed, that is, win–win or no deal. This acknowledges that there are times when the parties to the transaction cannot seem to come to terms. We suggest that many times it is better to go for no deal for the time being, rather than to settle for a lower form of a win–win compromise. Compromise breeds cynicism, and can put a mortgage on the prospects of a long-term relationship.

When you have no deal as an option in your mind, you feel liberated because you have no need to manipulate people, to unreasonably push your own agenda, or to drive too hard for a sale. You can be open. You can risk the vulnerability to really try to understand the deeper issues facing your customer. It is no longer an all or nothing game. It allows for the authentic dialogue necessary to determine if there is truly mutual benefit. If not, you leave the door open for future relationships without pushing the issue so far that you destroy the chance for future business. Often the short-term pressure of sales quotas undermines the opportunity to set the foundation of trust and authenticity needed for long-term relationships.

No deal also prevents win–lose, where you sell hard, get the sale, and the customer resents you, and cancels the order due to buyer's remorse, or worse, buyer's revenge, vowing not to do business with you again and spreading negative word-of-mouth to other potential customers. Another flawed practice is to overpromise just to get the sale, knowing you will underdeliver. The opposite challenge is lose–win, where you cut the price so low you resent the customer, and set a price precedent that will haunt you for the rest of the relationship.

The courage of character required to go for no deal, rather than compromise, is possible where there is self-confidence and a conviction to build potentially lifelong customers. The behavior flows from a predetermined motive and vision. Effective salespeople can afford the long-term perspective in customer relationships because they have paid the price and managed their personal and organizational resources and expectations so they are not pressured by short-term needs or quotas. Suggesting no deal when mutual benefit is in question actually improves your trust with the customer, and makes them more likely to want to do business with you in the future.

Effective sales professionals go for no deal the minute they suspect that mutual benefit is in question. This not only preserves the relationship and possible future business, but it sends a rare message to the customer—that the relationship and mutual benefit are more important to you than any mere transaction. Another benefit to salespeople is that it keeps them out of the obsolete linear "numbers game," a quantity paradigm created by investing only serious quality time with customers whose needs are clear and current, and where there is high probability of a long-term relationship. This is further enhanced by identifying in advance the characteristics of your ideal long-term customers and targeting only those that meet your criteria. Think what your personal satisfaction level for sales would be if most lengthy interactions led to a strong, lifelong customer relationship. This approach eliminates the stressful burnout of battling objections with marginally qualified prospects in win–lose situations.

Joint venture alliance selling or partnering is the highest form of long-term relationship selling (e.g., Miller and Heiman 1987). It creates an interdependent, long-term, and mutually beneficial relationship. Wal-Mart is an excellent example of this level of relationship. They even have customers on their board of directors. This shifts your position with the customer from a dispensable vendor to an indispensable resource and partner. It may involve writing a win–win agreement for your relationship with the customer to clarify expectations, identify desired results, and determine accountability. The mutual involvement and commitment of teams from both organizations elevates the relationship to the point that price, competition, and other issues become less relevant. You become a valued resource to the customer.

### Adaptation: Listening

A critical skill required to manifest and maintain a long-term customer relationship is empathetic listening. Listening not with the intent to reply but with the intent to understand. It is the fifth of the Seven Habits of Highly Effective People (Covey 1989). Seeking first to understand requires a very deep shift in paradigm. Most salespeople do not listen with the intent to understand, they listen with the intent to reply. They are speaking of preparing to speak. Sales effectiveness would increase enough to significantly increase the nation's entire economy if salespeople could do this one thing—let the customer talk. As Pascal observed many years ago, "We are generally better persuaded by the reasons we discover ourselves than to those given to us by others." Patrice Nagasawa, a Nordstrom salesperson, said, "The day I stopped worrying about selling and started listening to the customer was the day it all fell into place for me. When you are young starting out with this company you want to sell. But the more you talk, and the less you listen, the less you are going to do" (Spector and McCarthy 1995).

Effective salespersons know that customers buy for their reasons, not ours (Miller and Heiman 1987). They apply the principle of seeking first to understand, and work to diagnose before they prescribe. Imagine going into your eye doctor's office and having him or her say, "Here, try these glasses, they look good on you," without giving you an eye exam. You would not have any confidence in his or her prescription without a diagnosis. So it is in relationship selling—we must first understand the customer's problem or need before we can suggest a solution or opportunity.

The early Greeks had words for these sales characteristics: ethos, pathos, and logos. Ethos is your personal credibility, the faith people have in your character and competence, or your trustworthiness. Pathos is empathic understanding, the trust they feel, the emotional bank account. Logos is the logic, the reasoning part of the presentation. Most sales communication is in reverse; we pitch first, then attempt to overcome objections.

When you present your ideas clearly, specifically, visually, and most important, in the context of a deep understanding of the customer's perceptions and concerns, you significantly increase your influence. The presentation, or the prescription, begins with an acknowledgment of understanding. Only when you understand the concern and position of the customer should you attempt to link their needs to your benefits. Empathy lifts you to a greater accuracy, greater integrity, and greater authenticity in your presentations. Customers feel that. It puts you both on the same side of the problem looking at possible solutions together. They know you are presenting ideas, having taken all known facts into consideration, and will benefit everyone. You present benefits in the context of their needs.

Recently, Procter & Gamble developed a strategy to adapt to customer needs by organizing its salespeople and other employees into multifunctional teams that interface with a counterpart team in the customer's organization (Lucas 1996). Each customer has a fully dedicated team consisting of salespeople and experts in a variety of functional areas such as marketing, finance, logistics, and technology. Together, the team of experts and salespeople build well-aligned relationships with customers.

IBM is healthy and growing again, after stumbling in the early 1990s. "The primary reason for our success is simple—we are listening to our customers," notes a senior sales executive (Yarbrough 1996). The company's focus is on "account relationship." To operationalize account relationship, salespeople specialize and focus on a particular industry. For example, salespeople focusing on the banking industry take classes at the Wharton School of Business. The objective is for salespeople to understand the customer's needs better than the customer.

Since the railroad industry became deregulated more than a decade ago, Union Pacific has developed and trained its sales force to ensure customer satisfaction. A national account manager notes, "Now we can take the time to listen to and service our customers" (Cohen 1996). Every month, Union Pacific surveys a sample of its customers to measure the company's performance in such areas as delivery, pricing, and billing. If a customer is dissatisfied, the salesperson designs an action plan to address the issue. Salespeople are evaluated on how well their action plans solve customer problems and increase customer satisfaction. The company's profits have increased with higher customer satisfaction levels. Union Pacific ranks first in profitability in the seven-company railroad industry with net income increasing an average of 13 percent a year for the past decade.

### High Contact Intensity

Hewlett-Packard, Sales & Marketing Management's Best Sales Force of 1996, continues to find ways to provide salespeople with as much time as possible in front of customers, and as little time as possible in "non-value-added-activities" (Brewer 1996). Using technology, the company frees its salespeople from time-consuming paper work and helps them manage valuable customer information. In addition, field support specialists increase salespeople's "value-added time" by handling administrative tasks for salespeople and following up with customers. The field support specialist becomes an extension of the salesperson. Customers know, understand, and appreciate the extra attention they receive from the sales team.

## Social Bonds

The Mutual Life Insurance Company of New York (MONY), Sales & Marketing Management's Best Sales Force of 1995, asked its top producers to find ways to improve their sales performance (Brewer 1995). The result of this request was the creation of a "customer intimacy marketing plan" in which agents work on ways to spend more time with customers in both formal and informal settings. Agents are encouraged to "get close to clients" by taking them, either individually or in groups, to the symphony, ball games, or to fine restaurants. This allows clients to meet each other as well.

## Shared Technology

Intel's sales force is almost exclusively engineers. In an intensive two-year training program, Intel salespeople learn about products and develop consultative selling skills (Yarbrough 1996). In the field, salespeople use their expertise to consult with customers. For example, Intel salespeople, working with a development team of Toshiba and Intel engineers, helped create a single cable (Universal Serial Bus) which connects all computer peripherals for a Toshiba PC. "We are not only acting as consultants, but we also get the chance to work with customers on what the future of the industry will look like," says an Intel sales manager (Yarbrough 1996, 60).

## FUTURE RESEARCH

Although relationship selling is not a new phenomenon, our understanding and level of knowledge remain somewhat elementary. Therefore, we suggest several directions for further research. First, research is needed to develop better measures of salesperson performance in long-term exchange relationships (Biong and Selnes 1996). Researchers would do well to develop performance models that include relational, financial, and other relationship management considerations.

Second, relationship-selling concepts need to be refined (Wilson 1995). Although a number of relationship-selling concepts have been identified conceptually and empirically, additional research is needed to purify definitions and operationalize concepts. Furthermore, the search for additional determinants of relationship selling must continue.

Third, contingency frameworks should be developed and explored to help scholars model relationship selling in different situations (Biong and Selnes 1996; Wilson 1995). Situation variables such as balance of dependency (Buchanan 1992), maturity of the relationship (Ring and Van de Ven 1994), and company cultures may influence the effect of various salesperson behaviors on the relationship.

Further investigation of relationship selling may provide additional insights into one of the more fundamental problems in marketing: the nature of buyer–

seller relationships. These are clearly areas of future study for researchers of relationship selling.

## MANAGERIAL IMPLICATIONS

The reasons for moving from traditional, transactional selling toward relationship selling are compelling. The conceptual models, empirical findings, and anecdotal evidence provide incentives for sales organizations to develop and maintain long-term relationships with buying firms. Such relationships create value for buyers and sellers (Wilson 1995). Furthermore, to the extent that the relationship contributes to product differentiation and creates barriers to switching, it can provide a competitive advantage for the seller (Day and Wensley 1983; Jackson 1985).

Sales then is a function not so much of closing sales but of opening relationships. Your motive of mutual benefit frees you to be real, to be authentic. The passion and spontaneity generated creates an almost irresistible rapport with customers. They sense that they can trust you and that it is safe for them to risk disclosing their deepest concerns. Communicating genuinely with no pretense allows for creative and innovative solutions that the exchange would be too awkward to allow under typical circumstances. The experience for the customer is in such sharp contrast to what they have had with your competitors—they feel so understood, they want to do business with you.

The benefits of long-term relationships with customers are obvious. It costs approximately five times as much to get a new customer as it does to keep an existing one. Repeat business is a hallmark of relationship selling. Another outgrowth of happy customers is referrals. "You can have as many customers as you want, but you have to take care of each one of them on an individual basis. Ninety percent of your new clients come from referrals from current clients who appreciate the job you have done" (Spector and McCarthy 1995). Referral sales are a leading indicator of your emotional bank account with your customers.

Carl Sewell, owner of Sewell Cadillac in Dallas and author of *Customers for Life*, told us a few years ago that he figures each one of his customers could potentially buy $322,000 worth of vehicles in his or her lifetime. He teaches his staff to treat each customer accordingly—even if they are buying a fifty-cent bolt, treat them as if it were a $332,000 bolt.

## REFERENCES

Alderson, W. 1965. *Marketing Behavior and Executive Action*. Homewood, Ill.: Richard D. Irwin.

Anderson, E., and B. A. Weitz. 1990. Determinants of Continuity in Conventional Industrial Channel Dyads. *Marketing Science* 8 (Fall): 310–323.

Anderson, E., L. M. Lodish, and B. A. Weitz. 1987. Resource Allocation Behavior in Conventional Channels. *Journal of Marketing Research* 24 (February): 85–97.

Anderson, J. C., and J. A. Narus. 1990. A Model of Distributor Firm and Manufacturer Firm Working Partnership. *Journal of Marketing* 54 (January): 42–58.

————. 1984. A Model of the Distributor's Perspective of Distributor–Manufacturer Working Relationships. *Journal of Marketing* 48 (Fall): 62–74.

Bagozzi, R. 1975. Marketing as Exchange. *Journal of Marketing* 39 (October): 32–39.

Biong, H., and F. Selnes. 1996. The Strategic Role of the Salesperson in Established Buyer–Seller Relationships. Working paper, report nos. 96–118. Marketing Science Institute, Cambridge, Mass.

Borys, B., and D. B. Jemison. 1989. Hybrid Arrangements as Strategic Alliances: Theoretical Issues in Organizational Combinations. *Academy of Management Review* 14 (February): 234–249.

Brewer, Geoffrey. 1996. The Best Sales Forces. *Sales and Marketing Management* (November): 38–42.

————. 1995. Best Sales Force Awards. *Sales and Marketing Management* (October): 53–54.

Buchanan, L. 1992. Vertical Trade Relationships: The Role of Dependence and Symmetry in Attaining Organizational Goals. *Journal of Marketing Research* 29 (February): 65–75.

Cohen, A. 1996. Best Sales Force Awards. *Sales and Marketing Management* (October): 56.

Covey, S. R. 1989. *The Seven Habits of Highly Effective People*. New York: Simon & Schuster.

Crosby, L. A., K. R. Evans, and D. Cowles. 1990. Relationship Quality in Services Selling: An Interpersonal Influence Perspective. *Journal of Marketing* 54 (July): 68–81.

Dahlstrom, R., K. M. McNeilly, and T. W. Speh. 1996. Buyer–Seller Relationships in the Procurement of Logistical Services. *Journal of the Academy of Marketing Science* 24 (Spring): 110–124.

Day, G. S., and R. Wensley. 1983. Marketing Theory with a Strategic Orientation. *Journal of Marketing* 47 (Fall): 79–89.

Doyle, S. X., and G. T. Roth. 1992. Selling and Sales Management in Action: The Use of Insight Coaching to Improve Relationship Selling. *Journal of Personal Selling and Sales Management* 12 (Winter): 59–64.

Dwyer, F. R., P. H. Schurr, and S. Oh. 1987. Developing Buyer–Seller Relationships. *Journal of Marketing* 51 (April): 11–27.

Emshwiller, J. R. 1991. Suppliers Struggle to Improve Quality as Big Firms Slash Their Vendor Rolls. *Wall Street Journal*, 16 August, B1–B2.

Frazier, G. L., R. E. Spekman, and C. R. O'Neal. 1988. Just-in-Time Exchange Relationships in Industrial Markets. *Journal of Marketing* 52 (October): 52–67.

Ganesan, S. 1994. Determinants of Long-Term Orientation in Buyer–Seller Relationships. *Journal of Marketing* 58 (April): 1–19.

Gronroos, C. 1994. From Marketing Mix to Relationship Marketing: Towards a Paradigm Shift in Marketing. *Management Decision* 32 (2): 4–20.

Hakansson, H., ed. 1982. *International Marketing and Purchasing of Industrial Goods: An Interaction Approach*. Chichester, U.K.: Wiley.

Hallen, L., J. Johanson, and N. Seyed-Mohamed. 1991. Interfirm Adaptation in Business Relationships. *Journal of Marketing* 55 (April): 29–37.

Hallen, L., N. Seyed-Mohamed, and J. Johanson. 1988. Adaptations in Business Relationships. In *Research Developments in International Marketing*, ed. P. W. Turnbull and S. J. Paliwoda. Proceedings of the 4th IMP Conference, IMP Group, Manchester, United Kingdom.

Han, S., and D. T. Wilson. 1993. Antecedents of Buyer Commitment to a Supplier: A Model of Structural Bonding and Social Bonding. Unpublished paper, Marketing Department, Pennsylvania State University, University Park.

Han, S., D. T. Wilson, and S. Dant. 1993. Buyer–Seller Relationships Today. *Industrial Marketing Management* 22 (4): 331–338.

Hardwick B., and D. Ford. 1986. Industrial Buyer Resources and Responsibilities and the Buyer–Seller Relationships. *Industrial Marketing and Purchasing* 1: 3–25.

Heide, J. B. 1994. Inter-Organizational Governance in Marketing Channels: Theoretical Perspectives on Forms and Antecedents. *Journal of Marketing* 58 (January): 71–85.

Heide, J. B., and G. John. 1990. Alliances in Industrial Purchasing: The Determinants of Joint Action in Buyer–Supplier Relationships. *Journal of Marketing Research* 27 (February): 24–36.

———. 1988. The Role of Dependence Balancing in Safeguarding Transaction-Specific Assets in Conventional Channels. *Journal of Marketing* 52 (January): 20–35.

Hunt, S. 1983. General Theories and the Fundamental Explananda of Marketing. *Journal of Marketing* 47 (Fall): 9–17.

Ingram, T. N. 1996. Relationship Selling: Moving from Rhetoric to Reality. *Mid-American Journal of Business* 11 (Spring): 5–13.

Jackson, B. B. 1985. *Winning and Keeping Industrial Customers: The Dynamics of Customer Relationships*. Lexington, Mass.: D. C. Heath.

Kalwani, M. U., and N. Narayandas. 1995. Long-Term Manufacturer–Supplier Relationships: Do They Pay Off for Supplier Firms? *Journal of Marketing* 59 (January): 1–16.

Kotler, P. 1972. A Generic Concept of Marketing. *Journal of Marketing* 36 (April): 46–54.

Lagace, R. R., R. Dahlstrom, and J. B. Gassenheimer. 1991. The Relevance of Ethical Salesperson Behavior on Relationship Quality: The Pharmaceutical Industry. *Journal of Personal Selling and Sales Management* 11 (Fall): 39–47.

Lucas, A. 1996. The Best Sales Forces. *Sales and Marketing Management* (November): 60–61.

Lyons, T. F., A. R. Krachenberg, and J. W. Henke, Jr. 1990. Mixed Motive Marriages: What's Next for Buyer–Supplier Relations. *Sloan Management Review* 31 (Spring): 29–36.

Macneil, I. R. 1981. Economic Analysis of Contractual Relations: Its Shortfalls and the Need for a "Rich Classificatory Apparatus." *Northwestern University Law Review* 75 (6): 1018–1063.

———. 1980. *The New Social Contract: An Inquiry into Modern Contractual Relations*. New Haven, Conn.: Yale University Press.

———. 1978. Contracts: Adjustment of Long-Term Economic Relations Under Classical, Neoclassical and Relational Contract Law. *Northwestern University Law Review* 72: 854–902.

Miller, R. B., and S. E. Heiman. 1987. *Conceptual Selling*. New York: Warner Books.

Milliman, R. E., and D. L. Fugate. 1988. Using Trust-Transference as a Persuasion Technique: An Empirical Field Investigation. *Journal of Personal Selling and Sales Management* 8 (August): 1–7.

Moorman, C., G. Zaltman, and R. Deshpande. 1992. Relationships between Providers and Users of Marketing Research: The Dynamics of Trust within and between Organizations. *Journal of Marketing Research* 29 (August): 314–329.

Morgan, R. M., and S. D. Hunt. 1994. The Commitment–Trust Theory of Relationship Marketing. *Journal of Marketing* 58 (July): 20–38.

Newman, R. G. 1988. Single Source Qualification. *Journal of Purchasing and Materials Management* 24 (Summer): 10–16.

Noordewier, T. G., G. John, and J. R. Nevin. 1990. Performance Outcomes of Purchasing Arrangements in Industrial Buyer–Vendor Relationships. *Journal of Marketing* 54 (October): 80–93.

O'Neal, C. R. 1989. JIT Procurement and Relationship Marketing. *Industrial Marketing Management* 18: 55–63.

Ring, P. S., and A. H. Van de Ven. 1994. Development Processes of Cooperative Interorganizational Relationships. *Academy of Management Review* 19 (1): 90–118.

Schurr, P. H., and J. L. Ozanne. 1985. Influences on Exchange Processes: Buyers' Preconceptions of a Seller's Trustworthiness and Bargaining Toughness. *Journal of Consumer Research* 11 (March): 939–953.

Shapiro, B. P. 1987. Specialties vs. Commodities: The Battle for Profit Margins. Working paper, Harvard Business School, Harvard University.

Spector, R., and P. D. McCarthy. 1995. *The Nordstrom Way: The Inside Story of America's #1 Customer Service Company*. New York: John Wiley & Sons.

Stigler, G. J. 1951. The Division of Labor Is Limited by the Extent of the Market. *Journal of Political Economy* 59 (3): 185–193.

Swan, J. E., F. I. Trawick, Jr., D. R. Rink, and J. J. Roberts. 1988. Measuring Dimensions of Purchaser Trust of Industrial Salespeople. *Journal of Personal Selling and Sales Management* 8 (May): 1–9.

Swan, J. E., and J. J. Nolan. 1985. Gaining Customer Trust: A Conceptual Guide for the Salesperson. *Journal of Personal Selling and Sales Management* 5 (November): 39–48.

Trevelen, M. 1987. Single Sourcing: A Management Tool for the Quality Supplier. *Journal of Purchasing and Materials Management* 23 (Spring): 19–24.

Vlosky, R. P., and D. T. Wilson. 1994. Technology Adoption in Channels. *Relationship Marketing: Theory Methods and Applications*, Conference Proceedings, Ed. J. N. Sheth and A. Parvatiyar, Center for Relationship Marketing, Emory University.

Webster, F. E., Jr. 1994. *Market-Driven Management: Using the New Marketing Concept to Create a Customer-Oriented Company*. New York: John Wiley & Sons.

———. 1992. The Changing Role of Marketing in the Corporation. *Journal of Marketing* 56 (October): 1–17.

Williamson, O. E. 1985. *The Economic Institutions of Capitalism*. New York: Free Press.

———. 1975. *Markets and Hierarchies: Analysis and Antitrust Implications*. New York: Free Press.

Wilson, D. T. 1995. An Integrated Model of Buyer–Seller Relationships. *Journal of the Academy of Marketing Science* 23 (Fall): 335–345.

Wilson, D. T., and V. Mummalaneni. 1986. Bonding and Commitment in Supplier Relationship: A Preliminary Conceptualization. *Industrial Marketing and Purchasing* 1 (3): 44–58.

Wilson, D. T., P. K. Soni, and M. O'Keeffe. 1995. Modeling Customer Retention as a Relationship Problem. Working paper no. 1995–13, Institute for the Study of Business Markets, Pennsylvania State University, University Park.

Yarbrough, J. F. 1996. The Best Sales Forces. *Sales and Marketing Management* (November): 46.

Chapter 3 ————————————————————

# Relationship Selling: New Challenges for Today's Sales Manager

Kenneth R. Evans, David J. Good,
and Theodore W. Hellman

Historically, the role of the sales manager was to direct the selling effort to achieve short-term (e.g., monthly, quarterly) sales results. Implicit in these types of environments is a tendency to focus on goods–services sales, and the types of sales management systems designed to accomplish these performance expectations. However, with the emerging emphasis on sales and marketing programs dedicated to customer solution strategies, the previous expectations of the field sales manager to direct and encourage short-term tactical behavior have assumed a longer-term, more integrated, strategic focus.

Transactional sales are evaluated and encouraged in single exchange contexts where buyers and sellers have become socialized to maximize single exchange situations. The impact of this socialization is illustrated through the constant emphasis on price discounting by sellers, the usage of excessive expense accounts to win over buyers, and an environment where effective selling means lower prices. These exchange contexts are often characterized as win versus lose. However, changing market conditions have challenged buyers and sellers to identify means to work toward integrated solutions, which often result in long-term relationships. These relational sales contexts require sellers to focus on the application of the goods and services as opposed to the transaction. The long-term objective of relational sales should be to assist the customer to succeed in the marketplace. The seller works with the buyer seeking to enable them to win in the market. While the opportunity exists to establish relational exchanges in a number of sales contexts, the management tools and conventional roles of sales managers are frequently not suited to these new strategic business challenges.

In today's markets, successful sellers have developed strategic and managerial practices that support both relational and transactional exchange contexts with buyers. Thus, the need exists to engage in behaviors with clients where customer relationships can be formed by focusing on customer problem solving, while simultaneously selling goods and services in markets where transactional demand persists. In this setting, the coexistence of multiple strategies (e.g., balancing the needs of large national accounts, and smaller, often single transaction accounts) commonly occurs.

While customers frequently must earn the privilege of being a relationship partner through high sales volume over time, what this may have to do with fitting strategies to customers' needs is tangential at best. In short, any field sales organization must address, if not integrate, selling practices dedicated to both transactional and relational market exchange contexts. Therefore, it is based on this premise that this article addresses—the challenge of structuring a sales organization that is capable of supporting both transactional and relational selling, as well as the requisite changes in sales management practice imposed by the integration of relationship selling. Paramount to this challenge, however, is understanding current practices of sales managers.

## SALES MANAGEMENT PRACTICES

Various market contexts dictate distinctive sales management practices. At one extreme are activities that permit focused sales behaviors, while at the other extreme are sales actions that concentrate on supporting problem-solving behaviors. However, conventional textbooks on sales management (e.g., Stanton, Buskirk, and Spiro 1995; Churchill, Ford, and Walker 1993) and common business practices focus predominantly to a large extent on tools reflective of transaction-oriented field sales forces. This focus includes the creation, motivation, and control of sales organizations with the intent of accomplishing specific short-term sales objectives. This is opposed to the design of optional supervision and rewards for a sales organization dedicated to solving customer problems, enabling customer success, and resourcing customer relationships. While limited work in team sales has sought to discover how sales organizations may design improved customer relationships, considerable development needs to take place both academically and in practice to identify characteristics and develop techniques for managing successful relationship sales strategies. Consequently, recognizing distinctions between relational and transactional selling is not only vital from the standpoint of meeting customer needs, but also in terms of the accountability of the sales staff, including its management.

Transactional activities are likely in discontinuous environments, or situations where the selling conditions are seen by buyers and/or sellers as one-time events. In this setting, customers typically have identified their needs, and as a result, they seek vendors with suitable product quality at acceptable prices. Based on this knowledge, the involvement and time of buyers in these purchase-related decisions is usually limited to assuring that the product meets specifications and negotiating the terms of sale. Satisfaction with the exchange is also determined by a single transaction, as opposed to a network of exchanges where contentment is derived from cumulative effects of past, present, and future transactions. Qualities of the exchange, such as commitment, transaction specific assets, and trust, may be of lesser importance in these short-term situations, where the product qualities and costs serve to determine the majority of seller satisfaction. Characteristic of business organizations that have transformed their sales operation from a transactional to a relational sales orientation is Procter and Gamble (P&G). Until the late 1980s, P&G's sales focus was on the design and implementation of transactional exchanges dedicated to increasing their sales, relying on very little input from clients. As such, the sales organization within P&G was fashioned to encourage and reward salespeople who engaged in these selling behaviors. To support these activities, P&G's structure was hierarchial in nature, aligned by geographical divisions. Consequently, this structure provided an excellent environment for high levels of control, with sales managers acting as inspectors, constantly focusing on calibrating individual performance.

Because multiple P&G divisions often serviced the same account under transactional selling, customers were prone to expedite transactions with any given P&G sales representative. As a result, buyers and P&G salespeople were conditioned to operate in this transactional, arms-length buying–selling environment, where sellers took orders and aggressively pursued shelf space, while buyers pushed for the lowest prices and sought the highest shelving allowances possible, such as in the form of vendor fees for premium shelf facing. Organizational structures that facilitated transactional selling strategy were built and supported, leading to an organizational and marketplace bias toward an exchange context that made it very difficult for the buyer and seller to work together to achieve mutual objectives.

In contrast, relationship selling represents collaborative efforts between buyers and sellers, where the interaction is designed to create added value from this synergy. The customer focus under P&G's transactional orientation was primarily price. To foster collaborative relationships, the exchange context was realigned, where the underlying purpose was to focus on dimensions that add value beyond price. In this relational setting, buyers and sellers strategically behave as though they are engaged in a long-term attachment, though the relationship does not have to be, nor is it essential that it be intended to be, long-term (e.g., when a firm purchases major capital equipment). Thus, the quality of the exchange originates from the added value obtained from the interaction between parties working together to achieve a collaborative objective. Consequently, relationship accountability, as opposed to transaction specific objectives, becomes the core focus of relational selling. Customer Business Development Teams now utilized by P&G are particularly congruent with this approach. These multifunctional teams are constructed with personnel from a variety of functional areas (e.g., logistics, systems, finance, or product supply) and organizational levels. What P&G has attempted to do is redesign its selling effort to coordinate with customer's business planning needs, and P&G sales efforts are mirror images of one another resulting in a seamless interface.

It is no less appropriate to attempt to develop extensive problem–solution strategies with clients desiring transactional exchange, rather than to focus on sales where more extensive solution strategies are warranted. In short, the "one-size-fits-all" approach to sales management must be expanded to provide for differentiation across assorted customer exchange contexts. As sellers seek to differentiate themselves among one another, it is imperative to adhere to legal constraints, such as protection against price discrimination (e.g., Robinson Patman Act). For instance, in the case of price, sellers are constrained from differentiating among customers of products of like grade and quality; thus, customized programs directed toward improving customer service and/or reducing operating costs can become very effective in establishing new performance standards for buyer–seller relationships. For many companies, relational selling has provided them with a means of establishing an enduring, meaningful, and truly distinctive differential advantage with key customers. Whatever approach a seller selects in servicing the market, it is important to match the seller's approach to the buyer's expectations. A relational approach with a transactional customer is no more effective than a transactional approach with a customer who has relational expectations.

## TRANSACTIONAL SELLING TOOLS IN A CHANGING ENVIRONMENT

In support of transactional selling, the *performance evaluations* of salespeople and sales managers tend to focus on narrowly defined time periods (e.g., monthly), with *compensation systems* having a major variable component (i.e., high in commissions and low in salary) (e.g., Anderson and Oliver 1987). Sales management tools also typically focus on *close supervision and exclusive control of sales behaviors*, with relatively short-term horizons. For instance, sales managers may schedule weekly meetings with salespeople to regularly discuss sales quota results.

Contrasting transactional strategies, and consistent with the emergence of relationship-oriented strategies, many of the sales management tools necessary to support this new orientation are not in place in many selling organizations. As a result, numerous transactional tools persist, or have been poorly adapted to support this new strategic focus. For example, managers may use weekly meetings to review short-term sales results, even when salespeople are expected to build and maintain long-term relationships with clients. In this environment, an orientation toward transactional selling is particularly troublesome when sales management tools serve to reinforce or motivate behaviors which are ill suited to the customer's needs (e.g., accelerating a decision when a long-term strategy is appropriate, or engaging in a lengthy customer needs analysis when an immediate purchase is desired). To some extent, these limitations in the development of sales management tools for relational sales forces are due to the lack of sufficient performance measures. For instance, a multimonth investment in diagnosing a potential customer's problem exhibits no bottom line sales performance. For this reason, transactional tools tend to receive continued emphasis due to the control features inherent in short-term quantitative performance measures.

It should be recognized that many firms seeking transition from a transactional to a relational marketing strategy are often harnessed with inadequate staffing and training to execute the desired strategy. It is imperative that an organizational commitment be made to organize and support a relational selling effort. For example, P&G's decision to utilize relational selling strategies was accompanied by many changes (e.g., the use of cross-functional marketing teams) that, in effect, realigned the firm. This restructuring was important to ensure that the organizational strategy was consistent with P&G's customer focus. This reorientation of the sales and marketing efforts of the firm requires extensive resource and strategic commitments, particularly when past behaviors and supporting tools have been designed for transactional exchanges with customers. The relational sales orientation, therefore, requires organizational structures, behavioral, and performance–reward systems that are in many ways inconsistent with the transactional exchange orientation.

However, in spite of the challenges deploying a relationship-oriented sales force, in many cases the benefits outweigh the managerial ambiguities. In this context, the purpose of the following section is to examine how the evolving role of sales managers have contributed to their more extensive strategic involvement in the marketing efforts of the firm.

## EVOLUTION OF STRATEGIC RESPONSIBILITIES IN SALES ORGANIZATIONS

As previously noted, field sales managers traditionally assumed tactical roles within their firms. However, the emergence of several key inter- and intraorganizational changes has refocused the field sales manager into a more strategic role. First, *financial pressures* have increasingly required executives above the field sales manager (e.g., director of sales or marketing manager) to become more versatile. As organizations continue to downsize, engineering human resources more precisely to satisfy marketplace conditions, marketers will have to expand their expertise beyond functional boundaries. This will cause sales executives to broaden their focus to include wider organizational issues (i.e., becoming cross-functional) beyond traditional sales functions. Yet, while executives continue to be responsible for sales output, by necessity (e.g., a lack of time and availability) they will increasingly be removed from specific decisions and activities involving sales personnel. Hence, pressures on executives to become more diverse directly places tension on field sales managers to become more strategically oriented.

Sellers and buyers have also found occasions when it is advantageous to transition from transactional attachments to more complex and potentially long-term attachments. For example, when P&G determined in the late 1980s that the number of retailers was becoming smaller and their buying and selling capacities were becoming larger, the need developed to create strategies that would more closely align this newly concentrated buyer capacity with P&G's offerings. As part of this strategy, it was determined that, despite the historically successful use of a transactional orientation, the need existed to create partnerships with these large-scale buyers, characterized by collaboration and codevelopment of P&G and the retailer's and wholesaler's strategies. Accordingly, because the nature of these relational attachments begins with identifying individual customer needs, it is necessary to motivate and empower local sellers to respond to client needs. Hence, the *engagement of customer relationships* is a strategic endeavor requiring decisions and commitments that reflect resource allocations and monitoring at the field sales level.

Adopting relational selling specifies a different set of opportunities supported through a broader array of organizational resources, changing the role of sales managers, and resulting in greater expectations of strategic formulation and execution among local managers. In the P&G example, the need existed to redirect how salespeople did business. Clients became integral in the design of collaborative strategies that sought to add value for the customer, while contributing to profitable sales for P&G. An example of this collaborative strategy is P&G's continuous inventory replenishment system, wherein P&G manages the stocked inventory for the retailer or wholesaler in certain high volume categories. In contrast with past practices, this system has increased customer product turnover by 20 to 30 percent, and inventory is often sold at the retail level before the client actually pays for it. The result of the program has been an increased appeal of P&G brands among resellers, even though many of these brands may sell at equal or higher prices than their competitors. Of course for this program to be successful, customers must allow P&G to have critical data on inventory levels, and trust that inventory replenishment would operate in the customer's best interest. The focus of this new business environment suggests that as clients and markets change, the strategic use of relationships by field sales managers must be facilitated by *the willingness of the marketing organization to make appropriate resource investments* that encourage relational linkages with customers. To illustrate the depth of commitments, factors that have become the strategic focus of relational selling are as follows:

• A selling orientation toward solutions, not products.

- Determining how value is established for buyers when the product is purchased.
- The development of smooth communication processes between buyers and sellers.
- A willingness to explore alternative solution criteria.
- The strategic construction of buyer trust.
- Ensuring reciprocal treatment.
- Creating commitment on the part of the supplier.
- Demanding transaction satisfaction for buyers and sellers.
- Having the buyer rely on supplier system for stability (Can I replace you, and still deliver the products of the same quality?).
- Making teams more valuable to the buyer, and individual sellers less key.

The current limited availability of control mechanisms that effectively assess the performance of relationship selling constrains the application and development of this strategy. In the case of P&G, a system is in place where key criteria are mutually agreed upon between P&G and the customer, which enable the customer to be successful in the marketplace. These criteria then serve as a score card against which performance of P&G and the customers are measured on a regular basis.

As markets continue to demand specific products to fit recurring needs, not all markets will demand a relationship focus. Accordingly, the key to successful sales management often rests with the ability to develop a *strategic equilibrium between transactional and relational sales opportunities*.

## TRANSACTIONAL AND RELATIONAL
## STRATEGIC EQUILIBRIUM

The simultaneity of transactional and relational strategies within sales organizations presents a situation where one strategic focus may overshadow the other, disrupting the balance required in the marketplace. For example, if transactional exchange activities produce 70 percent of the revenue in a sales district, the manager may allow this selling approach to be assigned disproportionate resources. Similarly, the manager's leadership style and the organizational climate of the branch office may also assume a transactional focus. Thus, while a sensible deployment of resources would seek to support the exchange condition demands (i.e., both transactional and relational), the predominance of one sales behavior tends to dictate the sales management culture of a given sales organization. The inertial qualities of familiar management tools and techniques are therefore likely to pervade in any organizational setting. Where a dominant role of transactional exchange does exist, challenges arise when this pervasive management orientation is misaligned with market needs.

Organizations designed for transactional selling may not be suited for relational strategies (Cravens 1995), so occasions arise where inter- and intraorganizational conflicts minimize selling effectiveness. For example, training, performance monitoring, assessing effectiveness, quota setting, and hiring practices of salespeople are likely to require different methods and processes, based on whether the environment is transactional or relational. Ingram (1996) addresses this problem when he notes those engaged in transactional selling focus on making customer contact, selling the product, closing the sale, and providing appropriate follow-up activities. In contrast, relational selling revolves around the salesperson initiating, developing, and enriching client relationships. The differences required of salespeople in these environments further emphasizes this issue, since about 80 percent of the importance in transactional selling is weighed toward overcoming the objections of customers and securing agreements to purchase. This can be compared to relational selling, where 80 percent of the selling is devoted to identifying client needs, codeveloping a joint business plan, and providing support, while matching seller abilities and buyer needs (Brooksbank 1995). Therefore, the lack of congruency between transactional and relational strategies and related organizational–management practices presents a number of unique management challenges, since it is difficult to freely interchange resources between transaction and relational sales organizations, even under conditions demanding both selling approaches.

## Relational and Transactional Selling: Organizational and Strategic Uniqueness

The dimensions of relational and transactional marketing and sales strategies offer unique conditions, often requiring a different set of processes, operating mechanisms, and control systems. The magnitude of these differences suggest they also require different personnel infrastructures, as aptitude, task, and management environments may not be compatible. For instance, to maximize overall strategic and operating effectiveness, transactional organizations are likely to be more horizontal and informal, with an emphasis on individual autonomy. In addition, relational sales organizations will focus on greater salesperson empowerment, higher levels of functional collaboration, and greater levels of customer-specific functional expertise.

The diversity resulting from implementing several strategies simultaneously within sales organizations creates environments of conflict and role ambiguity. If expectations are not explicit, salespeople may lack sufficient management direction regarding how to best invest their time with a client (e.g., building a relationship or creating immediate sales), which, in turn, fosters interorganizational conflict. Thus, as organizations assess opportunities for transactional and relational sales strategies, managers must also consider how these conditions contribute to role conflict and ambiguity within and across sales functions. For instance, should two sales organizations exist, or if not, where and under what conditions can they be joined? Such linkages might occur, for example, where "outside" salespeople and telemarketers work for the same organization, concentrating on different accounts. However, despite the uniqueness encouraged by these strategies, their implementation is greatly improved when each strategy advances or compliments the other.

Transactional selling as a complementary strategy suggests it is not "outdated," but an appropriate approach that can be properly balanced with relational strategies. Further, this balancing supports the differential marketing advantages of utilizing the proper exchange strategy at the appropriate time in contemporary markets, which in turn presents field sales managers with a daunting task. Hence, employing relational selling should not be an all or nothing decision, as transactional and relational selling should be used in cooperation and concert to enrich both strategies and environments.

In this setting, there remains a need to understand how managers and organizations can facilitate realignment of the sales function to incorporate relational exchange. That is, the predominance of organizations entertaining and/or incorporating relational sales strategies suggests there is a need to search for management tools that support relationship selling behavior in an environment dominated by transactional activities. Fortunately, existing management practices with national accounts may prove a source of reference and expertise in designing relational sales strategies.

## Previous Relational Selling Experiences: National Accounts

The strategic use of national accounts demonstrates opportunities to translate existing sales management tools used in relational contexts. For instance, when one customer produces disproportionately high revenue, the importance of this client frequently requires working closely over time with this buyer. In turn, for some organizations, this client may be assigned national account status.

To ensure the development of these types of relationships, selling organizations frequently have special internal systems designed to support these accounts. Facilitating mechanisms often include different types of compensation (e.g., salary with annual bonuses), measurement systems (e.g., group quotas that are based on the productivity of the entire selling team), and career paths (e.g., salespeople working with only one customer, requiring him or her to focus on building a strong relationship with this client). From these experiences, the internal mechanisms applied to national accounts may provide strategic directions to sales organizations interested in engaging in relational selling, while minimizing learning time required to align the sales force with the demands of a relational exchange environment. Concurrent with these experiences, it is also important to fully comprehend the impacts of utilizing relational strategies.

## CONSEQUENCES OF RELATIONAL SELLING

The realignment by sellers to incorporate a relational sales orientation can be expected to produce a number of key consequences (Dunn, Friar, and Thomas 1991) that are in part driven by the interrelationships that exist between the organization, training, employee selection, compensation, supervision, and evaluation in a sales force (Avionitis and Boyle 1989). The impact of this uniqueness is illustrated by the time and processes required for P&G to move from a transactional sales organization in the mid-1980s, to a relationship driven firm by the early 1990s. In a setting where upper management had the authority and resources necessary to engage in such changes, this transition took five years, many organizational, personnel, and structural changes, and an ongoing commitment to constantly revisit progress, before the adoption of relational selling could be considered fully implemented and begin to achieve potential. Therefore, the consequences of adopting relational selling includes rethinking specifically the roles of sales managers, sales organizations, and selling processes.

### Sales Managers

From the sales manager's perspective, it is important to assess under what conditions customer–seller attachments are appropriate for relational linkages. This strategic matching of relational and transactional selling to the appropriate account requires a *close working relationship between the sales manager and salesperson* accompanied by the *proper allocation of sales force resources* relative to the most effective exchange configuration. That is, managers must be able to determine what accounts are most likely relationship candidates, and in turn, support this decision with appropriate resources. Key to these issues is also the accompanying development and deployment of *performance measures* that permit sales managers to assess the relative impact of exchange activities of salespeople.

Coalitions that require relationship exchanges with the customer place *different demands on the sales and buying organizations* than transactional exchanges. For instance, sellers must be able to marshal cross-functional support from production, logistics, and customer service in the event that specific needs arise in a relational account. Often sales require team efforts where the salesperson serves as the team leader of a multifunctional sales group dedicated to diagnosing and solving a customer's needs.

Frequently the result of these buyer–seller relationships is the establishment of a *close bond between the customer and the firm's salesperson*. For instance, in recognition of the sensitivity of these close working relationships, IBM offers major accounts the opportunity to interview a number of IBM salespeople encouraging them to pick the one that best fits their preferred style of interaction. Salespeople in these close working relationships find themselves in the role of buyer advocates within the sales organization. The inherent danger in this salesperson juxtaposition is that sales personnel may become too closely aligned to buyers, losing sight of their long-term profitability objectives within their own organization.

Because of differences in the degree to which buyers and sellers are relationally attached (i.e., ranging from awareness, exploration, expansion, commitment, and dissolution [Dwyer, Schurr, and Oh 1987]), the sales manager must *structure field sales strategies that direct efforts toward the proper stage in the relationship.* For example, the level or stage of a client relationship can be used to dictate the type of selling contact a client receives. If a client is in the early or formative stages of a buyer–seller relationship, telemarketing might be the appropriate sales contact technique, since it is inexpensive, and allows wide market coverage in a short time with less skilled salespeople. As clients become positioned where opportunities develop to build relationships, this may be conducive to personal visits by salespeople. As relationships begin to experience deterioration (e.g., sellers can no longer secure key products), it may become strategically sound to engage direct marketing to retain existing but faltering clients as long as possible at a minimal cost.

The *role of salespeople may change* as they assume increasing responsibility, as the relationship manager (Crosby, Evans, and Cowles 1990) directing investment decisions, asking, for example, should we invest more resources in this buyer? Should we use more skilled sales staff that we can take the relationship to a new level? To meet new opportunities, sales managers will have to *invest more in salespeople* to ensure their continued professional growth. Concurrently, inherent in the design and execution of a relationship exchange strategy is concern over salesperson turnover. Efforts therefore need to *focus on salesperson retention*, including stock options, profit sharing, and other long-term incentives that align the reward system with long-term employment and performance, as opposed to the traditional transactional exchange reward models. Should a salesperson leave the sales organization, the potential exists that he or she could take his or her customer relationships and/or knowledge of the customer to a competitor. Through the use of team sales efforts and other client support services that extend beyond salesperson contact, sales managers will seek to design relationships with customers that insulate the customer relationship from salesperson turnover. However, the dilemma with this solution is that it may diffuse the effectiveness of the salesperson, and introduce the possibility of various efforts by the sales organization working at cross-purposes.

Another outgrowth of relational sales is sales managers will become *more coaching oriented*, reducing the "overseer" mentality sometimes possessed. This suggests the necessity of building relationships with clients that will extend attachments between salespeople and their managers, requiring intrafirm relationships similar to what is desired with customers.

The *training and development* of salespeople is also different under relationship selling. For instance, on-the-job training and sales coaching need to be structured to teach and reinforce how salespeople can develop relationships that will evolve into sales results. In contrast to previous training and development objectives, the focus will be on the long-term cultivation of accounts, attempting to bridge factors such as trust and commitment into sales opportunities.

The *career ladder* of salespeople and managers will also be impacted as the need escalates to match personal and professional qualities of salespeople to buyers in relationship-exchange environments. Salespeople with little interest in long-term associations and who have a need for short-term reinforcement are probably better suited for transactional accounts. In contrast, individuals who enjoy close-working client relationships and who are satisfied with intrinsic rewards might be more appropriately assigned to work with relationship accounts. For instance, at P&G, sales managers have become responsible for different clients under this structure. The need to foster client relationships has resulted in sales managers creating relational linkages directly with those client managers responsible for partnerships (e.g., CEOs), increasing the span of contact and authority of sales managers. Accordingly, sales managers are now part of a team representing their firm, and not just a supervisor of the selling effort. As such, job performance and job satisfaction can be expected to differ, based on the proper matching of strategic sales exchange focus and motivations of the sales staff.

## Sales Organizations

Given the variability in the relative benefit of establishing client relationships, *the mechanisms for assessing the value of the relational exchanges* are critical to this strategic venture. Hence, any assessment of relationship selling should begin with the understanding that in the short-term, the *initial costs may be disproportionate* to expected returns. These elevated costs may be the result of realigning selling processes, mechanisms, and structures to incorporate this strategy. However, these investments are necessary, and failure to anticipate these adjustments will likely lead to premature reductions in sales support, contributing to poor long-term results. Therefore, a major challenge of upper management is to identify the explicit nature, magnitude, and duration of these costs.

To evaluate the performance of relational accounts also calls for changes in *formal measures used to evaluate salespeople, managers, and organizations.* While relational performance measures are probably poor indicators (e.g., trust and commitment) of sales outcomes on a short-term basis, individual and group performance measures will be needed that extend beyond the historical quantitative values to include more difficult to measure qualitative factors (Dunn and Thomas 1986) that are crucial to sound relationships.

For example, the degree to which a salesperson can improve client satisfaction, or the extent to which a sales district has been able to build customer trust, may become key assessments. Thus, this will require changes in how firms evaluate return on investment (ROI), as well as other organizational functions (e.g., how cost accounting is performed). As part of this change, there will also be a need to balance various performance systems for salespeople and managers who share transactional and relational accounts.

Another organizational change involves the need to *integrate national accounts approaches* to relationship selling. Among firms already experienced with account management programs there will be opportunities to apply these principles in the broader relational exchange context. Accordingly, relational selling also encourages strategic coupling across business functions, often resulting in the need to form buyer–seller teams. These linkages are particularly useful in areas of product expertise that exceed the capacity of the salesperson to be an effective representative of the selling organization. For instance, since production engineers in buying and selling organizations may be connected to enhance communication effectiveness, sellers are turning with increased frequency to the use of teams to execute relational exchange with clients. Hence, the extensive use of multifunctional teams (e.g., P&G's teams are often composed of sales, product management, logistics, and systems personnel) can be designed to broaden the understanding of client needs. At P&G, these multifunctional teams view customers as trading partners, creating seamless, mirror linkages between the buyer and seller. In addition to more solid marketplace relationships, these teams lowered logistics costs, increased cash flow, and enriched information exchange between the parties. In turn, this created a repositioning of P&G, where it now focuses on the design and execution of strategies dedicated to assisting customers in succeeding in the marketplace.

The use of relational selling also has a number of consequences in terms of the *structure of the firm.* For example, relational selling strategies must be structured to allow salespeople and sales managers to locally manage account relationships, molding offerings around specific buyer requirements. As such, *salespeople need autonomy* to make decisions that are appropriate strategically to enhance relationships with buyers, and the long-term objectives of sellers.

From an organizational standpoint, it is also necessary that firms develop a *better understanding of the conditions under which relational marketing should occur.* For example, the past experiences of selling firms have resulted in sellers generally understanding the conditions, expectations, and needs of transactional types of selling and buying. Consequently, *knowledge grounded in data banks* must be developed concerning relational selling that can be interpreted to make better strategic decisions at the organizational and field levels.

The nature of costs derived from relational selling suggests a *broader arena for strategic planning purposes* than traditional transactional strategies may provide. For instance, it has been proposed that one method sellers can strategically use to develop better relationships with clients is to acquire knowledge about their customers. While this may provide sellers with a strategic advantage (Smith and Owens 1995), the resource investments required to support these activities certainly have to be considered as part of the decision process. To satisfy the investment costs and anticipated returns, buyers and sellers must be able to assess the relative value of entering into a relationship exchange. An analogy might be drawn from a social context, where the risks of an intimate relationship heightens vulnerability, as opposed to the lower risk involved in just companionship. This also can be illustrated in a business context by Mackay Envelopes, where the demonstration of awareness and sensitivity between partners is seen as a similar context to that which occurs in marriage (Mackay 1988).

The utilization of relational selling also requires the *ongoing commitment of both the seller and buyer*. Consequently, it is critical to establish relational bonds at the highest managerial levels in the buyer–seller organization. Developing relationships at the senior management level allows for a cascade effect where sellers are able to achieve full alignment with the buyer from top to bottom. These relationships in turn contribute to stronger intraorganizational bonds among buyers and sellers responsible for ongoing implementation of the relationship. Buyers must invest in these relationships as well. Many customers are called upon to invest time and other resources in the design of highly effective strategic relationships, particularly with key vendors.

When transactional and relational selling strategically coexist, *management must determine how these differences will be organizationally defined*. Will variances exist in sales organizations (e.g., two different organizations); control systems (e.g., separate objectives for each type of selling); management (e.g., managers specializing in one type of selling); and selling (e.g., salespeople only selling to relational accounts)? This may require a revisiting of the type of salespeople and managers employed in field and executive sales positions.

The extent of these consequences suggests the need for cultural changes within the organization. P&G discovered that some of their salespeople (including some of their better transactional performers) were inappropriately equipped to sell in relational environments. To meet the challenges of this new environment, changes in rewards and recognition, training, supervisory techniques, and objective setting had to be implemented as part of the new relational selling strategy. However, not all of these salespeople and managers could make the necessary adjustments to the new environment, resulting in turnover. Unfortunately, many of these people were excellent transactional performers who had an outstanding history of performance. However, from a positive perspective P&G had found a new way of cultivating long-term success, allowing remaining and new salespeople and managers opportunities to build more effective customer linkages.

## Selling Processes

Integration of relationship exchange as an element in the firm's strategic sales orientation also impacts selling processes. For example, under conditions of relational selling, the salesperson has broader responsibilities in dealing with accounts. Consequently, the balancing of activities within these accounts (relational versus other transactional accounts) requires different *support mechanisms*. Under these conditions, P&G has had to closely examine and restructure many of the processes used to prepare salespeople. To meet this challenge, P&G began emphasizing internships. Internships increase the likelihood of a long-term career match. Salespeople tend to get off to a faster start. It is this combination of career fit and early sales success that results in increased retention.

Also, salespeople are provided more freedom and empowerment in determining tactics, actions, and strategies, as the accompanying selling systems must allow for distinctiveness among relational accounts. Hence, salespeople and managers need to have *the authority to commit various resources* in an effort to attract and retain specific relational accounts (e.g., the ability to approve expenses on accounts).

The roles of the parties in these relational exchanges may also change, as *the buyers may act as sellers, and sellers act as buyers*. For instance, because the value of relationships will change, escalating in worth for some, and decreasing for others, buyers may have to assume the role of seeking out relationships, while sellers more closely evaluate and assess the worthiness of client attachments. Such experiences will require buyers and sellers to more responsibly assess what actually determines the value added by relationships, and in turn, to determine the worth of existing and potential attachments.

Also, requiring sales managers to be involved with strategic, long-term decisions within the framework of their immediate sales district or organization will change the processes used to establish marketing *forecasting*. Organizations that use "bottom up" forecasting processes will increasingly rely on the strategic decisions and assessments of local sales managers. Organizations that rely on "top down" forecasting will, in turn, have to be more inclusive of input from their field sales managers. In addition, while alternative forecasting techniques, such as scenario-based planning and panels of experts, may displace some of these traditional planning models, and the processes used to link activities with expected future conditions will be impacted through a commitment to relationship selling.

The need for clear and precise communication channels between sales managers and upper management needs to increase. *Effective communication processes* will clarify upper management's understanding of sales manager responsibilities regarding strategic activities and resource commitments relative to transactional and relational sales contexts. As an illustration of resource adjustment, P&G customers are now willing to reveal sensitive business data without the need to have legal counsel present. P&G attributes this freer exchange of information to its new strategic alignment with its customers, where the focus is on mutual development of the customer's business.

While it is difficult to assess the value of relationship-exchange customers, it is likely initial investments in these accounts may result in less than desirable returns. Thus, relational selling often requires a long-term strategic orientation that *trades off short-term performance*, requiring selling organizations to have processes that allow for the *measurement of success* consistent with the goals of relational selling. It is necessary therefore to have processes to weigh investments, returns, and opportunity costs (e.g., Would we be able to maintain this level of sales without a relational attachment?) within the relational framework. For example, at P&G the key to this approach rests with ensuring that continuity with the client is maintained. While this continuity can be obtained through a variety of mechanisms, their approach is to preserve the understanding of the customer by moving people to other assignments within the team. This broadening of the salesperson's exposure through intrateam reassignment allows individuals to advance their careers without disrupting customer–team continuity.

## FUTURE EXAMINATIONS

As many of the issues raised in this chapter attest, a number of questions remain as to how selling organizations can best adapt to different selling situations. Under what conditions can firms achieve an effective balance between transactional and relational strategies? Is it necessary to create independent sales cultures and/or organizations dedicated to relational and transactional sales, or can they coexist? For instance, how does the sales function interface with other functional units when it simultaneously executes transactional and relational strategies in the field? It would also be useful to determine what managerial, personal, and professional qualities are best suited to working in transactional and relational sales environments.

From a customer perspective, it would be beneficial to identify those factors that contribute to a client moving from transactional to a relational exchange with the seller. In turn, this would generate a number of related questions. For example, how are transactional customers converted into relational customers? What are the dangers of aggressively converting customers into relational accounts? When is it good business practice to retain a transactional strategy with select clients? What role should relational customers play in performance evaluation of the sales staff? How can selling organizations encourage customer input into performance evaluation processes, while maintaining objectivity among the field sales staff or teams?

While the need exists to empirically test many of the issues addressed in this article, this testing should not be limited to only the seller's or buyer's side of the dyad. That is, understanding the benefits of relationship strategies, as well as comprehending the balance of relational and transactional strategies, cannot be delimited to the context of only sellers and buyers. Given the two-sided nature of selling, particularly in relational sales, methodologies need to be employed that capture the buyer–seller dyad, where the relationship, as opposed to either the buyer or seller, is the unit of analysis.

## CONCLUSION

Relational selling may not be selected as the primary or even secondary strategy of choice. The impacts of the decision to incorporate relational selling needs to be weighed against the potential returns, financial and organizational investments, and the responsibilities encumbered by organizations, sales managers, and salespeople required for its implementation. Only careful consideration can determine the appropriateness of strategies, and the degree to which they should be implemented. For many sales managers, it may be necessary to ensure that relational and transactional strategies coexist in the same environment.

Should a firm seek to incorporate relational strategies, management must ensure that the necessary control mechanisms are in place to provide the philosophical, strategic, and operational direction of the firm, from salesperson upward. For instance, P&G's decision to utilize relationship selling to meet increased competition and to reduce costs fostered many changes throughout the organization. The new P&G team configuration is technically more complex from an internal organizational standpoint, but the primary benefit is that the customer views P&G as considerably less complex.

For many organizations, a focus on customer relationship strategies may be premature until sales management practices are properly aligned with the intended strategic orientation. Reliance on sales quotas that focus performance on short-term behaviors may be in direct conflict with long-term relationship objectives. Strategic realignment of the selling effort toward long-term customer relationships calls for a reexamination of common sales management tools such as sales quotas, compensation methods, and evaluation methods and measures to assure they are consistent with relational selling objectives of the firm.

In summary, the purpose of this article has been to address the impacts of relationship selling on the strategic role of sales managers in contemporary exchange environments. Faced with the challenge of balancing transactional and relational strategies, this chapter examines how sales organizations and field managers need to carefully assess the significant implications cultivated from relational selling, as well as encouraging their coexistence.

## REFERENCES

Anderson, E., and R. L. Oliver. 1987. Perspectives on Behavior-Based versus Outcome-Based Sales Force Control Systems. *Journal of Marketing* 51 (October): 76–88.

Avionitis, G. J., and K. A. Boyle. 1989. Linkages between Sales Management Tools and Practices: Some Evidence from British Companies. *Journal of the Academy of Marketing Science* 17 (Spring): 137–145.

Brooksbank, R. 1995. The New Model of Personal Selling: Micromarketing. *Journal of Personal Selling and Sales Management* 15 (Spring): 61–66.

Churchill, G. A., Jr., N. M. Ford, and O. C. Walker, Jr. 1993. *Sales Force Management*, 4th ed. Homewood, Ill.: Irwin.

Cravens, D. W. 1995. The Changing Role of the Sales Force. *Marketing Management* 4 (Fall): 49–57.

Crosby, L. A., K. R. Evans, and D. Cowles. 1990. Relationship Quality in Services Selling: An Interpersonal Influence Perspective. *Journal of Marketing* 54 (July): 68–81.

Dunn, D. T., Jr., J. H. Friar, and C. A. Thomas. 1991. An Approach to Selling High-Tech Solutions. *Industrial Marketing Management* 20: 149–159.

Dunn, D. T., Jr., and C. A. Thomas. 1986. Strategy for Systems Sellers: A Grid Approach. *Journal of Personal Selling and Sales Management* 6 (August): 1–10.

Dwyer, F. R., P. H. Schurr, and S. Oh. 1987. Developing Buyer–Seller Relationships. *Journal of Marketing* 51 (April): 11–27.

Ingram, T. N. 1996. Relationship Selling: Moving from Rhetoric to Reality. *Mid-American Journal of Business* 11 (Spring): 5–12.

Mackay, H. B. 1988. Humanize Your Selling Strategy. *Harvard Business Review* 17 (March–April): 36–47.

Smith, D. C., and J. P. Owens. 1995. Knowledge of Customers' Customers as a Basis of Sales Force Differentiation. *Journal of Personal Selling and Sales Management* 15 (Summer): 1–15.

Stanton, W., R. H. Buskirk, and R. L. Spiro. 1995. *Management of a Sales Force*. Chicago, Ill.: Richard D. Irwin.

# From Individualism to Teamwork

# Chapter 4

# Customer Relationship Strategy and Customer-Focused Teams

## Keith A. Chrzanowski and Thomas W. Leigh

Sales force decisions are increasingly strategic in nature. A "seachange" in buying strategies and processes of at least the more sophisticated customers has dictated a reevaluation of the strategic role of the sales force. As has been noted, "the world of selling must accommodate a dramatically changed world of buying . . . yet, all too often, sales forces are populated by dispirited Willy Lomans and managed by short-term oriented and narrow perspective executives" (Shapiro, Slywotsky, and Doyle 1994, 1).

As firms become more marketing-driven, the nature and quality of the sales forces' relationship with customers is stressed. Market-driven firms systematically segment their customers in terms of how customers *prefer to buy and relate to their suppliers*. This is an elegantly simple notion; yet it is quite complex in terms of its sales force design and application implications. Customers seemingly vary in their supplier relationship preferences, along a continuum from purely transactional to highly collaborative (Anderson and Narus 1991; Wotruba 1993). Moreover, there are many exchange variations along this continuum. Hence, the traditional, or "generalist," selling model is no longer adequate, either in terms of its customer value delivery or its cost-effectiveness. The sales generalist, who calls on all customers and prospects, sells all products, and manages all tasks in the selling process, suffers competitive disadvantages of scope, focus, expertise, effort, and time resources relative to the "specialized" selling models employed by market-driven firms.

The emphasis in market-driven firms is on customizing strategic selling approaches to fit the buying processes and relationship requirements of targeted customer segments or even individual accounts. In our view, this is a dramatic shift in the organizational role of the sales force. In essence, *customer relationship strategy*, or the *general set of targeted customer segments and attendant strategic selling models required to effectively and efficiently build competitive advantage in these segments*, literally becomes a "boardroom topic" (Shapiro, Slywotsky, and Doyle 1994, 1). Customer access and relationship considerations become part and parcel of both strategic and marketing plans, rather than the tactical domain of field sales management. Sales force issues influence market entry, product development, customer segment prioritization, marketing campaign, and channel selection decisions. Sales force competencies are considered to be a core corporate asset to be selectively nourished and leveraged.

Our purpose in this chapter is to explore this notion of customer relationship strategy in the context of the health care industry. We risk preaching to the choir to some degree. However, our sense is that health care, with its simultaneous emphasis on value-added patient care and cost control, is a vanguard industry. Our specific focus is on the distribution business of Allegiance Healthcare Inc. (until recently a division of Baxter Inc.). During the 1990s, the business model for this firm was radically reconfigured in an attempt to cope with the political and marketplace emphasis on managed care. This required rethinking the division's strategic direction, with particular emphasis on customer segmentation, customer relationship strategy, selling models and processes, organizational structure, sales force role and culture, salesperson knowledge and mindset, and reward systems. Particularly important to this new strategic thrust was the emphasis on strategic partnership accounts and the employment of customer-focused teams as the customer relationship approach. We will stress these particular issues in our discussion. However, it is important to remember that Allegiance is representative of a firm that moved from a generalist to a "hybrid" selling model as it attempted to serve multiple customer segments. Hence, we will initially overview the changing health care environment, especially the emergence of managed care, as a context for these changes in customer relationship strategy.

## HEALTH CARE INDUSTRY CHALLENGES

The dilemma in health care is to balance quality care for patients, cost of service delivery, and patient access to care. The relative rank of these imperatives has changed over time. *Technical quality*, in terms of product-based medical solutions, was dominant in the 1960s. *Access* to medical care was aggressively expanded, largely through government spending programs, in the 1970s. Rapid growth in health care expenditures in the 1980s led to *cost reimbursement capitation* and a focus on the specific costs of medical applications. At the risk of oversimplifying, the products of medical science spawned patient demand and challenged the economic and political systems' capacity to pay.

*Managed care* is an approach aimed at simultaneously providing quality patient care, broadened distribution, and reasonable cost. While the jawboning of the Clinton administration provided the immediate stimulus for public pressure for health care change, rapid advancements in the private sector quickly outpaced the political channel. In essence, the health care costs facing large firms (such as Ford or Exxon), as well as the government's Medicare and Medicaid programs, motivated health care providers (including pharmaceutical firms, hospitals, physician practices, distributors, drug retailers, and insurance companies) to adopt managed care as a business model. From Allegiance Healthcare's perspective as the leading medical supply distributor, managed care meant a shift away from selling product-solutions on a transactional basis. A more strategic partnership orientation was indicated. Managed care is in essence the adoption of an administered, rather than a market-based, solution to the health care dilemma of simultaneously providing quality, access, and low cost. In business terms, it requires a focus on the entire health care delivery system, or supply chain, in the belief that optimal health care solutions can only be approached through the collaborative efforts of all players in the health care delivery system.

The business implications for Allegiance are summarized in Figure 4.1. The essence of the new paradigm is the emphasis on total quality management and total delivered cost instead of the purchase price of a product itself. From a supply chain perspective, the transactional business model ignores a variety of costs, notably purchasing (and sales call time), receiving, inventory, space, handling, paperwork, processing, leakage, and so forth. These costs may account for as much as 50 percent of the revenue dollar spent on

**Figure 4.1**
**Implications of Changing Healthcare Models from Allegiance's Perspective**

| Transactional Business Model | | Managed Care Business Model |
|---|---|---|
| Revenue Focused | ⟶ | Capitation/Cost Focused |
| Provider Driven | ⟶ | Payor Driven |
| Nationally Focused Programs | ⟶ | Regional/Community Focused Initiatives |
| Purchase Volume Incentives/Rebates | ⟶ | Managed Cost Shared Risk/Reward Partnerships |
| Transactional Focus | ⟶ | Total Delivered Cost Focus |

patient solutions. The promise of managed care is that cooperative exchanges will yield quality patient care while reducing many of these supply chain costs. For example, a simple transactional exchange for a heart catheter would involve negotiations between a supplier salesperson and a buyer or purchasing committee. Once a price per catheter is negotiated, an order would be delivered to the hospital. The hospital would be responsible at that point for a variety of activities, including receiving, stocking, processing, distributing, accounting, financing, and disposing. Moreover, the hospital is responsible for designing its management, information, and distribution systems on its own. The human time costs, expertise costs, and financial costs of doing so can be considerable (i.e., as much as 50% of the patient revenue dollar).

Managed care solutions directly target these supply chain costs. The belief is that joint actions of the manufacturer, distributor, and hospital will yield novel business applications and lower systemwide costs. Moreover, these benefits will be shared by the partners. For example, cooperative efforts by Allegiance and a cardiology hospital might yield a just-in-time, paperless, and accurate delivery system that reliably satisfies physician and patient medical care practice needs with minimal transactions, inventory, or accounting costs. Each party would benefit from the systemwide savings according to prior agreement. Each party is thereby motivated to share information, expertise, ideas, and time to benefit the partnership.

It is important to note that similar changes are occurring in a variety of industries. In terms of supply chain perspectives, a hospital can be thought of, metaphorically, as Wal-Mart or Kroger. Alternatively, it could be a simile for a shopping mall, with specialty stores and general service areas. Hence, the category management issues that package goods companies (i.e., Procter & Gamble and Lever Bros.) face in selling to Wal-Mart and Kroger are analogous to the paradigm shift faced by Allegiance. Similarly, the challenges presented to Black & Decker in marketing DeWalt Industrial Tools through Home Depot and Loew's favor a partnership perspective. Thus, the lessons to be learned from Allegiance's experiences are quite general.

## THE TRANSACTIONAL BUSINESS MODEL

The transactional business model for Allegiance's healthcare distribution division included the following elements:

- Very broad product line of more than 100,000 items.
- Products and services offered to all customers, regardless of size or purchase commitment.
- Customers were shielded from manufacturer's price increases to protect existing business positions.
- Large investment in inventory to benefit clients, including the full range of high and low demand products.

- Regional distribution system to maximize service and availability to customers.
- Liberal financial and services payment schedule.
- Sales force organization according to product specialty and geography.
- Revenue generation focus in terms of regional goals and compensation systems.

This business model fit the health care industry requirements of the 1960–1980s, with its particular emphasis on product-focused solutions. The sales force was organized by product specialty, within geography (see Figure 4.2). This sales force structure places a premium on product expertise. Sales personnel are literally product-solution specialists who are relied upon by physicians, nurses, pharmacists, and lab technicians for their product and service expertise. Sales personnel establish personal relationships with customers on a department-by-department basis. This selling approach is rewarded by the customer as long as quality solutions are the top priority. For example, the health care system in the 1960s rewarded high quality patient care for those who could afford to pay (the wealthy or insured). Similarly, the 1970s rewarded firms that provided solutions because "health care is everyone's right" at whatever cost, and so the salesperson who provides expert patient solutions was valued. Of course, firms such as Allegiance rewarded these expert salespeople handsomely. Sales personnel were compensated based on the revenue and gross profit dollars they generated. Sales personnel who developed their product expertise, cultivated hospital department relationships, allocated their time and effort to priority accounts, and limited their territory expenses (car and entertainment), earned six-figure incomes. Moreover, their hospital customers appreciated them for their product-solution expertise and personal

**Figure 4.2**
**Geo-Product Type Organization Structure**

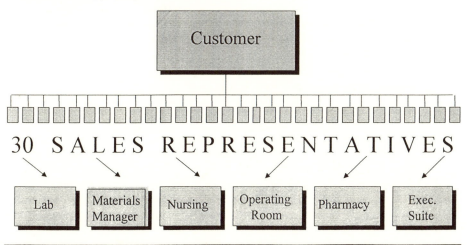

qualities, with only limited regard for cost. Senior sales personnel, who were compensated on a full commission basis based on territory gross profit dollars, earned between $100,000 and $250,000 annually.

This 1980s sales force model relied heavily on regional vice presidents for leadership and management. Regional vice presidents were in charge of the field sales force, distribution, and manufacturing. Coordinating with the Corporate Sales and Marketing Group in Chicago was required to adequately serve multihospital systems that cut across regional sales territory boundaries. Regional vice presidents received annual management objectives (MBOs) and operating targets from divisional headquarters. Their goal was to "marry up" the corporate mission and financial goals with the regional action plans to drive success. Literally, the regional vice president had to be able to lead the field team to a consensus plan and generate acceptance of individual performance goals and contributions. While regional vice presidents varied in their leadership styles from the very numbers-oriented to the very people-oriented, considerable direct supervision, coaching, and personal motivational support was required to ensure that territorial performance objectives were met.

The rising importance placed on cost controls, especially through the capped reimbursement system and radical changes in how hospitals made buying decisions as they moved to apply managed care principles, pressured the profit margins of distributors, such as Allegiance, Stuarts, and Owens and Minor. Hospitals increasingly established formularies, elevated the role and status of purchasing, provided their own product analysis and expertise, carried fewer product lines, and restricted salesperson access to key department personnel such as physicians and nurses. Moreover, the number and importance of multihospital systems increased as managed care companies expanded and merged. Finally, as purchases of medical products and supplies were centralized, the focus of decision-makers shifted from scientific and product-solution issues to a total health care systems perspective. The generalist selling paradigm, with its emphasis on product expertise, personal relationships with key hospital department professionals, and revenue-based targets and rewards was no longer functional in light of these changes. At the organizational level, this was signaled by declining pretax rates of return as low as 5 percent and the negative returns suffered by the typical medical distributor. Clearly, a new marketing and selling system was in order.

## THE NEW MANAGED CARE PARADIGM

Maintaining leadership among medical product and supply distributors required a radical transformation of the Allegiance Healthcare business model. This transformation incorporated many of the considerations suggested for firms to "become more market driven" (Webster 1994; Day 1992). Particularly important, given our sales force perspective, are the following strategic elements:

- Segment the market according to customer buying models, processes, requirements, and managed care sophistication.
- Profile specific hospital accounts according to their customer relationship preferences and capabilities along the transactional to collaborative continuum.
- Developing product and service bundles to fit key market segments and provide "best value" choices to selected customers.
- Adopt a total supply chain focus and partnership approach with selected suppliers in order to cut inventory, selling, paper and processing costs, and so forth.
- Establish "cost-plus" or "listless" pricing agreements where indicated.
- Develop a customer relationship strategy that recognizes the varying selling model requirements of transactional, relationship, and collaborative accounts.
- In particular, develop a customer-focused team selling model to develop competitive advantage with collaborative accounts.
- Tighten pricing and compliance with service fee and financing agreements to cut investment costs.
- Align Allegiance and customer organizational structures, processes, and systems to emphasize shared reward and risk payoffs.
- Avoid overinvesting in service and selling activities with transactional accounts.

The common theme in this strategic shift is the belief that more and more health care business will flow through managed care enterprises; hence, the winning distributors will be those who learn how to provide enterprise solutions, collaborate with suppliers and customers, and align organizational knowledge assets, processes, and resources to these partnership requirements.

Our subsequent discussion will emphasize the new customer segmentation model, the characteristics of the customer relationship strategy typology, the general and specific selling models indicated by these segments and account priorities, the customer-focused team model specified for collaborative accounts, the strategic human resources systems, and process requirements to implement these new selling approaches. Throughout we will articulate the practical issues encountered as the organization adapted over a five-year time horizon.

## SEGMENTING THE HOSPITAL BUSINESS

Market segmentation emphasized strategic considerations relevant to the industry evolution toward the managed care business model. Hospitals and their management teams varied considerably in (1) their degree of managed care sophistication, commitment, and capabilities; (2) their sophistication and leadership in developing integrated health care systems and processes; (3) their understanding and acceptance of partnerships (or win–win) versus transactional (or adversarial) orientations toward suppliers; (4) their willingness to adopt new buying and operating strategies and processes, especially those related to a total cost versus purchase-price focus; and, (5) their present and potential financial viability in terms of share or "lives" covered, profitability, and financial strength. Allegiance Healthcare's penetration of these segments and accounts varied considerably as well due to the "generalist" selling strategy previously noted.

The segmentation scheme developed by grouping specific accounts according to these criteria is presented in Table 4.1. The five emergent segments vary along the transactional to collaborative relationship continuum (Anderson and Narus 1991). *Strategic partners* are leaders in the managed care and strategic partnership movement. They are tough customers, but are sophisticated in taking a total health care system and business management orientation. Because they are leaders and have high penetration levels in their

**Table 4.1**
**Hospital Segmentation Scheme**

| Customer Attribute | Collaborative ← | |
| | Strategic Partners | Emerging Partners |
| --- | --- | --- |
| • Managed care sophistication and commitment | Leaders in integrated health system or merger movement | EDI & process oriented |
| • Progressiveness and commitment to health care systems | Leading edge players of the future | Open to adopt; uses value link (or prime vendor) |
| • Acceptance of and capability to conduct partnership strategies (win-win exchanges) | Fully committed & capable; demonstrated partners | Partnership oriented (may not be ready) |
| • Adoption of total delivered cost versus purchase price orientation | Total supply chain cost focus | Service and value oriented (still price sensitive) |
| • Progressive management and purchasing decision making (top to bottom) | Very progressive | Recognizes need but requires operational guidance |
| • Financial viability | High or potentially high | High potential & financially sound |
| • Baxter penetration and current position | High penetration | Low to medium penetration; value Baxter resources |

own markets (often nationwide), they are the core customers for firms such as Allegiance Healthcare. They are collaborative in orientation and business practices.

*Emerging partners* and *potential partners* are the hospitals that will likely adopt collaborative approaches as the industry evolves. In fact, educating these accounts is facilitated when distinctions are noticed in the business models of their strategic partner competitors. These firms are early adopters among hospitals; however, they require considerable education and coaching. Emerging partners are more partnership oriented and knowledgeable than potential partners. Potential partners are lacking full commitment to a primary distribution supplier. A key distinction is that emerging partners need to

**Table 4.1** (*continued*)

| Potential Partners | Contract Customers | Transactional Base Customers |
|---|---|---|
| Customers strategy is not clearly articulated (worried) | Unsophisticated in market orientation and operations | Little interest or understanding (usually small rural facilities) |
| Management looking for guidance | Requires a lot of service and attention | Patient Solution Oriented |
| Uncommitted or lacking full commitment to primary distribution suppliers | Prefers multiple suppliers & Market-based purchasing (contract oriented) | Not loyal |
| Service and price oriented | Product & price oriented; usually transactional | Prefers bidding process (often government institution) |
| No clear champion of managed care practices | Purchasing off divisional contracts | Price-driven |
| Medium to high Potential (financially surviving) | Low to medium potential | Low to high potential |
| Medium penetration | Low to medium penetration | Low to high penetration |

learn how to develop and implement collaborative relationships, whereas potential partners required that top management be educated as to the general nature and possibilities offered through partnerships. Potential partners do not have champions supporting the adoption of managed care. While Allegiance penetration in these accounts in each case is low-to-medium, emerging partners are generally high priority accounts and potential partners are only selectively high priority on an account-by-account basis.

*Contract* and *base* customers are relatively unsophisticated transactional hospitals. They are relatively unaware of health care environmental pressures, or feel they are insulated from them in their local markets. Contract customers require a lot of service and attention, especially to specific department decision-makers. They play suppliers against each other to cut product purchase prices. Base customers are price sensitive and are not loyal. They often use a formal bidding process. Generating a profit in these segments requires careful attention to service resource investments and tight expense controls.

Recognition that hospitals varied considerably in their customer relationship orientations, supply chain and health care systems sophistication, distribution and sales securing expectations or requirements, and financial viability forced Allegiance to reconsider its strategic priorities and resource investments. The strategic choice is between focusing on one segment and developing a narrow customer relationship model, or cultivating a "portfolio" of customer relationship segments, each with its own customer relationship strategy, or selling model (Anderson and Narus 1991). Given the current base of business in all five segments, the portfolio model seemed prudent. However, greater emphasis was to be placed on the more collaborative customers in the belief that this was the health care model of the future, and that this is how Allegiance's resources could be most profitably employed. Allegiance Healthcare's leadership position in distribution systems, service delivery, and sales force expertise would provide competitive advantage in the collaborative segments.

## CUSTOMER RELATIONSHIP STRATEGIES
## AND PROGRAMS

Managing a customer relationship strategy that covers the full range of collaborative-to-transactional customers is difficult. Segment and account-within-segment priorities must be clearly articulated to, and accepted by, key personnel (especially sales personnel). The key elements of the customer relationship strategy by customer segment are summarized in Table 4.2. *Strategic partners* are the strategic priority, with a goal of penetrating and differentiating the business and selling model to achieve 100-percent customer satisfaction and joint profit improvement. The "One Allegiance" customer-focused team concept is the core strategic element in order to develop collaboration with clients on a strategic, operational, systems, and key personnel relationship basis. These customer-focused teams are assigned the best people available, with an emphasis on technical and business knowledge, creativity, flexibility, and customer service orientation. Customer-focused teams are fully staffed from top to bottom to match up with client buying groups and requirements. Full investment of resources is intended as a basis for developing cutting-edge health care solutions and a leadership position.

*Emerging partners* are also high priority, as these are the hospitals that are likely to emulate their strategic partner peers in the future. These accounts will receive full attention of customer-focused teams to support rapid adoption of leading edge health care systems and solutions. The strategy is to use recognized sales force experts to creatively guide and coach these emerging partners to full strategic partnership status. Intensive service and resource investments here are indicated to achieve 100-percent customer satisfaction and mutual profitability.

*Potential partners* are those which, while they share many organizational attributes with strategic and emerging partners, are not yet "believers" in the collaborative model. Hence, longer-term education and account development are the key strategic issues. These accounts will be assigned senior salespersons who will focus on building top-to-bottom relationships and coaching top executives as to market trends concerning partnership approaches, the total cost orientation, and Allegiance Healthcare's evolving capabilities. These senior account executives are asked to be judicious in servicing these accounts, to improve profit margins and cut expenses where possible, and to improve the product mix. These accounts may be reassigned to an account team if they adopt a more collaborative orientation.

*Contract* customers are low priority, but are potentially profitable accounts *if service mix and resource allocation investments* are appropriately managed. Essentially, the goal is to retain the more profitable accounts while selectively reducing costs overall. In particular, the distribution strategy is to be deemphasized in favor of a manufacturer strategy (i.e., products manufactured by Allegiance are to be stressed for their slightly higher gross margins). Over time, some accounts in this segment will likely be lost due to Allegiance's *relative* lack of attention and investment. The existing sales territory system can adequately manage these customers.

*Base* customers are the transactional customers who emphasize competitive bids, product pricing, and being "open-to-buy." These customers are low priority and will receive minimum resource investments. However, while the goal is to redeploy resources from this segment to the others, the need is to gradually and professionally do so. In particular, many accounts may be profitably shifted to the network sales system (i.e., call 1–800 to place an order or schedule a personal sales call). Corporate products are to be stressed and financial agreements enforced to maximize gross margins. Again, many of these accounts may be switched to regional distributors as Allegiance reduces resource support.

**Table 4.2**
**Customer Relationship Strategy by Customer Segment**

| Customer Relationship Strategy Characteristics | Collaborative ← | |
| | Strategic Partners | Emerging Partners |
| --- | --- | --- |
| • Strategic priority | • Highest priority (Maintain; penetrate; differentiate) | • Second priority (penetrate/enable) |
| • Partnership focus | • Establish cutting edge hospital | • Provide cutting edge solutions & education |
| • Selling approach | • Customer-focused team (Baxter One concept) | • Full team complement as needed to support customer development |
| • Relationship strategies & investments | • Build relationships at all management levels | • Open all doors; develop coaches in key influence areas |
| | • Joint strategic planning | • Develop specific account plan for each customer |
| | • Set mutual goals & profit targets | • Focus on total cost strategy & move toward mutual goal measurement |
| | • Assign best sales people and invest resources | • Tenured team leaders with technical expertise assigned by account |
| | • Assign field account administrator & FSR coverage | • Dedicated service reps; full EDI linkages. |
| | • Use knowledge, creativity, service, and flexibility as value-added | • Creativity & education is key; service & flexibility are important |
| | • Manage the Churn strategy | • Work with customer to meet their goals; improve profit where possible |
| | • Implement full EDI Link | |
| | • Achieve 100% customer satisfaction | • Validate customer requirements and achieve 100% satisfaction |

## CUSTOMER-FOCUSED SALES TEAMS

The transition to the new distribution paradigm for Allegiance Healthcare was complicated by the need for multiple selling models. In particular, the new distribution paradigm required the design and development of a customer-focused team selling model to fit the requirements of the more collaborative customers. As we will see, the transition from a generalist sales force approach was neither immediate nor easy.

The customer-focused team strategy was called "One Allegiance." The fundamental element of the strategy involved forming organization-to-organization, or "wall-to-wall," relationships with strategic partner accounts. The "One Allegiance" approach involved four sales strategy elements: focus on meet-

| | | Transactional |
|---|---|---|
| Potential<br>Partners | Contract<br>Customers | Base<br>Customers |
| • Solid Account<br>  (Selectively invest & protect) | • Potentially profitable with tight<br>  resource controls | • High risk accounts |
| • Educate and coach key<br>  executives as to possibilities | • Provide education concerning<br>  market trends & competition | • Professionally limit resources |
| • Assign account manager to<br>  manage resource commitments | • Assign account manager<br>  (territory model) | • Stress network sales system where<br>  possible |
| • Build personal relationship in the<br>  departments | • Focus on executive suite to direct<br>  account behavior | • Provide professional rationale for<br>  minimizing |
| • Review customer strategy<br>  regularly for changes | • Monitor customer periodically for<br>  strategy changes | • Communicate reasons for service<br>  selectivity |
| • Improve account profitability &<br>  cash flow | • Reduce expense base where possible | • Minimize investments |
| • Assign experienced account<br>  managers | • Assign experienced or junior sales<br>  personnel | • Stress call 1-800 for account sales<br>  call |
| • Be cautious about over-servicing | • De-emphasize distribution strategy,<br>  focus on manufacturing strategy | • Focus on DSO, DIOH, and other<br>  systems |
| • Education regarding Baxter<br>  capabilities is key | • Consider strategic distribution | • Focus on corporate manufactured<br>  products |
| • Work with customer to refine<br>  their goals | • Be sensitive to MHS issues | • Enforce terms & financial agreement |
| • Retain customer & satisfy key<br>  requirements | | • Maintain Baxter reputation for<br>  professionalism |

ing a wide variety of customer service and product needs; the adoption of a consultative selling strategy focused on total supply chain solutions and cost savings; the employment of customer-focused teams to provide the full range of expertise and service needed to provide total system solutions; and, a shift from a divisional to a customer-oriented regional organizational structure. At the same time, top management stressed decentralization of the entire sales force structure, elimination of at least two levels in the reporting hierarchy, and improvement in organizational responsiveness to customer requirements and requests. The intended outcome was a customer-focused organization in which each and every employee was committed to customer satisfaction and cost efficiency. The goal was to meet and exceed customer requirements.

## CUSTOMER-FOCUSED TEAM STRUCTURES AND ROLES

The customer-focused team structure is presented in Figure 4.3. The lead executive is the *Customer and Account Manager*. Account managers are the business managers in their market or region. They manage the relationships with strategic partner, emerging partner, and potential partner accounts in their region, including accountability for revenue generation, resource investments and costs, and customer satisfaction. They are accountable for profitability as measured in an "economic value-added" sense. Because account managers have several customers, a key strategic concern is allocating team resources among the specific hospitals in the customer-focused team's regional portfolio.

Given the new decentralized and streamlined organizational structure, account managers are strategic-level in responsibility. They report directly to the Vice President of Sales and Marketing and are only one step removed

**Figure 4.3**
**The "One Allegiance" Customer-Focused Team Structure**

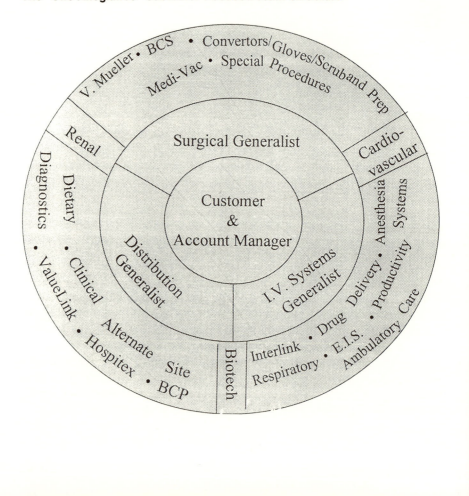

from the Regional or Divisional President. Hence, strategic thinking ability, planning skills, organizational knowledge and political skills, business management experience in marketing, operations, distribution, and finance, and leadership skills and enthusiasm are required for executives seeking to fill these new roles. However, sales skills are also critical. Account managers are responsible for developing relationships with the hospital, especially at the executive suite level. They spend about 70 percent of their time in front of customers. Moreover, they facilitate sales team product specialists in their direct selling roles. Hence, sales expertise in the sense of problem-solving ability, creativity, product-solution knowledge, reliability, and selling skills is also a high priority. As we will see, many previously exceptional sales people did not successfully meet the requirements for this new role.

Account Managers have direct and indirect responsibility for a variety of team members. Key direct reports include the Sales Generalists, Surgical Generalists, Distribution or Order Fulfillment Generalists, and I.V. (Intravenous) Systems Generalists. Other team personnel include Product Specialists and Field Service Representatives (FSRs). We will describe each of these team roles briefly below. It is important to recognize that these teams were not fully dedicated to a specific account. Given the multiple selling model approach, the regional nature of most hospitals, and the need to use sales team personnel as cost efficiently as possible, most sales team members served a variety of customers and reported to several account managers. The complexity of these reporting structures lengthened the amount of time involved for teams to mature in their customer service capabilities.

*Sales generalists* served to integrate the Allegiance product offering and the services of supporting specialist organizations into system solution. The sales generalist is literally the sales conduit for the "One Allegiance" system. The sales generalist is responsible for relationship management and lead generation with the major departments in the hospital (materials management, operating room, pharmacy, and catheterization lab). The sales generalist has direct sales responsibility for "best value products" (BVP), medical–surgical products, best value lab products, preferred supplier products, admission kits, and distribution services. Given these integrative responsibilities, sales generalists are vital in assisting the account manager in controlling key profitability drivers such as product mix, margin management, pricing integrity, service contract compliance, and customer satisfaction. Sales generalists were also responsible for "best value product" standardization agreements, and for managing the supply pipeline for Allegiance products shipped indirectly through alternate distributors to customer-focused (CF) team customers. Clearly, sales generalists are the key "solution" salespeople on the account; account managers must learn to rely and trust sales generalists in order to focus on the strategic issues of relevance to top management at the hospital.

*Surgical generalists* have primary responsibility for Allegiance Custom Sterile (ACS) sales and maintenance. They develop and manage relationships with key operating room and surgical service department decision-makers. They coordinate the customer service representatives and materials management personnel in ensuring customer satisfaction with ACS products and service agreements. Open communication and coordination among account manager and other team members is a key aspect of the surgical generalist role.

*I.V. systems generalists* are the product and service managers of the I.V. business. They coordinate I.V. contracts, service, and pricing for Allegiance Healthcare and Baxter Healthcare Division products (as part of the divestiture, Allegiance remains a prime distributor of Baxter Healthcare products). They are responsible for value-added product and service selling. They serve as the drug delivery specialist for the pharmacy department. They are charged with maximizing customer responsiveness and improvements in client performance results. Communications and coordination with account team members is critical to ensuring customer satisfaction.

*Distribution or order fulfillment generalists* are responsible for all key distribution service requirements, including appropriate fill rates, invoice accuracy, breadth and depth of product line offerings, flexibility in meeting client needs, and customer responsiveness. In addition, distribution generalists are responsible for value-added service systems such as quality-enhanced distribution (QED), procedure-based distribution systems (PBDS), and Value Link. Finally, distribution generalists are specifically responsible for the clinical laboratory and medical–surgery disciplines. Distribution sales reps are critical in supporting the efforts of the customer-focused team in its efforts to provide a seamless solution for the customer.

A variety of *product specialists* (renal, cardiovascular, and biotech) provide specific product expertise for both Allegiance and Baxter Healthcare products. These product "experts" develop, provide, and coordinate customer in-service training programs, and also directly provide systems implementation expertise, as well as diagnose and communicate specific customer technical needs and speciality product requirements for the entire CF team. They serve a variety of account teams on a need basis.

*Field service representatives (FSRs)* are primarily responsible for order–problem resolution, including back order problems, identifying substitute products to fit patient applications, shipping error problem resolution, and return goods disposition. They are also responsible for accounts receivable management to ensure payment terms are met and account receivable "aging" dollars are at prescribed minimums. They facilitate accurate pricing by acting as a gatekeeper between the sales organization and central contracts. Finally, they coordinate the new and lost business process and customer product standardization.

## HUMAN RESOURCE STRATEGIES AND PROGRAMS

The human resource implications of the managing customer relations (MCR) paradigm were considerable. In the first place, it was imperative that all employees understand the need for the new MCR strategy and their particular role in its achievement. Achieving commitment to change on a personal basis was the focus of early human resource programs. These early sessions stressed communicating the vision for the new partnering approach and involving employees in setting the agenda for change (Larson and LaFasto 1989).

Second, the fact that the sales organizational structure was to be *customer-within-region* had important personnel and reporting implications for employees. In particular, the use of regional account-based teams meant a shift away from revenue production by individuals to sales team efforts, new jobs for new and tenured employees alike, new reporting relationships and expectations, expanded job responsibilities for most employees, new knowledge and skill sets, and a new "shared value" system focused on customer satisfaction. Educating and coaching employees was the key to align their efforts with the intended strategy.

Third, the MCR paradigm required the adoption of a new 7-Step Selling Process (see Figure 4.4). This new MCR selling process places considerable emphasis on diagnosing and profiling hospital accounts for an appropriate "fit" with the customer relationships strategy model. Once an account is suitably classified into one of the five customer types, a detailed account strategy and plan could be developed and presented to the customer. For collaborative customers, this account plan would be jointly negotiated from a "solution"

**Figure 4.4**
**The 7-Step Managing Customer Relations Selling Process**

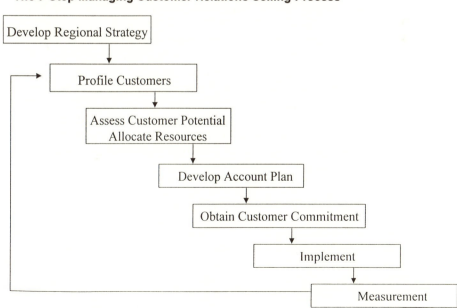

and "total delivered cost" perspective. A key aspect of this agreement was the service bundle promised, service expectation levels, and customer-focused team roles and responsibilities throughout the hospital. For these relationship accounts, defining a mutual interest in the ongoing partnership was the key to value enhancement and shared cost reductions.

Acceptance of this new selling process required education and training. More important, sales personnel had to feel comfortable that these changes were necessary. While the firm understood how difficult it would be for some salespersons to adapt their selling approach and style, it was clear that willingness to change was the crucial issue for most sales personnel. The MCR model also created new service-level expectations for key customers, new pricing models and responsibilities, and increased decision-making authority for sales teams and geographic sales personnel. These changes required the adoption of new "mindsets" and values by both sales and service personnel alike.

Finally, the new MCR system presented significant measurement challenges. Periodic business reviews were required for customers and account teams. Clearly, measures beyond revenue and gross profit were necessary. Business reviews involve evaluating the status of the account in light of segmentation profiling, account relationship status, customer satisfaction, and profit–cost position. These data points are essential for account prioritization, sales force strategy and effort, and service resource investments. In addition, the employment of customer-focused teams required the development of team performance measurement systems and standards. Financial targets based on revenue and/or gross profit dollar production were inadequate given the new focus on customer satisfaction, cost control, and selective resource investments in customer services. Moreover, individual contributions to team and regional goals needed to be recognized and rewarded.

In the interest of brevity, our review of the human resource strategies and programs will highlight six areas: (1) the problems of building commitment to the collaborative model; (2) the collaborative leader program; (3) core competencies of the sales force; (4) knowledge and skill development programs; (5) performance management and 360° feedback process; and (6) the MCR compensation systems for the sales force. These human resource strategies and programs represent the major steps in a process of change. We will conclude with a brief overview of transitional issues and outcomes of this organizational change process.

### Establishing Commitment to the MCR Model

A major issue in achieving an organizational transformation of the degree indicated in the MCR model is the commitment of leaders and employees to the vision itself. As Larson and LaFasto (1989) note, effective leaders (1) establish a clear and elevating vision of the future; (2) articulate and demonstrate an agenda for change; and (3) unleash the energy and talents of team members. In a sense, this is a continuing process; such is the case with the transition to the MCR model. The sequence of formal change events to date has included (1) a paradigm breaking program to establish the partnering vision; (2) a "getting connected" program designed to build the collaborative structure and capacity to work in teams; (3) the continued use of task forces and programs to institutionalize the partnership discipline in daily practices; and (4) the availability of home office and regional human resource managers as "free agents" to support account managers and teams as necessary. At this point, the key requirement is staying focused on the customer and maintaining openness of communication among the team members.

The setting event for the organizational change process was a five-day program entitled "Partnering: Creating Customers for Life," developed in conjunction with Pecos River Learning Centers. The purpose of this program was to establish the reality of partnering as the health care industry's and the firm's future. Over a period of time, twenty-five hundred sales personnel completed this program. A series of experiential exercises were designed to involve participants in the process of defining the vision, establishing an agenda for change, and providing them with a forum to suggest strategies, action programs, and tools for change. For example, all salespersons completed a prework guide designed to help them profile their customers according to the transactional, consultative, or partnership format. Specific exercises were designed to facilitate learning for key partnering processes, including prioritizing customer accounts for partnerships; strategic questioning sequences to use in conversations with "executive suite" hospital personnel; methods for conducting a value-chain analysis; and approaches for negotiating mutual goals and service agreements in a partnership context. A variety of process-oriented tools were presented to enable sales personnel to develop specific account plans for implementation upon return to the field.

The second phase of the change process was a program entitled "Getting Connected." The purpose of this seminar was to build the capabilities of the sales force in collaborating with customers and teammates alike. Again, through a series of nine seminars lasting nine hours each, all sales personnel were trained in collaborative problem-solving skills. The Connect Model© (Larson and LaFasto, forthcoming) was designed to teach the collaborative process of surfacing and resolving team issues while minimizing the chances of eroding team relationships and effectiveness.

Current programs focus on reinforcing the partnership model, with particular emphasis in the organizational and personal issues involved in working collaboratively. A variety of task forces have been established to examine organizational structure, systems and processes, the partnering culture, and training and facilitation programs. According to Frank LaFasto, Corporate Vice President of Organizational Effectiveness, "everything starts with the goal . . . but the key to success is the discipline of working collaboratively on a day-to-day basis" (personal communication, June 4, 1997).

## Collaborative Team Leadership

The current initiative in collaboration focuses on team leadership. Based on principles identified by Larson and LaFasto (1989), a collaborative team leader instrument was developed as a diagnostic tool. Six general leadership principles were targeted: (1) ensuring a collaborative climate ("Does our team leader create a safe climate for team members to openly and supportively discuss any issue related to the team success?"); (2) focus on the goal ("Does our leader articulate our team's goal in a clear and inspiring way?"); (3) building confidence ("Does our team leader build the self-confidence and enthusiasm of team members?"); (4) demonstrate sufficient technical knowledge ("Does our team leader understand the technical issues we face in achieving our goal?"); (5) setting priorities ("Does our team leader keep our team focused on a manageable set of priorities?"); and (6) managing team performance ("Does our team leader effectively manage performance issues within our team?"). These leadership characteristics are operationally measured by multi-item scales (Larson and LaFasto 1996).

The collaborative team leader instrument is used as a diagnostic feedback tool for account managers. Self-assessment using the instrument is a vital part of the leadership development process. To facilitate the development of collaborative leadership skills, account managers are brought together for a collaborative team leader seminar. Specific workshops and role-plays are designed to exemplify effective team leader practices. Human resource personnel are available for individual account manager coaching and feedback concerning collaborative leadership processes.

## Core Competencies of the Sales Force

The shift to the MCR model required a reconceptualization of the core competencies of the sales force. For *transactional selling*, regular call patterns, scripted or organized selling presentations, price negotiating skills, and closing tactics are key success factors. For *solution selling*, core skills include product and application knowledge, expertise in diagnostic selling, as well as process skills in relationship management, service excellence, customer satisfaction, and competitive analysis. However, *strategic partner selling* involves a fundamental shift to strategic thinking, customer orientation, and organizational focus. Sales personnel, particularly account managers, must think strategically about: (1) what the nature of the relationship with a strategic customer should be; (2) how to build and advance this relationship; and (3) how resources can be most productively employed to satisfy strategic partnership goals. In partnership contexts, transactions and solutions support the strategic partnership. Thus, while product and solution-selling knowledge are important in collaborative selling, their role and thrust are more strategic in nature.

In light of these multiple selling models, the transition to the MCR model required (1) the development of a set of core competencies, particularly for the account manager and sales generalist roles; (2) evaluations of the current competency and developmental potential of the present staff for filling the new MCR roles; and (3) helping employees manage their transitions to their new individual and team roles. A key issue in this change process was how to source the account manager role. Given the team leadership role required, it was not obvious how many previously lead salespeople would be willing and able to adapt to this new role. As it turns out, many salespeople did not successfully make the transition.

The core competencies for the MCR selling model are presented in Table 4.3. Each core competency is identified by a set of three or four behavioral roots or anchors. These behavioral roots facilitate understanding and role clarity, provide a clear basis for evaluating employee competency and potential, signal developmental needs and programming requirements, and provide a basis for the 360° performance feedback system. It is important to note that these competencies are more consistent with executive roles than they are with field-selling roles. Hence, account manager roles could be sourced with executives from a variety of organizational backgrounds. Specific selling skills could be developed through field training and coaching.

To identify candidates for the various account roles, employees were evaluated on the core competencies as well as a related set of specific functional competencies. This evaluation process was tough because the individuals under review were almost universally successful in the older selling paradigm. Salespeople and functional department employees were evaluated in terms of their current and future promotability (i.e., clearly promotable at that time; ready for an expanded role at same level; exceptional performer in current role; solid contributor and development potential; not a good match for company requirements; or not performing satisfactorily). This process yielded a set of candidates for the selling team roles (about 50 percent of the sales personnel who applied for the account manager roles were selected).

### Knowledge and Skill Development Programs

Specific human resource training programs targeted five key positions: account managers, sales generalists, lab specialists, field service representatives, and customer service representatives. These courses had two purposes: (1) to lay a foundation for change, so that key team members would be capable and willing to change and learn; and (2) to provide a sound conceptual grounding for understanding the organizational changes and the fundamental skills required. In essence, cognitive knowledge concerning new roles (i.e., know what and know how) as well as the rationale and motivation for change (i.e., know why and care why) (Quinn, Anderson, and Finkelstein 1996) were targeted. To illustrate this training, we will briefly review the account man-

**Table 4.3**
**Core Competencies for the Collaborative Selling Model**

| Core Competency | Sample Behavior Roots |
|---|---|
| 1. Business acumen | • Regularly stresses financial implications of actions/decisions. <br>• Demonstrates awareness of how strategies and tactics work in the marketplace. <br>• Assesses the implications of decisions on other components of the organization (financial, business, market customer, people, etc.). |
| 2. Customer focus | • Puts customer first. <br>• Anticipates future customer needs and wants and works to provide products, systems and services to meet their needs and expectations. <br>• Actively listens to and communicates with customers. |
| 3. Flexibility and adaptability | • Actively seeks new ideas, approaches and processes to create an environment that challenges the status quo. <br>• Makes effective decisions in uncertain conditions. <br>• Maintains effectiveness under changing circumstances and priorities. |
| 4. Interpersonal skills | • Initiates open and appropriate communication with management, peers, staff, and others in the organization. <br>• Is candid and honest in expressing thoughts and ideas while remaining sensitive to others. <br>• Demonstrates an appreciation of people from different backgrounds, cultures and viewpoints. |
| 5. Leadership | • Conceptualizes a vision for area of responsibility and develops strategies to achieve the vision. <br>• Takes ownership for actions and results. <br>• Initiates action without being asked to do so. <br>• Selects, develops and empowers others to achieve goals. |

6. Learning application
- Continuously seeks knowledge and applies to new situations (life-long learner).
- Assimilates data, identifies and analyzes complex conceptual/technical issues.
- Identifies and evaluates innovative/creative alternatives and realistic solutions to problems.
- Weighs the impact of a decision through the use of knowledge and expertise; takes appropriate calculated risks.

7. Maturity
- Reflects and learns from past mistakes and still takes risks in the future.
- Channels time and energy into areas one can impact versus general areas of concern (circle of influence versus circle of concern).
- Demonstrates good judgment and appropriate business conduct (common sense and good manners).

8. Process orientation
- Demonstrates organizational skills by completing multiple projects simultaneously.
- Mobilizes and effectively utilizes resources (people, funding, materials, support, time) to accomplish goals.
- Continuously seeks ways to improve processes and meet customer requirements.

9. Results orientation
- Achieves the results she/he committed to accomplish.
- Monitors progress of self and others and redirects efforts when goals are not being met.
- Understands and balances short-term and long-term impact of decisions and actions.
- Recognizes the difference between effort and results.

10. Teamwork
- Works collaboratively with others as both a member and a leader.
- Provides constructive feedback to others.
- Builds feeling of inclusiveness for all team members.
- Works effectively in situations involving shared accountability and responsibility.

ager and sales generalist programs. It is important to recognize that organizational change of the degree indicated by the new MCR strategy requires several years of field experience for true collaboration to develop among account managers and their teams.

The training curricula shared a common focus in the MCR process. Core business knowledge topics common to all programs included finance for profit, managed cost essentials, distribution fundamentals, and corporate contracts. Account managers received an extra day on pricing issues. Subsequently, the account manager program stressed leadership and business management skills, including consultative selling (2 days), account team leadership essentials (2 days), managing self and others through change (1.5 days), influencing customer behaviors (1 day) and interviewing skills (0.5 day). The account manager program was capped by product training (1 day), advance sales presentation skills (1 day), and account planning and profitability (1 day). The total program length of fourteen days, and the significant financial investment in training, signaled the importance of the new company vision.

Following the general MCR business knowledge topics, the sales generalist curriculum stressed product specialty knowledge. Surgical products and services were stressed for almost a week. Attention was also paid to understanding the decision influences and processes of key hospital departments. Leadership and selling skills concluded the program, including team excellence (1 day); managing the self through change (1 day); and facilitating customer negotiations (1 day). Sales presentation and computer skills (one day each) capped the program.

All employees received training to facilitate the transaction to the MCR and team-based structure. In every case, about a week was invested explaining the MCR strategy, process, and rationale. The latter part of each program stressed specific knowledge, skills, and attitude (KSAs) relevant to each team role.

### Performance Management and the 360° Feedback Process

The collaborative selling and team-based model required a major change in the performance management system. The central elements of the new performance evaluation process are (1) focus on the "shared values" of the firm as expressed in the customer relationship model; (2) the employment of a multisource, or 360°, feedback model; and, (3) agreement among participants, as both giver and recipient of feedback, that customer, salesperson, and organizational development are enhanced through open and honest dialogue. To ensure the integrity and confidentiality of the multisource feedback process, an external firm was employed to manage the process.

To implement the performance evaluation system, all employees were oriented to the purpose, process, and procedures involved. In particular, employee roles as feedback givers and recipients were targeted. As feedback givers, employees were asked to "provide open and honest feedback concerning performance relevant to the shared values of the firm" (i.e., respect, responsiveness, and results). Consistent with the notion of 360° feedback, employees evaluated their bosses, their peers, and themselves. As feedback recipients (the tough side of the process), employees were asked to support the "shared values" culture, champion the multisource feedback process, exhibit openness to feedback, and take responsibility for developing and acting on a personal development plan for each feedback cycle. The fact that developmental programs, succession planning, and opportunities for personal advancement are built into the annual performance planning cycle is critical for employee acceptance of this role in the process.

The 360° feedback instrument measures the "shared values" of the firm in terms of the following: (1) respect (integrity and respect for individuals); (2) responsiveness (quality, teamwork, empowerment, and innovation); and (3) results (accountability, results orientation, performance standards, and vision). Each shared value is measured in terms of behaviorally oriented scales (five-point scales, anchored by "applies to a very great extent" and "applies to a very limited extent"). Sample items are presented in Table 4.4. To supplement these scale ratings, open-ended feedback is collected by asking employees to describe "one thing the individual does well" and "one thing the individual should do differently," in terms of respect, responsiveness, and results. These feedback summaries are collected once per year as a basis for performance appraisal and developmental planning.

**Table 4.4**
**Sample 360° Feedback Instrument Measures**

| Shared Value | Illustrative Survey Items |
|---|---|
| A) Respect: | |
| • Integrity | A1) Behaves honestly and ethically in all business situations. |
| • Respect for individuals | A4) Develops relationships that are characterized by trust. |
| | A8) Encourages others to develop their skills and abilities. |
| | A11) Accepts feedback openly and non-defensively. |
| B) Responsiveness: | |
| • Quality | B1) Demonstrates commitment to meeting or exceeding customer. |
| • Teamwork | B4) Solicits input from others in solving problems requirements and making decisions. |
| • Empowerment | B8) Gives others the freedom they need to do their jobs. |
| • Innovation | B11) Coaches others as needed on how to get the job done. |
| C) Results | |
| • Accountability | C1) Holds others accountable for the results of their actions. |
| • Results Orientation | C4) Sets high personal standards for his/her own performance. |
| • Sets Performance Standards | C8) Creates a clear vision based on the firm's business strategy. |
| • Vision/Long Term | C11) Demonstrates long-term strategic thinking beyond the current plan year. |

## Sales Compensation

Reconsideration of the compensation system focused on three questions: (1) What can the firm afford to pay?; (2) What is the market value of individuals with the competencies required to fill the account manager and team roles?; and (3) What behavior does the firm wish to provide incentive for? These compensation questions arise as a direct consequence of the recognized need to downsize the organization and cut selling expenses relative to the industry, while at the same time facilitating the organization's transition to the team-based partnership selling model.

Selling expenses were recognized to be out of line with the industry. A major issue was the direct expense per distribution salesperson and account manager, which averaged over $125,000 and $175,000 respectively. The commission-driven sales model was not as relevant in a contract and partnership selling environment. Hence, while meeting customer requirements with the new customer relationship model was the first priority, cutting selling expenses by at least 20 percent was also targeted. To do this, the current field sales force structure was downsized (by approximately 20 percent in head count), compensation pools were reduced and several sales administration positions were eliminated (sales directors, V.P. Sales, and secretaries). A field sales administrator (FSR) was added to each sales territory to enhance management of customer services (DSO, credits, back orders, and pricing administration). In essence, customer responsiveness and the interface between account managers and distribution teams was enhanced as the sales force was downsized.

Establishing the market value of key personnel required for the customer relationship strategy required an industry benchmarking study. This was conducted internally by examining comparable positions of the new selling roles at other firms. The overall conclusion was that compensation levels were in excess of 125 percent of industry norms.

The team-based partnership selling model itself presented several compensation challenges. First, each team member had a distinct role to play in the customer relationship process. Hence, different compensation mixes were required to provide suitable incentives to encourage each team member to meet the particular requirements of his or her role. Second, the benefits of the new partnership selling model, in particular providing total business solutions, finding ways to cut costs for both parties, and maximizing customer satisfaction, were best realized through teamwork. Hence, the compensation system required team-based incentives. Third, to encourage individuals to excel in their roles, especially the generalist and lab representatives, the compensation system needed a variable portion (i.e., commission) and allowances for "upside" earnings beyond established quotas. Last, the compensation system had to be linked to specific performance measures, including financial targets such as revenue, gross profit dollars, economic value added, receivable turnover, product margin and mix, and cost controls. As the customer relationship strategy model suggests, rationalizing selling and service models to fit customer requirements is intended to enhance both customer satisfaction and financial performance. The conundrum in partnership selling is achieving win–win outcomes for both parties.

The account manager has a compensation mix that is 80 percent fixed and 20 percent variable. The variable portion is a team-based bonus based on the degree to which the team achieved its financial targets. As was mentioned earlier, 360° feedback evaluations and customer satisfaction results drive increases in the fixed portion over time (i.e., merit salary increases). The team bonus portion is intended to keep the account manager focused on executive suite relationship and team leadership, rather than specific solution selling and product mix initiatives.

The sales generalist's compensation mix is 40 percent fixed, 30 percent variable, based on territory performance, and 30 percent variable, based on team performance. To encourage individual motivation and excellence, sales generalists have additional upside earnings potential in excess of the performance standard equated to 100 percent compensation. The fixed salary and team portions of the compensation plan operate similarly to the account manager system. The variable territory performance is heavily influenced by economic value-added to encourage product mix, margin management, and cost control consistent with the account profile matrix.

Surgical and laboratory representatives are compensated in similar proportions to the sales generalists (40% fixed, 30% variable, 30% team, and significant upside potential). However, the variable portion is focused more specifically on revenue generation, gross profit dollars, product margins, and account receivables management (days of sales outstanding). A major problem in the older sales paradigm was the overinvestment in financing customer inventories and receivables float.

Field service representatives are rewarded with 90 percent fixed salary and 10 percent variable. The salary portion is designed to focus the FSR on customer service. Increases in salary from year to year are based heavily on customer satisfaction and team evaluations relevant to service delivery requirements. The 10-percent bonus was based on direct contribution in driving DSO credits.

This compensation system is relatively complex, though it in no way reflects the inherent complexity involved in the customer relationship strategy and collaborative team operations. Clearly, the major factors driving success in partnership selling are commitment to the values of the partnership sales culture and the account manager's ability to function as a collaborative leader. The compensation system is designed to align sales personnel to their team roles and reinforce the values of the collaborative selling model. The specific compensation elements and proportions are continuously reevaluated as MCR selling process evolves.

## CONCLUSION

Transition to the customer relationship strategy (MCR) model extended over several years. Several internal and external issues and outcomes deserve attention. Downsizing through attrition helped to minimize morale problems. However, a "survivor effect" was noted, that is, for survivors, the "work does not go away"; therefore, they felt somewhat pressed to add to what already were considered taxing responsibilities.

A related issue involved team development. Regardless of the amount of formal training in partnering and collaborative team decision making, it takes time for account managers and their teams to gel. For Dave Wietecha, previously experienced as a sales representative and regional manager, the team leadership and development process continued for almost three years. This is an indication of how much learning and experience is required to realize team capabilities and comfort levels. In fact, many successful salespeople under the old system did not adapt to the new collaborative team environment. Learning to sell collaboratively is a major challenge for all involved.

Several customer issues arose during the transitional process. Most important, Allegiance found that its partnership strategy was almost too far in front of most of the customer base. Hence, while Allegiance was correct in the sense of driving change in the industry, some visibility was lost in the marketplace. For collaborative customers, the amount of education required concerning the partnership vision was underestimated. On the other hand, the more transactional accounts received too little attention and education. This is a fundamental problem in balancing multiple customer segments and selling models.

A second issue involved inconsistencies in approaching and managing relationships with large collaborative accounts. The team selling model empowered teams to make many decisions they had not previously made. This unleashed a tidal wave of innovation in value-added services and cost reduction programs, as was intended. However, inconsistencies in the service offerings occurred among multihospital chains, as well as among competing hospital groups. These inconsistencies lessened as the teams stabilized and learned to work collaboratively.

Financial performance of Allegiance Healthcare over the transition period improved measurably in terms of sales growth, contribution margins, day sales outstanding, and inventory turnover. Stock market performance for Allegiance Healthcare has been strong. The customer relationship strategy, partnership selling approaches, and customer-focused teams are given substantial credit for these enhanced results.

## ACKNOWLEDGMENTS

We would like to thank David Wietecha, Boston Scientific (formerly account manager at Baxter Healthcare), Mark Vuturo, Regional Vice President of Operations, Frank M. S. LaFasto, Corporate Vice President of Organizational Effectiveness, William A. Donan, Corporate Vice President, and Allegiance Healthcare Inc., for their insights concerning the customer relationship strategy transition at Allegiance Healthcare Inc.

## REFERENCES

Anderson, J. C., and J. A. Narus. 1991. Partnering as a Focused Market Strategy. *California Management Review* 33 (3): 95–113.

Day, G. S. 1992. *Market-Driven Strategy: Process for Creating Value*. New York: Free Press.

Larson, C. E., and F. M. J. LaFasto. Forthcoming. Working draft of book in process.

———. 1996. *The Collaborative Team Leader Scale*. Deerfield, Ill.: Allegiance Healthcare.

———. 1989. *Teamwork: What Must Go Right/What Can Go Wrong*. Thousand Oaks, Calif.: Sage Publications.

Quinn, J. B., P. Anderson, and S. Finkelstein. 1996. Managing Professional Intellect: Making the Most of the Best. *Harvard Business Review* (March–April): 71–80.

Shapiro, B. P., A. J. Slywotsky, and S. X. Doyle. 1994. Strategic Sales Management: A Boardroom Issue. Boston, Mass.: Harvard Business School, Case # 9–595–018, 1–23.

Webster, F. E., Jr. 1994. *Market-Driven Management*. New York: John Wiley & Sons.

Wotruba, T. R. 1993. The Evolution of Personal Selling. *Journal of Personal Selling and Sales Management* 11 (3): 1–12.

# Chapter 5

# Strategic Account Strategies

Lawrence B. Chonko
and Herbert F. Burnap

Decades ago, a relationship between a sales organization and a buying organization might have been described as a series of "muggings," in which the buyer sought a relationship by mugging sellers to offer rock-bottom prices. Several events changed this notion of buyer–seller relationships. First, the Arab oil embargo of 1973 resulted in the top management of buying organizations expressing much more concern about the nature of supplier relationships. The oil embargo led purchasing executives to move away from the typical adversarial relationships that described buyers and sellers. Buyers moved from a mentality of the "one-night stand" to one of longer-term relationships with suppliers. The second event occurred over a period of years, beginning in 1978. This was the beginning of a period of excessively high inflation and led purchasing executives to shift from an orientation of long-term supply relationships to one of cost control. The third event is not really an event. It is an orientation toward quality, which has led purchasing executives to demand quality from suppliers. The demands for quality have led to partnering relationships between suppliers and customers, the first step to quality being to seek out suppliers who can deliver on their promises every time. The result has been that many customers, like Motorola, General Electric, and Xerox, have streamlined their supplier base, vastly reducing the number of suppliers. They have also reduced the length of long-term contracts to a period of only a few years in an effort to promote complacency on the part of suppliers in providing quality.

While all of this was (and is) occurring, a natural conflict arose. This fourth "event" was that customer organizations precipitated change to centralization in an effort to drive standardization, reduce costs, and leverage buying power. Customers had nationally organized purchasing functions while suppliers retained a decentralized sales and supply function. However, customers became more and more cost driven, using purchase volume as leverage. Further, many individuals on the purchasing side became involved in transactions. Supplier companies found that local dealing with national customers was an inefficient and unacceptable way to conduct business. Moreover, as suppliers continued to use a localized approach, national customers perceived a lack of internal coordination on the part of suppliers. Local sales representatives failed to communicate with headquarters—but customers' purchasing executives communicated with both. The result was that sales objectives and customer purchasing goals often went unmet. Listed are several other events that foster strategic account marketing strategies.

• Trend toward partnering
• Breakdown of custom or tariff barriers via trade agreements
• Increasing sophistication of purchasing managers
• Era of bigger deals
• Increasing customer expectations of supplier organizations
• Demand for quality on a worldwide basis (e.g., ISO 9000)

All these phenomena led to the seeming explosion of strategic account marketing as a way of better servicing customers, meeting their increasing expectations, and of developing and maintaining long-term relationships with customers. And, as barriers to global marketing efforts such as national preferences, shipping costs and delays, tariffs, customers delays, local content laws, travel and communication constraints, and patent barriers have all been reduced, strategic account marketing has taken on a new stature in global marketing strategies.

A number of other factors have fueled the move to strategic accounts. These factors include changes in products, the resource situation, changes in the buying process, and changes in buying criteria. Each of these factors has had multiple impacts on the demands placed on salespeople, as shown in Table 5.1.

In light of the growing importance of strategic account marketing, this paper examines several issues related to strategic account marketing. These issues include (1) partnering; (2) barriers to effective strategic account service; (3) the role of the strategic account department in establishing criteria for qualifying strategic accounts; (4) strategic account manager's marketing responsibilities; and (5) the strategic account team.

## STRATEGIC ACCOUNTS DEFINED

Before we begin our discussion of strategic account strategies, it is necessary to define the term "strategic account." In general, there are three elements that define strategic accounts. First, strategic accounts are, simply put, strategic with respect to revenues, profits, and growth opportunities for the

**Table 5.1**
**Factors That Have Served As Catalysts for Strategic Account Marketing**

| Changes in products . . . | Determine what salespeople must do to avoid fast obsolescence |
|---|---|
| Shorter life spans | Gain more product knowledge—faster!!! |
| Proliferating products and product lines | Formulate differentiation strategies |
| Parity | Transform product knowledge into specific and diverse customer solutions |
| Less brand loyalty | Marshall product support resources |
| **The resource situation . . .** | **Demands that salespeople . . .** |
| Diminishing resources | Sell internally |
| Stiffer competition | Consolidate and increase knowledge of own company |
| Less management assistance | Cultivate and maintain solid key relationships |
| More complexity | Build a sales team inside and outside |
| More confusion | Keep sales team moving |
|  | Show individual initiative |
|  | Communicate the strategic account plan to the sales team |
| **Changes in the buying process . . .** | **Demand that salespeople . . .** |
| Greater number | Map a complex decision-making process |
| More diverse | Understand corporate culture |
| New decision-making groups | Understand the political situation |
|  | Understand cross-functional buying teams |
|  | Build relationships with decision makers at all levels |
| **Changes in buying criteria . . .** | **Demand that salespeople . . .** |
| Promote strategy | Build knowledge beyond the product and sales shell |
| Solve problems | Form customer partnerships |
| Foster long-term partnerships | Understand the customer's competitor |
|  | Balance short and long term |
|  | Build credibility at all levels |

future. Similarly, they are strategic with respect to the nature of the relationship (a partnership) between the seller and the buyer. Third, they are strategic with respect to the development of new products and services.

Strategic accounts can be differentiated from major accounts. A strategic account is more than just a large customer. A strategic customer may be defined by the high level of customer contact, the level of customer support required, and the structure of the supplier's account team. Further, a strategic account may represent the key to penetration of the account or dominance of the account. Finally, the strategic account is far more complex in terms of planning issues.

It may also be useful, at this point, to differentiate between the responsibilities of a strategic account manager and the responsibilities of the individuals known as national account managers:

- The strategic account manager's responsibilities are likely to be global (or at least multinational) in scope. The national account manager will be focused on local and national issues.

- The strategic account manager must be a practitioner of multifunctional business management. The typical national account manager's focus is on sales success and customer service. Typically, the national account manager is the team leader for a single function—sales, although the national account manager may also have responsibilities for the marketing function.

- The strategic account manager must be the empowered focal point for the entire customer service system.
- The strategic account manager must be equipped with general business skills.
- The strategic account manager must understand financial and information system issues.
- The strategic account manager cannot rely on selling skills alone for excellence in performance.
- The strategic account manager's resume of experience must be broad.
- The strategic account manager must have the confidence of top management in the supplier organization.
- The strategic account manager must have the confidence of top management in the customer's organization.

## PARTNERING

The term "partnership" may be a term as much abused as "quality." Simply put, a partnership is an agreed upon relationship between two or more parties who choose to cooperate in an enterprise and share its risks and rewards. Thus, a partnership represents a relationship that is based on cooperation. A partnership is a structured relationship with an overall goal of success of the enterprise. As partnering is discussed from the perspective of strategic account management, it must be stated that partnering is more than the evolution of long-term contractual relationships. Partnering requires a degree of cooperation that transcends preferred supplier status. Further, partnering requires an openness that appears unnatural.

Partnerships are the types of relationships that have provided many Japanese companies with their competitive advantage. The current business environment is one that makes it difficult and very time-consuming to assess the viability of a supplier whenever a purchase is to be made. It has become imperative that buyers know who are the most capable at all times in all purchasing classifications. Supplier relationships, from the buyer's perspective, guarantee that products and services can be procured at high levels of quality and competitive prices. Thus, purchasing has evolved into a continuous process of supplier assessment and relationship management. Buying, once the focal point of purchasing activity, now is almost a by-product of the relationship process.

The structure of a partnership is shown in Figure 5.1. The partnership requires a definition and a negotiation of an agreement that is acceptable to supplier and buyer concerning the enterprise in which they will cooperate. As can be seen in Figure 5.1, agreement must be reached on goals, operating principles, progress measurements, communications processes, problem-solving pro-

**Figure 5.1**
**How a Partnership Is Structured**

Agreement on Common Goals That
    Complement Each Other

⬇

Operating Principles for Results

⬇

Progress Measurements

⬇

Communication Processes

⬇

Problem Solving Processes

⬇

Quality Improvement Objectives

> All of these activities are enhanced
> by an environment which is
> open, honest, cooperative

cesses, and quality improvement objectives. The partnership must exist in an open, honest, and cooperative environment, which may seem counter to the lack of trust that seems pervasive in many business and government sectors. In short, before partnering can succeed, both the supplier's and the client's organizations must be practitioners of "internal" partnering (i.e., a culture of cooperation that overcomes functional barriers).

Figure 5.2, describes the partnership development process. The overall goal is to improve relationship quality and supplier performance as shown on the right side of Figure 5.2. In order to accomplish this, the supplier must be able to assess the customer's current culture and receptivity to the partnership concept. Based on this, the supplier can then determine the effectiveness of the existing customer relationship and the effectiveness of supplier performance as viewed by the customer. Clearly, the supplier must objectively make these customer assessments as the quality and effectiveness of subsequent relationships will be based on an objective and thorough review of the supplier's relationship history with other customers. Only after a satisfactory assessment of the relationship potential is made can an ongoing program of supplier–customer relationship development proceed through a process which produces results for the buyer and the supplier.

Partnership development represents a proactive strategy designed to foster excellence in customer relationships. It includes, but is not limited to, supplier certification which is often a reactive response (and a necessary response) to defects in a relationship. A relationship defect is a deliverable (e.g., a product or service) from a relationship development process that does not meet

**Figure 5.2**
**The Partnership Development Process**

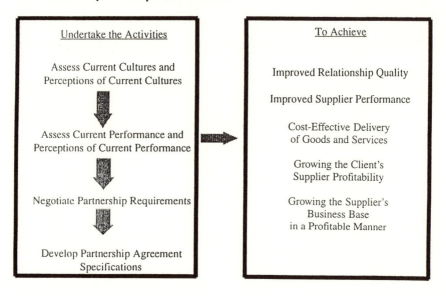

customer requirements for any reason. To have a successful partnership relationship, suppliers must excel at the proactive relationship building process and the reactive supplier certification processes.

## PARTNERSHIPS AS A FORM OF COMPETITIVE ADVANTAGE

"If you are not the lead dog, the scenery never changes." Finding and sustaining a competitive advantage has forever been at the heart of business strategies. Recently, attention has been given to the development of a distinctive set of capabilities as a means of generating competitive advantage (Hamel and Prahalad 1989). Capabilities consist of skills and knowledge that are linked together through business processes that produce outcomes in the marketplace. The essence of competitive advantage focuses on the identification and development of processes rather than on particular products or markets. In other words, products represent only temporary solutions to customers' problems. Tomorrow's problems will be different and require different solutions. Thus, companies must be capable of providing an ongoing set of products and services to solve dynamic customer problems. Companies that have a proven track record regarding the quality of relationship have a capability that can be translated into a competitive advantage.

Not all processes provide competitive advantage. Process are strategically significant only to the extent that they provide some superior value to customers, are difficult to imitate, and render the organization more adaptable to change (Day 1994). Further, the ability to continuously build new capabilities is at the heart of competitive advantage in industries where change is rapid. Liedtka (1996) refers to metacapabilities, or the skills and knowledge that underlie the process of capability building, as the means by which business can continuously recreate business related capabilities over time. Collaboration is described as one of those metacapabilities, defined as the process of decision making among interdependent parties. Collaboration involves joint ownership of decisions and collective responsibility for outcomes (Gray 1991). Collaboration allows organizations to learn and to work across the silos that have typified business structures. As noted above, the market environment that once demanded a line of business approach is changing and creating new demands on the line of business structure. As an aside, companies that have demonstrated excellence in internal partnering have one of the prerequisites to this metacapability of collaboration with other organizations.

Firms that have produced value through collaboration have identified a set of skills, a way of thinking, and a multifaceted support organization that other firms lack. These skills are those that have been rarely rewarded in most organizations including:

1. Listening with an open mind to the proposals of others versus selling one's solutions harder.
2. Acknowledging and using conflict productively versus suppressing and ignoring it.
3. Leading by supporting and facilitating versus managing through authority and fiat.
4. Designing new end-to-end value systems rather than tinkering with incremental fixes to current processes (Liedtka 1996).

Liedtka also examined best practices in collaboration and found the following factors contributed significantly toward the ability to achieve collaborative outcomes of real value: (1) a partnering mindset; (2) a partnering skillset; and (3) a supportive context that provides commitment, processes, and resources to facilitate collaboration. Figure 5.3 describes these three components of effective partnering.

## THE PARTNERING MINDSET

A key quality of successful partnerships is the partners' way of thinking. Successful relationships are characterized by a mindset with which partners approach their relationship. This partnering mindset consists of the following: (1) a view of partnership as opportunity, (2) a sense of at-stakedness, (3) a level of trust among partners, and (4) a readiness to learn from each other.

**Figure 5.3**
**Elements of Effective Partnerships**

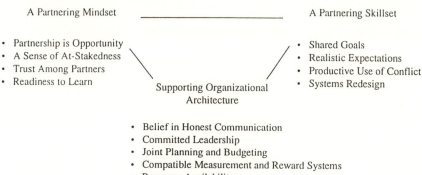

*Source*: Adapted from Jeanne M. Liedtka. 1996. "Collaborating Across Lines of Business for Competitive Advantage." *The Academy of Management Executive* 10 (2): 25.

## Partnership As Opportunity

Partnership as opportunity represents a different way of expressing the age old question, "Is the glass half full or half empty?," and discussing the optimist and pessimist viewpoint. Top managers set initiatives that are almost always viewed from a risk perspective by those who must implement those initiatives. That is, the risks of nonperformance are clear, but the benefits (particularly company-wide benefits) are often not very clear. Care must be taken, at the strategic level, to insure that the logic behind partnering via strategic accounts is clear, meaningful, and, above all, shared by all who will be involved in the strategic account strategy.

## A Sense of At-Stakedness (A Sense of Urgency)

In any successful collaborative relationship, the individuals involved in the partnership must have a sense that they make a difference to the organization. They must have a clear sense of the organization's strategic direction and the critical role that collaboration plays in achieving the strategic direction. Further, individuals must view themselves as having a personal stake in partnership outcomes—that they play a key role in producing an outcome that they care about. At-stakedness is akin to commitment—those who are committed to a venture do not allow uncertainties to undermine their commitment in making a partnership work. Those not committed tend to adopt a wait-and-see attitude—they wait and see what happens, as opportunity passes them by.

Oftentimes it is individuals at middle levels of the supplier organization that drive the organization toward strategic account partnerships. Unfortunately, much credit for partnership creation is claimed by top management. Those in the trenches (who may be the original drivers behind the partnership) are often told they will become a part of the partnership which immediately puts stress on the new relationship. If individuals are simply told to participate in the partnership, their level of commitment will likely not get beyond token acceptance (Reardon and Spekman 1994). What is desired is that all involved in the partnership see themselves as having some responsibility for making the relationship work. This is why it is paramount in importance to carefully choose those individuals who will ultimately manage the partnering relationship.

## Trust among Partners

Trust comes from performance. And, performance can only occur over some period of time. Of course, as a relationship begins, there is an element of faith in the competency of the individuals entering the partnership. Faith must be upheld by performance.

There is also a trust built among partners concerning the requisite skills to make the partnership function successfully. Presumably, each member of the partnership brings some unique skill to the table. The skills combinations are the basis of successful partnerships. No one has all the skills required for success. Each member must rely on the other to perform the skills needed to insure the success of the partnership.

A key element of trust is equity. Partners must learn to trust other partners' intentions. But, performance is still important. While outcomes are important as well, if the motives of those producing the outcomes are questioned, the partnership will have difficulty. Similarly, good intentions that never seem to reach performance fruition are also not conducive to the longevity of partnerships.

## Readiness to Learn from Each Other

No one member of the partnership has all the answers, despite what any of the individuals may think. While each partner must belief that he or she has something to contribute, it is equally important for each partner to believe that he or she has much to learn. The process of give-and-take that develops from these attitudes can lead to tremendous results—every member of the partnership develops new skills so that they can become even more productive members of the partnership. Key elements of learning in a strategic account organization include the following:

1. Feeling free to challenge existing ways of thinking in all functions and in all work done by other groups.
2. Treating mistakes as learning opportunities, moving first to control any damage and then conducting debriefing sessions to "correct" errors and avoid repeating mistakes.

3. Allowing appeals to move to the next level if a group cannot achieve consensus.

4. Indefinite continuance of the educational process, recognizing that learning is just as relevant to the day-to-day business operations as the good management of time.

## THE PARTNERING SKILLSET

A second key quality of successful partnerships lies in the partners' skillset. This skillset includes the following: (1) creating shared goals and realistic expectations, (2) using conflict productively, and (3) redesigning systems.

### Shared Goals and Realistic Expectations

The customers' interests are paramount and the entire culture of any organization must revolve around putting those customers' interests first. Without shared goals, partners are relegated toward the mutual pursuit of individual self interests (Liedtka 1996). Both customers and suppliers must have a mutual vision, mission, and a strategic plan to make the partnership happen. That mission should incorporate the achievement of long-term objectives of both the supplier and the customer by building a complete partnership that leads the respective partners to better serve mutual customers. While the pursuit of self interests is important for all partnerships, by itself it provides a shaky foundation for the formation and management of partnerships. In the long run, collaboration is difficult at best if there is no common ground. The customer can provide that common ground.

Shared goals represent results to be achieved. Along the way, there must be realistic expectations concerning the contributions to be made by each partner. The process by which expectations are set can vary, but it is clear that the negotiations must be joint in nature. Each individual must have some idea of the expectations for a particular individual and then, through negotiations, agreement as to adjustments for those expectations must be reached.

### Using Conflict Productively

Successful partnerships view conflict as opportunity. Clearly the opportunities vary, but they tend to revolve around two aspects. First is the opportunity for individuals to use their skills to develop ways to resolve conflict. Second, if creative conflict-solving approaches are employed, there is also an opportunity to realize positive outcomes as a result of the conflict resolution process.

### Redesigning Systems

Successful partnerships are also skilled at redesigning processes. Much can be said about process redesign, reengineering, and other terms used to describe radical organizational change. Suffice to say that successful partnerships hold little sacred when it comes to how things are done. This does not mean that they endorse a policy of change for change sake. Rather, their change policy is to consider all change as a viable option until demonstrated otherwise in the decision process. Successful partnerships undertake systems redesign with the customer as the focal point.

## SUPPORTING ORGANIZATIONAL ARCHITECTURE

Successful partners have benefited from the support of a larger organizational architecture that valued what the partners were striving for and gave them the resources to succeed. Organizational architecture may be defined as all the elements of design of the social and work systems, including formal structure, the design of work practices, operating cycles, and processes for selection, socialization, development, and reward (Nadler et al. 1993). Supportive organizational architecture includes (1) a belief in honest communication, (2) committed leadership, (3) joint planning and budgeting process, (4) congruent measurement and reward systems, and (5) resource availability.

A key consideration here is the market orientation of the strategic account marketing organization and the customer. An important question revolves around the degree of alignment between the marketing orientations of the buyer and seller. The degree to which the two organizations agree on how to approach the marketplace will affect the ease with which a partnership can be formed, and the degree to which that partnership can be successful.

Another key factor in the organizational architecture is the positioning of the relationship manager. For strategic accounts, this will likely be the strategic account manager in the supplier organization. The position occupied by the strategic account manager as partnership manager should enable him or her to effectively marshal resources in support of the partnership.

### A Belief in Honest Communication

Stated succinctly, all issues, simple or complex, must be dealt with honestly and openly. Only a climate where there is support in bringing issues to the table will foster open and honest communication. This means that confidentiality of sensitive data can still be a priority of the team. Partners should honor their companies' confidentiality and avoid discussions of information that is not public knowledge outside of the team. However, the team also has a trust of each individual's commitment to "do the right thing." And, each team member supports others as individuals and deals with disagreements as business issues rather than personal issues.

### Committed Leadership

Top managers must be committed to the success of the partnership. Such a commitment represents a total "buy-in," and proactive participation of top management from both organizations. This seems obvious, but many top managements allow things to happen, and then laud the successes but avoid the failures, not being committed in either case. Top managers must also hold others to their commitments. Failure to keep commitments or to hold others to their commitments is akin to subterfuge, and under circumstances of lack of top management commitment, partnerships will not succeed.

### Joint Planning and Budgeting Processes

Most commitments are obtained in planning and budgeting processes. As such, these processes represent key opportunities to obtain and incorporate input from all individuals. Successful partnerships assume that all individuals will be involved in planning and budgeting and, therefore, do not deal with issues of participation. Few things can be more damaging to a partnership than a unilateral decision to change the parameters of a partnership.

### Congruent Measurement and Reward Systems

People will do what they are rewarded for, not what we ask them to do. If rewards are based strictly on financial self-interests, partnerships will struggle. If rewards are based on activities that link the individual and partnership success, then the partnership has a much higher likelihood of success.

A critical element of partnership success is to insure that individuals do not spend inordinate amounts of time haggling about how to divide reward pies. Time spent dividing dollars within the company is not time spent in the customers' best interests. While there are many ways to do this, it is imperative that some mechanism(s) be established to prevent people from raging about whether or not their contribution was greater than someone else's.

### Resource Availability

Top management must provide the resources needed to ensure the success of the partnership. Resources are not just financial. They include the education required to impact the mindset of and skill levels of each partner. They include investments in information and other technologies required by the partnership to perform at excellent levels. They include the provision of time to allow the partnership to develop and grow (Liedtka 1996).

## INTERNAL BARRIERS TO EFFECTIVE STRATEGIC ACCOUNT SERVICE

Five barriers to effective strategic account service are presented below. These are (1) lack of teamwork, (2) lack of focus, (3) varying capabilities, (4) unclear authority, and (5) inadequate systems and support.

## Lack of Teamwork

If continuity is lacking, it is impossible to build an effective team. Considerable coordination is needed to meet customers' multilocation needs. Coordination between local salespeople and strategic account managers is key. Too often, local salespeople people view things from the perspective of "How much can I sell this week?" This perspective is in conflict with the national perspective of developing long-term relationships with customers. Local salespeople tend to be "event driven." Strategic account management is relationship driven. The differential focus can create confusion for customers and put the supplier–customer relationship in jeopardy.

A further problem is one that is not limited to strategic accounts, but manages to rear its ugly head in strategic accounts. Organizations and individuals still struggle with who gets credit for certain accomplishments in dealing with strategic accounts. Rethinking the compensation plan and/or the organization structure may result in some resolution of who receives credit for what performance. Without such thinking, the larger result is the "at risk" status of the strategic account.

## Lack of Focus

Strategic accounts can suffer from a lack of focus. Sales representatives often complain about excessive workload that comes from having too many accounts to service. The result is often reduced attention given to the strategic account. These salespeople face the traditional problem of allocation of time to various accounts. From the strategic customer's perspective, they will often acknowledge that supplier salespeople are busy. However, they are quick to change that perspective when a particular need arises and the strategic account sales representative is not available to service that need.

Lack of focus is a common problem in today's business environment where supplier organizations have downsized the field sales organization. In such cases, strategic account managers discover that it is difficult to find a local sales representative who will provide the expected level of service to a "smaller" buying location of a strategic customer. Local sales representatives often have a "full plate" of sales opportunities with their existing accounts and are unwilling to invest the time required to build a long-term relationship with a local division of a strategic account. When this occurs, the long-term goals of the strategic partnership can suffer as a result of the lack of continuity of effort toward the local elements of the strategic account.

## Varying Capabilities

Both field sales representatives and strategic account managers have varying capabilities. Strategic customers who view salespeople as becoming complacent because salespeople have a large part of their business will often seek salespeople who are more aggressive and proactive in servicing their accounts. Further, supplying organizations have been remiss in recruiting sales support personnel. Some sales support personnel are recruited right out of college. Others come from within the company, but are often those salespeople who performed at subpar levels while servicing their own set of customers and prospects. Finally, another root cause of varying capabilities lies in the variety of training programs afforded strategic account managers. These range from extensive programs that recognize the unique nature of the strategic account manager position to programs that promote a person to strategic account manager on the basis of past performance, assuming that past good performers will continue that good performance.

### Unclear Authority

When strategic account managers are unclear about their authority, the decision-making process is affected. Strategic customers do not want to have every decision approved by the supplier's home office. When strategic customers have needs, they want those needs serviced immediately, if not sooner. That strategic account managers are often unclear about their authority is sometimes caused by the perception of the lack of top management support. The lack of clarity regarding authority may also result from the organizational structure (i.e., unclear reporting lines). This lack of clarity creates difficulty for strategic account managers when they seek the cooperation of local salespeople. Strategic account managers often have influence, but without proper authority, the local salespeople can be left to their own devices and will often focus on sales instead of on building relationships. In both cases, the lack of authority undermines the strategic account relationship as strategic customers seek decisions and representatives of the supplying organization cannot provide it.

### Inadequate Systems and Support

This is a problem for many firms who have adopted a strategic account strategy, even the so-called high-tech firms. Very often, strategic account salespeople are selling state-of-the-art technology to their customers. However, the technology and information provided in support of their efforts is considerably less sophisticated than that which they are selling. Further, companies adopting a strategic account strategy often overlook the need for support that comes from gathering the sales team together and seeking some consistency in their approach to servicing the strategic account. These problems are compounded by the age-old problem of budget. Many strategic account managers are reluctant to spend money on support resources, as the impact of these expenditures is immediately felt on the bottom line, but the impact on revenues may be long term, and impossible to directly ascertain.

## CRITERIA FOR QUALIFYING STRATEGIC ACCOUNTS

Up to this point in this chapter, we have focused on the role of partnering and its implications for the supplying organization and the strategic account manager. We deviate in this next section and view strategic account management from the perspective of a strategic accounts department. In determining which accounts should be strategic accounts, several factors must be taken into consideration. These are highlighted in Figure 5.4.

### Size of Account

Clearly, strategic accounts will be large accounts, with size being determined by volume. Some minimum volume must be established, and existing and potential accounts that do not meet those minimums do not qualify for strategic account status.

1. What should be the minimum volume for strategic account status?
2. Should different minimum volumes be established for existing customers and potential customers?
3. What is the product–service mix that will be needed to create a long-term relationship with the strategic customer?
4. What return on investment of resources is required?

### Multiple Locations

Strategic accounts most often are those that have multiple buying locations. The existence of multiple locations requires coordinated support for those involved in purchasing decisions. However, when discussing strategic accounts on a strategic level, the mere fact that the strategic account has multiple locations is not sufficient justification for elevation to strategic account status. Companies interested in partnering on a strategic level must move from a multilocation mindset (e.g., allowing each location to buy independently, treating each location separately) to a strategic mindset that realizes the buying synergies that can occur as a result of a activity on a national or global scale.

### Centralized Purchasing

Most strategic accounts have a centralized purchasing function. The bottom of Figure 5.4 provides further insight into establishing priorities for the designation of strategic accounts. As can be seen, all accounts are classified according to their potential value and to the probability of achieving that potential. Potential value was discussed earlier. The probability of achieving that potential value is affected by several factors, including the following:

1. *The propensity of the customer to outsource and/or partner with suppliers.* Clearly, companies seeking to establish strategic accounts must obtain in-depth historical information concerning outsourcing and partnering activities of customers that are being considered for strategic account status. Once again, when considering a strategic customer for strategic account status, the strategic account must have a strategic focus, or at least a regional focus (e.g., Europe, South America, or Asia).

2. *The supplier's current relationship with a customer.* This would include an assessment of the supplier's current sales programs, recent history of sales programs, level of contact with the customer, and other signals from the customer that might be pertinent to the decision to elevate a customer to strategic account status.

3. *The strength of competitors' positions and competitive offerings.* In ascertaining competitive strength, consideration must be given to customer needs being served and the number of organizations that are currently servicing those needs. Further, the quality of competitive sales programs must be examined for identification of recent success and failures. The level of contact competitors have with customers is also an important consideration.

## STRATEGIC ACCOUNT MANAGER RESPONSIBILITIES

Strategic account managers will have many responsibilities as they seek to service strategic accounts. These responsibilities can be divided into four areas as shown in Table 5.2. As can be seen, strategic account managers are charged with considerable responsibility.

**Figure 5.4**
**Criteria for Establishing Account Priorities**

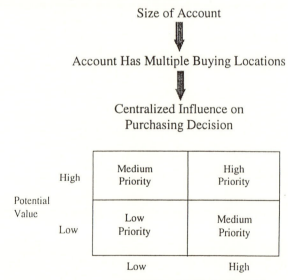

## Strategic Account Planning and Support Responsibilities

Organizations that have employed a strategic account management strategy have discovered the need for a centralized support function such as a strategic accounts department that serves as a clearinghouse and focal point for the overall program. Central to the functioning of a strategic accounts department, account planning and support responsibilities are classified into the following four areas: (1) account qualification, (2) account planning support, (3) contract administration, and (4) administrative support. Responsibilities in each of these areas are presented here:

### Account Qualification

- Work with field salespeople to ensure that required information is in place for proposed changes to the strategic and strategic account lists.

### Account Planning and Support

- Assist in the development and refinement of the strategic account planning process.
- Assist strategic account managers in the application of the account planning process to each strategic and strategic account.
- Serve as the primary driver of strategic account marketing activities.

**Table 5.2**
**The Strategic Account Management Challenge**

| Responsibility | What It Means | Qualities Needed |
|---|---|---|
| Account Strategy | - Build, direct, motivate team effort | team builder |
| | - Plan sales activity of the total strategic account | organizer |
| | - Plan/establish the strategic relationship | leader |
| | - Identify/evaluate strategic opportunities | planner |
| | - Evaluate/prioritize opportunities | rapport builder |
| | - Set objectives | communicator |
| Investments/Operations | - Drive the "delivery" organization | action oriented |
| | - Establish the investment criteria | goal oriented |
| | - Drive staffing of new opportunities | implementation |
| | - Monitor/measure/control progress | coach |
| Account Quality Assurance | - Develop/implement account quality program | planner |
| | - Perform proactive problem/opportunity management | leader |
| | - Monitor/enhance customer satisfaction | organizer |
| Executive TQC Role | - Preview plan for best practice | experience |
| | - Add value through internal influence | judgment |
| | - Initiate high level account contacts | credibility |

### Contract Administration

- Work with pricing to develop and maintain national and strategic contracts.
- Conduct profitability analysis.
- Develop and maintain sales reporting systems.
- Interface with all business units involved in strategic and/or strategic accounts.

### Administrative Support

- Provide assistance and support to strategic and strategic account managers for the development of proposals and presentations to accounts.
- Provide assistance and support to strategic and strategic account managers for all communications to accounts.
- Interface with information systems for needed information and reports.
- Develop and implement account performance monitoring and evaluation.

## Strategic Account Planning and Development Support

A critical problem facing organizations with strategic accounts is the level of support received from national account coordinators. A lack of support does indeed limit the strategic account manager's ability to further penetrate the account. The lack of support also makes the strategic account more vulnerable to inroads from competitors. As competitive inroads are made, the strategic account becomes more difficult to defend. Basically, the strategic account manager must be a master strategist.

Figure 5.5 overviews the account planning and development process, after the account selection (or targeting) process is competed. At each stage of the process, support, or lack of, can be a major factor in the strategic account manager's ability to obtain and maintain relations with the strategic account. For example, in the first stage of Figure 5.5, salespeople often try to sell an account before gathering information on customer needs. A lack of support would manifest itself in salespeople having little information concerning what information is important to gather.

In stage two of Figure 5.5, salespeople often view the effort and time required to plan as "wasted" or unproductive. Planning is not viewed as a selling activity. Too often, this occurs because management does not require planning activity. Moreover, salespeople are not rewarded for their planning activities. Consequently, salespeople often overlook the importance of planning when evaluating what they are paid for, although some organizations make the accomplishment of strategic account plan objectives an integral part of the strategic account manager's compensation package. Further, management can provide negative reinforcement for such planning activities if they actively promote sales volume and say nothing about other sales related activities and objectives. A lack of support can occur as the "system" does not support or encourage sharing of what works and what does not work across national account coordinators.

In the third stage of Figure 5.5, when dealing with strategic accounts, there is often little or no review with national management. In all fairness, sometimes this lack of review falls on the responsibility of the strategic account manager. Field sales managers have a tendency to review, if they review at all, with a focus only on district, or regional, outcomes. They tend to ignore outcomes that are strategic in nature and activities that do not directly yield sales results. Typical compensation plans for field sales personnel, often being very short-term in nature, largely drive such behaviors.

At the fourth stage, implementation, unclear responsibilities, and poor communications can lead to inconsistent implementation of the strategic account plan across all locations. Often, field salespeople are not even aware that there is a contact for an account they are serving locally. Finally, at the monitoring stage, many organizations employ little more than sales results in their assessment of performance. One reason for this is the inadequacy of information systems established to support strategic account efforts.

## IMPLEMENTING AN ACCOUNT PLANNING PROCESS

To overcome some of these difficulties, implementation of an account planning process should include three key elements shown in Figure 5.6: (1) development of the account planning process, (2) training of managers and salespeople, and (3) provision of guidance and discipline to ensure that strategic account plans are developed and used.

### Development of the Strategic Account Planning Process

Any strategic account planning process must be based on a fundamental understanding of customers' needs. The planning process must champion an approach that positions the supplier uniquely to meet those customers' needs. Briefly, as with all planning processes, the strategic account planning process should be specific and actionable, and include objectives, activities, and action plans to meet those objectives, assigned responsibilities and accountabilities, and resource requirements. Information should also be provided to all those who will service a strategic account about the history of the strategic account itself.

**Figure 5.5**
**Strategic Account Planning and Development Process**

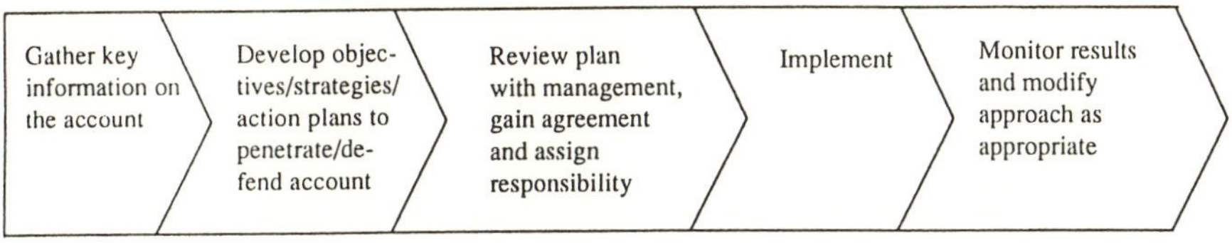

| Gather key information on the account | Develop objectives/strategies/action plans to penetrate/defend account | Review plan with management, gain agreement and assign responsibility | Implement | Monitor results and modify approach as appropriate |

## Train Managers and Sales Representatives

Training and education programs should emphasize the traditional selling and sales management skills required for success in sales. However, these all must be adapted to the needs associated with servicing a strategic account. Further, training education programs must emphasize the value that sales representatives and sales managers can provide in servicing strategic accounts. Because output with respect to strategic accounts is not as easily measured as output in traditional sales settings, some sense of worth and accomplishment must be instilled in strategic account people so that they understand what role they are playing and the importance of that role to the overall relationship and success with the strategic account.

## Provide Guidance for Plan Development and Implementation

Individuals called strategic account directors are largely responsible for the planning and implementation of strategic account plans. Strategic account managers provide much guidance and leadership concerning strategic account planning and implementation. Managers of strategic accounts require ongoing support to assist them in the development, refinement, and implementation of strategic account plans. Such support must be required of all strategic account managers. One form of support is to position the plan as a "contract" to ensure that managers have ownership in meeting their commitments to the strategic account. For example, some companies have implemented a senior executive sponsor program for strategic accounts. The purposes and responsibilities of a senior executive sponsor are as follows:

**Figure 5.6**
**Implementing an Account Planning Process: The Role of the Strategic Accounts Department**

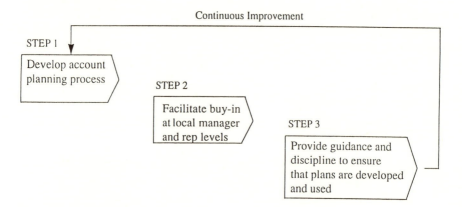

- Provide strategic account managers with a senior level advocate to further ensure that the needs of the strategic account are being met.
- Show the strategic account that the supplier organization is committed to a long-term relationship.
- Serve as a sounding board to the strategic account manager in the development and implementation of a strategic account plan.
- Assist the strategic account manager in securing resources if normal channels are unsuccessful.
- Provide all senior management with greater exposure to strategic customers.

The strategic account manager retains status as the key contact person for the strategic account. However, the executive sponsor serves as an advocate for the strategic account if needed. The sponsor meets periodically with the strategic account manager to develop and discuss plans, and to plan and implement programs designed to meet strategic account needs.

## THE STRATEGIC ACCOUNT TEAM

Figure 5.7 depicts the typical strategic account management team. While strategic account strategies may vary in terms the team configuration, Figure 5.7 depicts the four critical system requirements for servicing strategic accounts: (1) the strategic account manager, (2) local sales representatives, (3) customer service and support, and (4) strategic accounts organization management. The following identifies many strategic account functions that are to be performed by one or more members of the strategic account team.

- Monitor or control strategic account contacts
- Make high-level presentations to strategic accounts
- Maintain strategic account records

**Figure 5.7**
**The Strategic Account Management Team**

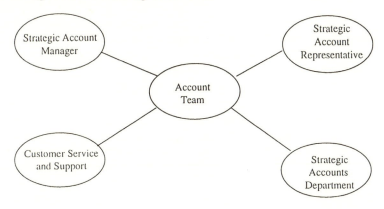

- Recommend corporate policies and procedures relating to strategic accounts
- Identify selling opportunities and sales potential of strategic accounts
- Coordinate communications among company units servicing strategic accounts
- Develop specialized communications for approaching strategic accounts
- Identify purchasing points, buying influences and preferred procedures for strategic accounts
- Engage in direct contact with key strategic account personnel
- Identify potential strategic account customers
- Develop long-term relationships with strategic accounts
- Assign strategic account goals
- Initiate contact with prospective strategic accounts
- Monitor competitive developments affecting strategic accounts
- Coordinate and expedite service to strategic accounts
- Negotiate long-term sales contracts
- Secure preferred supplier status
- Obtain product acceptance
- Be alert to possible duplication of coverage to strategic accounts
- Settle conflicts between strategic accounts and supplier units serving strategic accounts
- Determine pricing strategies
- Accept and resolve customer complaints
- Engage in routine service contact and follow-up

## SELECTION AND DEVELOPMENT
## OF STRATEGIC ACCOUNT MANAGERS

Success with strategic accounts will be limited if the organization places limited emphasis on selecting and developing strategic account managers. Selecting and developing strategic account managers includes identification and selection, training, coaching, and ongoing guidance.

### Selection

In most strategic account situations, organizations select the incumbent sales representative at the headquarters location to be the strategic account coordinator. In this selection process, little consideration is given to accounts' needs or the skillsets required to fully develop the strategic account, shown in Figure 5.8. To remedy this situation, detailed job descriptions including clear selection criteria must be developed based on the requirements of the strategic account manager position and the unique requirements of the customer (Wotruba and Castleberry 1993). The displaced incumbent sales representative must also be compensated with other volume and other opportunities.

## Training

Typical strategic account manager training is minimal, which can lead to a gap between skills and knowledge, and demands, as shown in Figure 5.9. Leadership training addresses some of the critical issues associated with strategic accounts. However, it is often assumed that the skill required by a strategic account manager is little more than an extension of the skills required when they were involved in traditional field sales, or, for that matter, strategic account sales. Companies thinking about strategic account management must develop a training program that enhances basic selling skills to meet the demands of the strategic accounts. This involves a clarification of the new responsibilities of the strategic account manager, the development of the skills required to implement a strategic account plan, the improvement in the ability to sell up in an organization, and the development of skills to marshal the resources needed to service the strategic account. The following summarizes the responsibilities of strategic account managers that must be discussed in training programs:

### Contact with Strategic Account
- Cultivate close relationships with key strategic account customer executives
- Serve as the supplier's primary spokesperson in negotiations with the strategic account
- Resolve all customer expectations and concerns in a timely manner
- Handle all questions and concerns from supplier personnel concerning the relationship with the strategic account

### Resources
- Ensure that the strategic account receives the proper attention from all units of the supplier involved in servicing the strategic account

**Figure 5.8**
**The Skills Required of a Strategic Account Manager**

**Figure 5.9**
**Skills and Knowledge versus Demands Gap**

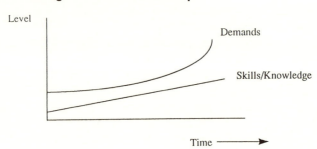

- The authority to discipline and/or replace field salespeople if there is justifiable cause
- Seek opportunities to bring together senior management of both the supplier and the strategic account

### Performance

- Measure performance against stated objectives
- Provide supplier upper management with periodic performance review
- Provide strategic account customer with periodic performance review

### Strategy

- Understand and document strategic account customer's needs, direction, and philosophies
- Develop a detailed account strategy plan that guides all decisions and focuses the supplier's resources on meeting the needs of the strategic account
- Establish objectives and benchmarks to measure supplier performance with the strategic account
- Review the strategic account strategy with upper management to gain commitment and resources
- Communicate strategic account strategy to the strategic account team
- Review and revise the strategic account strategy with the strategic account, when appropriate

## Coaching and Ongoing Guidance

Given that most companies have a lack of focus on strategic accounts, the guidance and coaching provided to strategic account managers is typically less than needed. Those placed with coaching and guidance responsibilities generally lack the ability to develop plans because their lack of experience tends to reduce their appreciation of the value of such plans in dealing with strategic accounts. Ongoing coaching and guidance should improve as strategic account strategies take on more of an organizational focus. This organizational focus must include strategic account training for the strategic account managers and others that will be involved in servicing the strategic account. Further, organizations will benefit from training provided to those who will be in coaching positions, so that they can improve their coaching and guidance counseling skills. One ultimate objective of coaching and ongoing guidance should be the institutionalizing of the strategic account mindset with all the members of the strategic account team.

## STRATEGIC ACCOUNT PLANNING ACTIVITIES

Field sales representatives must also be actively involved in strategic account planning. As with strategic account managers, improvements in supporting systems can assist field sales representatives in the areas of account planning, sales execution, delivery, and support.

### Account Planning

• Timely updates of account plans, so that field sales representative can assist strategic account manager in developing specific locations and achieving specific goals.

### Sales Execution

• Access to all proposals and call plans presented to executives to ensure delivery of a consistent approach.
• Simplify process for completing call reports and forwarding them to the strategic account manager.

### Delivery and Support

• Regularly scheduled meetings to aid in clarity of communications.
• Regularly scheduled meetings to aid in consistency of approach needed to service the strategic account.
• Up-to-date notification of all sales representatives of corporate decisions.

## SELECTION AND TRAINING OF FIELD SALES REPRESENTATIVES

Just as with strategic account managers, attention must be given to the selection and training of the field sales representatives who will provide service to the strategic account customer. As with strategic account managers, attention must be given to identification and selection, orientation and training, and communications and direction.

### Identification and Selection

Most organizations that have established strategic accounts have not developed clear criteria for the selection of field sales representatives. As a result, wide variations in the capabilities and experiences of field salespeople serving strategic accounts have been observed. Further complicating the selection process is the fact that strategic account managers often have little input into selection decisions and little recourse if a local field salesperson is not working out. To remedy this situation, organizations thinking of strategic accounts must develop clear selection criteria for field sales representatives. The strategic account manager, as well as regional and district sales managers, must all have inputs into and coordinate the selection decisions for strategic accounts. Selection must be based on strategic customer requirements as defined in the strategic account plan.

### Orientation and Training

Most organizations employing strategic account strategies have not set up training for the unique requirements associated with serving the multiple locations of strategic accounts. Such training can simply be added onto current training programs that highlight the general direction with and the importance of strategic accounts. The training must also include in-depth skills development for the role and responsibilities of local salespeople servicing strategic accounts.

### Communication and Direction

Infrequent and inconsistent communications characterize many organizations who have adopted a strategic account strategy. District, regional, and strategic account managers often provide inconsistent and conflicting information to salespeople concerning their responsibilities and accountabilities regarding strategic accounts. The strategic account plan must be made clear to all those who are involved in servicing the strategic account. Accurate communication requires periodic meetings to review the plan and discuss individual responsibilities in implementing the plan. At these meetings, the strategic account manager and field salespeople must review progress, discuss problems, and identify appropriate changes in the course of action in servicing the strategic account.

## OTHER MEMBERS OF THE STRATEGIC ACCOUNT TEAM

Figure 5.5 points out that there are many other important members of the strategic account team. Representatives from these areas provide support for strategic account managers and local sales representatives in a variety of ways, while also contributing much to the quality of the relationship with the strategic account. Following is a list of some of the activities that, collectively, fall under the responsibility of the strategic account department.

- Timely reporting of account plan completion status for all strategic account managers.
- Ability to consolidate account plan financial projections for budget development and resource requirements.
- Regular accumulation of strategic account qualification information to identify the best account opportunities.
- Access to all contract proposals to check for profitability.
- Access to all contract proposals to insure delivery requirements before acceptance.
- Summaries of call activity reports from strategic account managers.
- Summaries of call activity reports from local sales representatives.
- Monitoring of strategic account plan activity and account plan compliance.
- Coordination of design and production for the same strategic account across all locations.
- Periodic assessment of customer satisfaction through the use of interviews and surveys.
- Periodic summary reports to monitor progress against objectives as stated in the strategic account plan.

## RESEARCH QUESTIONS

We conclude with the presentation of some research questions, the answers to which would enhance our understanding of the requirements for the planning and implementation of strategic account management strategies by organizations.

- How can a strategic account program be best integrated into overall sales and marketing effort?
- What must be communicated between sales representatives, strategic account representatives, and strategic account managers?
- How can strategic account goals and missions be integrated into the goals and mission of the overall sales organization?
- What does it take to develop compatible working relationships between strategic account managers and regular management and field sales personnel?
- How can the skills of strategic account managers be used to the fullest potential?
- What training is needed to ensure that the strategic account unit fully uses its capabilities in servicing strategic accounts?
- What is (are) the optimum structure(s) for a strategic account unit?
- Is there a set of responsibilities that are universal to all strategic account managers in all situations?
- What strategic account activity must be monitored to ensure proper development of the relationship?

- How should a strategic account be staffed for maximum effectiveness?
- What knowledge do field level salespeople need in order to fully support the strategic account effort?
- How can potential resistance by field salespeople and the service organization be overcome?
- What information must be collected, analyzed, and used to monitor the success of strategic account relationships? to uncover problems? to identify opportunities?
- What specialized support is need for strategic account management?
- What are the appropriate types and levels of rewards for strategic account personnel and others involved in managing the strategic account relationship?
- How can the interests of various divisions in the company be balanced in the best interests of the company and the strategic account?

## REFERENCES

Day, G. 1994. The Capabilities of Market Driven Organizations. *Journal of Marketing* (October): 37–52.

Gray, B. 1991. *Collaborating*. San Francisco: Jossey-Bass.

Hamel, G., and C. K. Prahalad. 1989. Strategic Intent. *Harvard Business Review* (May–June): 63–76.

———. 1985. Do You Really Have a Strategic Strategy? *Harvard Business Review* (July–August): 139–148.

Liedtka, J. M. 1996. Collaborating Across Lines of Business for Competitive Advantage. *The Academy of Management Executive* 10 (2): 20–34.

Nadler, D., M. Gerstein, R. Shaw, and Associates. 1993. *Organizational Architecture*. San Francisco: Jossey-Bass.

Reardon, K., and R. Spekman. 1994. Starting Out Right: Negotiation Lessons for Domestic and Cross-Cultural Business Alliances. *Business Horizons* (January–February): 71–79.

Wotruba, T. R., and S. B. Castleberry. 1993. Job Analysis and Hiring Practices for National Account Marketing Positions. *Journal of Personal Selling and Sales Management* (Summer): 49–65.

# Chapter 6

# Horizontal Selling Alliances

## Donald W. Barclay, Judith M. S. Hatley, and J. Brock Smith

Customer-focused teams, global account management, strategic partnerships, and joint ventures are emerging as responses to changing customer decision-making processes, changing organizational forms, the globalization of business, and the opportunity to gain competitive advantage through superior relationships. Responding to this changing environment and leveraging opportunities can also be accomplished through adaptive distribution channels (Narus and Anderson 1996), comarketing alliances (Bucklin and Sengupta 1993), horizontal selling alliances (Smith and Barclay 1997), and other forms of cooperative interorganizational relationships. Here we focus on horizontal selling alliances as but one response to emerging market challenges. Horizontal selling alliances are formed between organizations to *jointly* sell to and manage relationships with customers. These alliances are typically at the same level in the market chain and have been referred to as "lateral partnering" by Morgan and Hunt (1994).

Marketing managers are adopting symbiotic marketing alliances such as comarketing and horizontal selling to face the challenges of complex and dynamic environments encompassing rapid technological change, global competition, and customer demands for more sophisticated and integrated solutions. Selling alliances allow firms to meet these demands by augmenting their own sales teams with external skills, resources, and technology. IBM, Digital Equipment, and Hewlett-Packard, for example, have developed cooperative agreements with a variety of hardware, software, and service specialists. They encourage their sales representatives to work with selling partners to jointly manage territories, develop customer solutions, and provide ongoing support. IBM has a formal Business Partner program with a variety of hardware, software, and service specialists (agents), where IBM sales representatives work with agent counterparts to provide joint customer solutions and ongoing support. Personal computer retail chains, such as ComputerLand, have developed marketing assistant programs that pay a commission to specialists, such as accountants or lawyers, to assist their salespeople in marketing and installing customer solutions and training users on the systems.

While more common among higher technology companies (e.g., 3M, DuPont, Xerox, and Nynex), selling alliances are also found in financial services, insurance, consulting, and advertising. Paychex, a payroll processing company, partners with accountants and commercial banks to gather leads in the small-business market. This partnering has helped Paychex sustain double-digit revenue growth for over thirteen years, while keeping sales force costs thirty percent lower than competition. Dissimilar companies which form the Rockwell conglomerate sell together to gain single-source contracts and preferred supplier status. This would not be possible with the companies working on their own.

The benefits that can be realized from selling alliances are numerous. For larger firms who often initiate the alliance, a key advantage is strategic flexibility. These firms can adapt quickly to technological and environmental change by aligning themselves with new partners without assuming the risk and cost of developing the expertise in-house. The partner firms, often smaller and more entrepreneurial, gain credibility and access to new markets, customers, and account opportunities. Both parties gain competitive advantage by leveraging each other's reputation and resources, preempting a competitor's access to those resources, providing more complete and integrated solutions to their customers, and having more sales representatives to cover accounts and territories. They develop collaborative advantage in contrast to more traditional product advantage in the marketplace.

This chapter explores issues faced by sales executives, sales managers, and sales representatives involved in horizontal selling alliances; discusses what we know about horizontal selling alliances; draws a picture of the implementation of horizontal selling alliances in technology, industrial, and financial services sectors; and ends with a set of questions that need to be considered by both managers and academics in this area. We start by providing some background on horizontal selling alliances.[1]

## HORIZONTAL SELLING ALLIANCES

A horizontal selling alliance (HSA) is a form of comarketing alliance (Bucklin and Sengupta 1993), where the specific focus is on joint selling as opposed to other dimensions of marketing such as complementary product development. The purest form of an HSA is between two distinct organizations, but selling alliances with the same challenges and advantages also form between distinct companies within conglomerates, and between distinct organization divisions or lines of business who consider themselves as basically autonomous.

A number of factors drive organizations to design and implement HSAs. From a market perspective, companies are driven towards alliances such as HSAs to gain competitive advantage through collaboration. Business customers are demanding more complete solutions to problems; to them piecemealing together parts of the puzzle is not an attractive proposition. With companies reducing supplier bases, it becomes imperative that those left in the game work with partners to develop total solutions. Companies looking to work with complementary partners are driven toward selling and other forms of comarketing alliances. Software is useless without hardware; some products are useless without service. Organizations are also driven towards HSAs to access emerging markets where joint solutions are more attractive than separate solutions from different vendors. This can be even more important in global markets where multinationals partner with local firms to gain preemptive market positions. In addition, selling partnerships can enhance an organization's reputation in the marketplace. Small software providers selling with the likes of Hewlett-Packard would be an example of this.

From an internal perspective, the need to maintain resourcing flexibility, work within resource constraints, and focus on core competencies makes HSAs attractive. HSAs allow an organization to stick to what it does better than anyone else and supplement its resources through other organizations. Given rapidly changing environments, HSAs are one way to continuously redesign virtual organizations as needs change. This is especially so in technology-based markets where change is rapid. This flexibility also provides a means to revisit and reconceptualize an organization's value-creating role. For example, IBM's working with Microsoft through product complementarity and selling partnerships allowed each company to redefine its role in the value-creation process.

In addition, there is an enabler emerging that is making the alliance route more feasible—information technology. Extranets, which are Intranets extended to partner organizations, are enhancing the capability of organizations to communicate and share information with each other, facilitating the alliance process. Access to partner product knowledge, sharing information across organizations about any interactions that a salesperson has with a customer, and passing on referrals are examples of how this technology can support and hence encourage horizontal selling alliances. Extranets are becoming part of the 'glue' which can hold selling alliances together at both the interorganizational and interpersonal levels.

As another piece of the background, we make the argument that HSAs are not the same as relationships formed within vertical distribution channels. What we know about managing distribution channel relationships may not directly apply. Horizontal selling alliances are different from, for example, manufacturer and distributor salespeople making joint calls on end-users. In vertical channel relationships, individuals are bound to their relationships by the coordinating forces of role expectations, contracts, and serial interdependence (where the output of one party is used as an input by another). These are often missing in HSAs, where partner relationships between salespeople tend to be voluntary, more interpersonal, and hence, more fragile. Most sales representatives have considerable choice of which, if any, individuals or organizations they want to work with. IBM marketing representatives, for example, often have a choice of three or four partner organizations, and possibly several different individuals, with whom they could work on a given piece of business. The roles the sales representatives adopt, the tasks they each perform, the coordinating mechanisms they deploy, and the decision-making approaches they use, typically vary from relationship to relationship, and often by customer situation. Thus, the onus is much more on the sales representatives to develop effective working relationships with their partners.

Coordination is particularly difficult since the partners often deal with multiple members of a buying center, over long sell-cycles, and face numerous sources of conflict, such as who maintains account control, who develops account strategy, and how to respond to competitors' activities. While selling alliances are often governed by formal agreements that outline expectations, responsibilities, resource commitments, and profit or commission sharing, it is often difficult to determine what needs to be done to generate the joint business, who has contributed most to the business, and the value of specific activities.

The implications of these characteristics are that relationships between partner sales representatives tend to be less structured than in vertical channel relationships, and not as well defined. Consequently, different issues may arise and different concepts, approaches, and techniques may need to be applied to understand and successfully manage HSAs. What are some of the more specific issues and challenges?

## THE ISSUES AND CHALLENGES

In any horizontal selling alliance, managers could express concern over a number of issues.[2] Questions about the appropriateness of forming an alliance, partner selection criteria and fit, the timing of when to initiate the alliance, the nature (terms, conditions, and governance) of the alliance agreement, and the pledges and guarantees required to offset nonexistent or emerging trust between organizations need to be answered. There could be skepticism about the rewards for participating, and the equitable distribution of these rewards. Managers may be concerned about impacting long standing customer relationships, forming alliances with organizations with whom one also competes, developing a partnering culture both at the interorganizational and sales representative levels, and working with partner organizations while still maintaining control over sensitive information. There may also be issues with respect to the potential for opportunistic behavior in the form of gaining market position at the expense of the partner, or building technological skills, and thus reducing dependence on the partner. Many of these issues are consistent with those identified in the management literature relating to the governance, structure, and control of similar types of alliances.

However, the overarching issue for sales executives, field sales managers, and sales representatives is understanding what accounts for observed differences in the effectiveness of HSAs. Executives focus on organizational performance dimensions, such as the organizational level issues of alliance partner choice and alliance formation, ongoing management, and evolution. They are also concerned that ineffective selling partner relationships might poison attitudes toward alliance partners and undermine management initiatives for alliance implementation. On the other hand, field sales managers and sales representatives are more concerned with how partnerships might affect their autonomy, account control, and personal sales performance. This leads to the need to discuss the issues and challenges associated with HSAs at both the interorganizational level *and* at the relationship level, that is, the sales representative-to-sales representative level (see Figure 6.1).

### Interorganizational Issues

Interestingly, when looking at existing horizontal selling alliances in the computer industry, there appear to be a limited number of concerns with relationships between the allied organizations at the interorganizational level. Sales managers have a relatively clear view of the objectives and benefits of the alliances and are generally satisfied with their partners. As one manager put it, "At the organizational level our relationship is very good. They have the name and reputation, quality people and products, and a tremendous amount of resources to throw at problems. We provide industry, application, and customer knowledge, technical support, field support, and software services."

Of the concerns that are raised, most come from smaller firms allied with large multinationals. Multinationals appear not to appreciate the differences in respective financial situations, scope of operations, or cultures. In a smaller firm, cash flow is a problem, the problem is sometimes generated by the larger partner; the abundance of paperwork and contracts can initially be burdensome, especially if the alliance crosses borders; and lack of consistency in large decentralized organizations can mean revisiting operations and terms and conditions with individual branches.

Sales representatives in smaller partner firms have some concerns at the organizational level. Simply not knowing who to contact for what, and what needs to be done for the larger organization can be confusing. Understanding a large organization's culture, internal politics, the motivations of the play-

**Figure 6.1**
**Horizontal Selling Alliance Issues**

*Stage in the Alliance*

|  | **Forming** | **Implementing, Managing, Evolving** |
|---|---|---|
| **Interorganizational** | • partnering mindset<br><br>• partner selection<br><br>• organizational compatibility<br><br>• role of contracts, pledges, guarantees<br><br>•<br>•<br>• | • managing imbalances<br><br>• goal setting<br><br>• conflict resolution<br><br>• reward systems compatibility<br><br>•<br>•<br>•<br>• |
| **Relationship** | • voluntary versus involuntary<br><br>• partner choice<br><br>• role of trustworthiness<br><br>•<br>•<br>•<br>•<br>• | • role of trusting behaviors<br><br>• open communication<br><br>• interdependence<br><br>• role of organizational differences<br><br>•<br>•<br>• |

*Level* (vertical axis label)

ers, and basic organizational dynamics can be imposing. On top of that, not knowing the partner organization's goals leaves representatives in the dark. Even if the goals are understood, however, there may be conflicts in the goals of the allied organizations.

Both sales representatives and managers express concern about turnover in territories and relationships, since it takes time to develop working relationships between partners and between the allied partners and a customer. Incentive programs also seem to get in the way of effective relationships, and can be a source of conflict. For example, a software representative only gets compensated when a sale of their company's product is made; this may not be in the best long-term interest of the customer if software from the hardware vendor is a better fit.

In summary, sales reps and managers can identify numerous organizational factors that might impede the development of effective HSAs. These observations are consistent with interorganizational exchange theories, which suggest that separations in structure, strategy, goals, culture, and technology must be overcome to actualize exchange (Levine and White 1961). These challenges become even more difficult when the gaps are exacerbated, as HSAs cross geographic boundaries in the global economy.

An interesting issue that emerges is how interorganizational issues might impact HSA effectiveness in two ways; one directly, and one through the effect that organizational-level determinants of success might have on the relationships between sales representatives charged with operationalizing the HSA in the field. We need to know more about this latter issue since, as discussed previously, this could be more serious in horizontal alliances than in more clearly defined vertical channel partnerships. Organizational structures and procedures, as well as a variety of individual differences, have been found to contribute to problems with interorganizational teams (Sims 1986). Goal incongruence and cultural dissimilarity have been found to impede the development of trust in channel relationships (Anderson and Weitz 1989). Do similar issues arise in HSAs?

## Relationship Issues

In selling alliances, individual sales representatives typically have a choice of partners and the degree to which they use partners. Consequently, to realize the benefits of selling alliances, sales representatives of the allied firms must want to work together as true partners in a specific sales situation. However, concerns about account control, and dealing with multiple partners, or partners who are also competitors, can create relationship stress that can affect effectiveness. Great variance appears to exist in the nature and effectiveness of selling partner relationships. In good relationships, reps work cooperatively, openly, and effectively as true partners. In poor relationships, reps withhold information from each other, point fingers when someone "drops the ball," question the competence, integrity, and standards of the partner, and express a high degree of frustration with, and negativity towards, the partnering concept.

In the context of relationship selling and relationship marketing in general, trust has been widely discussed as being of critical concern. This concern focuses on trust between seller and buyer. Trust is equally important in horizontal selling alliances, but it is trust *between* sales representatives in the alliance that is crucial. Trust in characteristics such as judgment and ability has been identified by almost all of the sales reps and managers in anecdotal studies of HSAs as being central to the successful dynamic of a relationship. The centrality of trust in facilitating exchange relations is well supported in relationship marketing theory (Morgan and Hunt 1994).

A variety of factors are reported by sales representatives and managers as contributing to misunderstandings, conflict, and a lack of trust in selling partner relationships. One recurrent theme is the difficulty of managing multiple partner relationships. Sales reps claim that they need a variety of partners to be effective in matching appropriate solutions to specific customer needs. However, the allied partner organizations are often competitors of one another and vie for the same business, in the same accounts. On occasion, prospects of one software supplier have been brought to computer seminars only to find that the seminar is being cohosted by another software supplier. Ownership of the customer is another key issue faced by sales representatives in HSAs. Giving up ownership to cooperate with a partner can be dangerous for two reasons. Giving up control means that the rep loses control over the behavior of the partner rep during the current sales opportunity. In the long term, customers might be lost if customer needs change and changes in allegiance result; trust comes into the picture as crucial.

The degree of conflict and lack of control, have been found to be important issues in the management of joint ventures, other forms of organizational alliances, and in distribution channels (Gaski 1984). How conflict is managed or resolved, however, may be even more pertinent in differentiating effective from ineffective sales partner relationships. Sales representatives appear quite cognizant that control, conflict, and conflict resolution or management are key in terms of the effectiveness in HSAs since they are, in effect, "sleeping with the enemy" by cooperating with potential competitors.

Issues of account control, multiple partners, and the possibility that today's partner could be tomorrow's competitor, also leads to concerns about information exchange. In good relationships, sales representatives report being more open with each other, especially about dimensions or degrees of cooperation and competition. Coordination is an additional driver of effectiveness. In better relationships, partners work out strategies and resolve conflict before meeting the customer and present a "common face." In poor relationships, reps argue in front of customers and propose different customer solutions.

Investing in poor relationships when a number of others are functioning well does not make sense to reps. Giving time to partners who pull their own weight, are competent, and consistently deliver value to the relationship and to customers does make sense. This indicates that it is important for sales reps to demonstrate value and demonstrate that they are needed by their partners; they need to show interdependence.

Finally, perceived fairness or equity has been identified as a factor in evaluating partnerships, with equity sometimes being shown through mutual recognition in front of peers and in front of each other's management. Concern for recognition is consistent with equity theory, which argues that individuals evaluate exchange outcomes in terms of "what is right," "what is deserved," or "what is fair," relative to comparison levels, rather than against expectations or specific targets (Walster, Walster, and Berscheid 1978).

These anecdotal reports provide insights into what might account for the effectiveness of HSAs. Sales representatives and managers identify several areas that may be particularly pertinent: *trust* at the organization and relationship level; *cooperation*; *constructive conflict resolution*; *open communication* between partners; *coordination* of effort; *interdependence* (mutual need recognition and demonstrated value); *commitment* (dedication and added value) to the relationship, territory, and customers; *equity* or fairness in the distribution of effort and rewards; and *organization compatibility* (such as compatible goals and systems) which sets the stage for the relationship to unfold.

## WHAT DO WE KNOW FROM RESEARCH?

Despite the increasing adoption of comarketing and selling alliances in industry, there has not yet been much empirical investigation of these alliances. Much of what we read captures anecdotally the managerial issues associated with such horizontal alliances, as discussed in the last section, but does not provide empirical evidence for the relative impact of these variables on the success of HSAs. The investigation of what drives horizontal alliance effectiveness has been primarily conceptual (Achrol, Scheer, and Stern 1990; Varadarajan and Rajaratnam 1986). While one empirical study by Bucklin and Sengupta (1993) makes a significant contribution towards understanding the effectiveness of comarketing alliances at the *interorganizational* level, there has been little investigation of effectiveness at the *interpersonal* level of the working relationships of allied sales representatives. What is least understood then are the important operational issues associated with the implementation of comarketing and selling alliances. As Liedtka (1996, 27) suggests, "Partnership must be conceived of as *both* an organizational partnership at the business unit level and as a personal relationship between individuals in the field." Let's look at what we do know.

### Interorganizational Level

In a framework of transorganizational strategic alliances, Achrol, Scheer, and Stern (1990) identify factors such as commitment, trust development, group cohesiveness, and motivation of alliance participants as being critical success factors. In Bucklin and Sengupta's (1993) empirical work on the comarketing of complementary products, key predictors of effectiveness were carefully selecting projects with joint payoffs; matching partners in terms of management style and culture; the length of prior history of doing business together; reducing power imbalances between the partners (or contracting if there are imbalances); reducing managerial imbalances in terms of disproportionate amounts of management talent being contributed by partners; and functional conflict resolution. Narus and Anderson (1996) echo some of these findings in their study of distributors forming alliances with other distributors to share complementary product lines and services, in that the focus on equitable reward systems, and trust and commitment built initially through pledges and guarantees, are keys to success.

Although based on working across lines of business under a corporate umbrella, Liedtka's (1996) qualitative study within professional service firms does capture some of the things that could make a difference in horizontal selling alliances. She found first of all that a partnering mindset is required. Partnerships must be viewed as an opportunity, as opposed to a threat; people must be willing to put a personal stake in the partnership; there must be a high level of trust among partners, based to a degree on capabilities; and there must be a readiness to learn from each other. Partnering skills are also required, including the ability to create shared goals and realistic expectations, using conflict productively, and redesigning systems and processes to cross business units. Finally, there must be the architecture in place to encourage partnering behavior. The supporting architecture involves an organizational culture of honest communication; leadership committed to partnering; joint planning and budgeting processes across the organizations; congruent measurement and reward systems; and the resources available, such as time, to actualize the alliance.

### Relationship Level

At the interpersonal relationship level of a selling alliance, Smith and Barclay have guided the research to date. In their work, trust has been identified as being *the* critical factor differentiating effective from ineffective selling partnerships. This may be especially so, given that at the territory level, sales representatives are free to choose their specific partners—the relationships are voluntary. Smith and Barclay's (1997) trust-based model of effective selling partner relationships conceptualizes trust as consisting of trustworthiness and trusting behaviors. Mutual satisfaction with the selling partner relationship was driven by perceived task performance, by the trusting behavior of communication openness, and by trustworthiness in the form of trustworthy character, motives, and judgment. Interestingly, differences across allied organizations in terms of differences in motivations, goals, and approaches to doing business, these often being driven by differences in the cultures, strategies, and systems of the partner organizations, did impact on how trustworthy a partner was perceived to be, but these effects did not generally have a big impact on satisfaction with the relationship. In Smith's (1997) study, open communication and trust again were found to differentiate successful from less successful relationships, but in addition, perceived interdependence of the partners was critical.

Liedtka echoes the importance of trust between individuals involved in partnerships, and found in her work with service firms that trust was conceptualized as absolute faith in the technical competence of partners and as trust of each other's intentions and ability to deliver. "In struggling partnerships, trust was demanded; in successful ones, it was earned" (1996, 27). Her conclusion reinforces the importance of the relationship level issues when she states that success "depends far more on the capabilities and commitment of the working partners in the field than on the directives issued from divisional or corporate headquarters" (24).

Netting out what we appear to know about selling alliance effectiveness at the interpersonal level, *trust*, and the constellation of related concepts—for example, commitment, perceived interdependence, and organizational differences are key to our understanding of effectiveness.

## WHAT DO WE KNOW FROM EXPERIENCE?

It is worth looking at attempts of specific organizations in different industry sectors to enhance selling alliance effectiveness, either across distinct business units under the same corporate umbrella, or across different companies. The discussion of the selling alliance phenomenon and the research reviewed above was largely in the context of technology-based companies. The issues and challenges were mainly gleaned from computer hardware firms allying with software firms to provide bundled solutions to customers. Repeating the insights from these experiences would be redundant. Instead, we look to a diversified industrial organization and to the financial services sector for additional experiences.

## AN INDUSTRIAL ORGANIZATION

We start with the Canadian subsidiary of a large multinational. This company is divided into a number of businesses; some related, some not. The impetus for forming selling alliances across business units originated with customers. First, some customers were demanding single point responsibility from the company, especially across closely related product lines. They were not going to tolerate a large number of salespeople from the same organization calling on them. The challenge came in how to respond to this situation in terms of coordinating selling activities, that is, allying across business units. Second, other customers were asking for "bundled" solutions to their challenges and problems. No more bits of this and pieces of that. They were asking, "What could this supplier as an entire organization do for us?"

The organization has certain things going for it. In general there is a shared set of values, and to some extent culture, across the business units. On the other hand, P&Ls are lined up against divisions, which makes compromises (for example, giving up margins to close a bundled deal) difficult.

Two approaches have been tried to work up alliances across the business units. In the first approach, an overall account manager was assigned to a major customer. This account manager had been a senior sales manager for an important division of the company. He now reports to corporate, not to a division, is on a unique compensation plan, and is evaluated on the general growth of the business with this major customer. He is given the task to work across all business units to pull the bundle together. Joint sales calls are made, joint account planning across divisions is facilitated, and a lot of informal selling is done internally to make the joint selling happen. Some of the keys that give this approach a chance of being successful are the reporting structure and compensation plan, which are "undivisionalized." In the United States, General Electric has implemented a similar approach in the automotive sector, where account managers in Detroit coordinate General Electric's sales efforts across lines of business to serve the needs of the large automotive manufacturers.

The second approach works much more on an informal team basis across a subset of related divisions. If a customer has a number of the company's sales representatives calling on it, the representative with the 'best' relationship with that customer becomes responsible for creating the selling alliance across the divisions. 'Best' is often defined by sales volume, but not always. Reps who develop true customer intimacy, but do not have the most at stake, sometimes become the alliance leader. What this approach means is that for one customer a sales rep is the leader, for another a team player in the alliance. Teams meet on a fairly regular basis to exchange information, develop new ideas, and develop customer account plans. Some of the issues generally associated with selling alliances are likely to arise in this approach. What if a team player feels that he or she owns the customer for his or her division? It is not easy to give up control to another rep. Will the alliance leader give more time and effort to their product line than to others? The issue of trust becomes critical with this approach.

Although it is too early to tell if these approaches make enough sense to expand their application (which would require more widespread organizational adjustment), they are at least worthy of our consideration.

### Financial Services

A large Canadian financial group, with a bank at its core, faced a different challenge which requires the close sales cooperation of loosely joined businesses. Gathered under the Royal Bank Financial Group (RBFG) umbrella is commercial banking (Royal Bank of Canada), personal banking (Royal Bank of Canada), a brokerage house (RBC Dominion Securities), a discount broker (Royal Bank Action Direct), and a trust company (Royal Trust). Many of these businesses were acquired as regulatory constraints lifted in the financial services sector. They have different histories, cultures, structures, ways of compensating salespeople, and inherently different perspectives on the role of selling in RBFG—vestiges of their former lives. For example, the investment brokers are highly motivated salespeople on commission; the personal bankers typically do not see themselves as salespeople and are on salary. Could RBFG leverage opportunities across these diverse businesses? If so, what would be the best way to get started?

A senior executive task force cutting across all businesses was formed to address these questions. Emerging from this was a decision to leverage across businesses to serve the crucial high-value client segment, the segment with the bank's most profitable customers. These clients demand advice across a broad range of products and services. RBFG has these products and services, but they need to be marshaled across very different businesses with very distinct cultures and objectives. The objective is to create a context where salespeople work together to meet these demanding clients' needs; selling alliances is the vision. To demonstrate leadership and commitment to making this happen, a "Vice President, Affluent Clients" was appointed to work through the issues. To give the selling alliance issue even higher profile, this vice president reports to the Senior Vice President, Sales in Personal Financial Services, Royal Bank. The new appointee was at the time with Royal Bank, but had come from Royal Trust, so she knew at least two of the cultures involved.

A number of issues surface in thinking about this vision around the affluent client. For example, certain businesses overlap each other in terms of product offerings. Both RBC Dominion Securities and Royal Trust provide discretionary wealth management services whereby a client signs on to a wealth manager who makes investment decisions on the client's behalf. On one hand, there is a need to cooperate to satisfy clients' needs, on the other there is a desire to compete to gain more of a client's 'share of wallet' for a given business unit. Some of the other issues are ownership of the customer, sharing compensation, compensating for 'lost' business if revenue is transferred to another unit, and the underlying motivation to sell across business units. RBFG knew that this was not an easy dilemma to solve, but they also knew that the financial group that figures out how to ally across its distinctive businesses to serve these clients will be in the driver's seat.

RBFG's approach was to start with a manageable objective. If they could only get one business to refer clients to another, that would be a start to eventual strong selling alliances across the entire financial group. The first step was to study the best practices throughout North America regarding rewarding, recognizing, and encouraging referrals. This led to a field experiment in which seventeen high potential markets were chosen across the country to study the impact that leadership, teamwork, coaching, compensation, and the relative location of one business unit to another would have on referral behavior. Compensation was varied in different markets by introducing cash awards, Royal Bank shares, points tied into the larger Royal Performance Recognition program, and points redeemable for merchandise.

Although it was concluded that leadership and teamwork seemed to have the greatest impact on results, a more tangible way of changing behavior to form selling alliances was deemed to be through rewards and recognition.

Quantitative results plus qualitative feedback from the field indicated that the direction to head toward was cash—the common denominator, especially considering the cash-oriented nature of the brokerage house. "Cash is king, and nothing else counts," was the claim of the representative from RBC Dominion Securities. This was not an easy conclusion at which to arrive. Royal Bank historically has not been a place where variable compensation is part of the fabric. Would people eventually accept the downside risk associated with variable compensation? It would also be a tough sell up the ladder, since the recommendation was counter culture.

Implementation of this referral program reveals a number of issues that need to be considered in heading toward any selling alliance formation. First, compensation sharing can be an issue. What if a number of people are involved in recommending that a client be served by another business within RBFG? Who gets the credit and cash for the referral? Superior salespeople recognize the key role that a front line customer service representative could play in initiating a referral, and will find informal ways to reward this behavior (i.e., sharing the cash or recognition points, or meals out). Second, legal restrictions may make it difficult, and in this case, difficult to reward stockbrokers for referring clients. Third, a help in creating effective selling alliances is information, so that everyone selling to a client, either separately or jointly, has access to client information. The need for an enterprise-wide database and client confidentiality can become an issue.

Fourth, the P&Ls of the RBFG are aligned with the businesses. What happens to a business that refers clients to another business? The impact on revenues can be enormous. This is true from the highest levels right down to the branch level. Businesses count on more referrals coming in than going out to make referrals worthwhile. This may not necessarily be the case. For example, it is more likely that a high-value client would be referred to RBC Dominion Securities than vice versa. A method of double counting may need to be designed to encourage behavior that results in moving revenue out of a business to another family member.

What about unexpected positives emerging from the field experiment and implementation process? There were a number of them. First, informal activities emerged that allowed representatives to get to know each other and each other's business, which led to the development of trust. Without this trust, it is unlikely that a salesperson will give up customer ownership. Some locations instituted weekly coffee times together where all businesses could meet, and at other locations invitations to attend one's business social functions were extended to other businesses.

Second, a number of more formal initiatives were undertaken. For example, trade fairs were organized where each business sets up booths and employees were encouraged to get to know the other businesses. Joint marketing ideas unfolded such as the sending of jointly-signed letters to clients. Salespeople have committed to sitting down with their partners once a week to review client profiles looking for opportunities to refer. Joint cold calls have been made. Salespeople attend and present product information at each other's sales meetings.

What can we learn from this experience? First, establishing selling alliances across businesses with different histories, cultures, and compensation philosophies is extremely difficult at both the organizational and individual levels. Second, it may pay off in the long run to start small in terms of encouraging the desired behaviors associated with selling alliances. Third, no matter what is done organizationally in terms of structure and leadership, two fundamental things need to be present: the compensation, reward, and recognition system; and the desire on the part of salespeople to want to work together. If the latter is there, salespeople will find creative ways, informal and formal, to get to know one another and one another's business leading to trust and further commitment. Fourth, a company must be prepared for surprises that surface during implementation, and making certain that the management commitment is there to carry it through.

## WHERE TO FROM HERE?

In considering the question of, Where to from here? we develop two perspectives. The first is, what managerial guidelines can be derived from what we know and what might be emerging in the area of horizontal selling alliances? The second perspective is, what questions should academics be addressing with respect to learning more about HSAs to guide managerial decisions?

### Managerial Guidelines

When thinking about successfully forming, implementing, managing, and evolving HSAs, managers need to consider the following questions:

- Do I have a clear rationale why I am considering HSAs? There is a multitude of market-based and internal reasons driving marketing managers towards HSAs. To which of these am I responding? Is it to ally with product complementors? Gain collaborative advantage? Access emerging markets? Focus on core competencies? Or for another reason?

- Do the partners have clearly defined objectives and payoffs envisioned for the HSA?

- Am I clear on the organizational similarities and dissimilarities that will impact HSA success such as reward system compatibility? Planning horizons? Have I thought through the impact that these will have at the organization-to-organization level, and also how these organizational attributes will impact the working of the sales representatives in the field?

- Have I identified power and managerial imbalances between the partners? Have I thought through contracts that might redress any imbalances, and ensure that issues such as the contribution of managerial time to the alliance is clear?

- Am I conscious of the need to put effort into the alliance at both the *interorganizational* level, in terms of, for example, selecting partners, or assessing organizational compatibility, and at the *relationship* level, between sales representatives? Since horizontal relationships are more voluntary, fragile, and informal than more traditional vertical relationships, am I aware of the relationship level perhaps being of utmost importance in HSAs?

- Is the *trust* there? Have I done all that I can to engender trustworthiness and trusting behaviors between the partners in general, and more specifically between the sales representatives actualizing the alliance? Do I understand some of the dimensions that are part of trust, such as open communication and good judgment?

- Am I open to seeing that as information technology evolves, especially Extranets, HSAs will be enabled by information, and that this may be a new 'glue' which binds alliances together and makes them more possible?

- Am I vigilant in spotting opportunities for the development of HSAs as markets become more global, as product complementors become critical in some markets, and as HSAs evolve in industry sectors where they may be limited in number today?

### Academic Questions

In general, research that helps managers provide better answers to the questions posed above would be of value. Research is also required which addresses the underserved quadrants in Figure 6.1, specifically in forming HSAs at the relationship level, and implementing, managing, and evolving HSAs at the relationship level. More specifically, academics might consider the following:

- We know something about what organizations should consider when forming alliances, but what should sales representatives consider when choosing selling alliance partners? Which of these attributes are accessible and visible enough to allow selection to be made? Trust is key, but how can they assess this before taking the plunge?

- What else at the sales rep relationship level drives effectiveness? There are a limited number of studies addressing this broad but important question, with the focus of research to date on trust and related constructs.

- We know something about forming alliances at the organizational level, but most of the research is in certain context, such as joint ventures. Are there unique dimensions of HSAs that make these findings more or less useful?

- Are there differences in the constructs that impact HSA success in situations where the partners are separate companies, versus the situation where they are autonomous members of a conglomerate?

- Do HSA success factors vary across industry sectors? Most of what we know comes from the technology sector. Are factors that result in success different in financial services? The industrial sector? Advertising?

- What happens when we move beyond two partners? In the future, more complex customer problems are going to demand more complex supplier-partnering arrangements, such as consortia. What additional insights do we need to move beyond the dyad?

- How will information technology, embedded, for example, in Extranets, impact what we believe to be core constructs such as trust in HSAs? Will technology increase trust? Decrease trust?
- What unique issues arise when we move HSAs into global contexts?
- Is there anything we can learn from sales approaches that do cross boundaries, but more within organizations as opposed to between? Do the insights gained through studying national account management and crossfunctional customer focused teams apply to HSAs? To what degree?
- Can we derive a better set of metrics to measure HSA outcomes and success? To date, most of the indicators have been partner perceptions of success, effectiveness, and satisfaction. Can we tease out the impact that HSAs have on harder measures of performance such as revenue? Market share? Share of wallet?

## CONCLUSION

Horizontal selling alliances are one form of new organizational configurations emerging in response to complicated, demanding, and increasingly competitive business markets. On the surface they make sense—jointly selling complementary products and services to better serve customers and to gain collaborative advantage over competitors. What we are discovering however, is that the doing is more difficult than the saying. Issues facing managers and sales representatives at both organizational and relationship levels leave many unanswered questions.

We believe that this chapter has highlighted the emerging importance of this comarketing approach, has identified a number of the issues faced in making decisions about the formation and management of HSAs, has indicated what we are learning about HSAs, and has left some questions for managers and academics to look at now and in the future.

## NOTES

We would like to gratefully acknowledge the financial support provided by the Social Sciences and Humanities Research Council of Canada, the Richard Ivey School of Business Plan for Excellence, and the George and Mary Turnbull Professorship.

1. The following background discussion draws heavily from work by Smith (1997) and Smith and Barclay (1997), both authors of this chapter. Sections have been reprinted with permission from *Industrial Marketing Management* 26, J. Brock Smith, "Selling Alliances: Issues and Insights," 149–161, 1997. Elsevier Science Inc.

2. This discussion of managerial issues draws heavily from work by Smith (1997) and Smith and Barclay (1997), both authors of this chapter. Sections have been reprinted with permission from *Industrial Marketing Management* 26, J. Brock Smith, "Selling Alliances: Issues and Insights," 149–161, 1997. Elsevier Science Inc. The insights are based on a series of interviews with executives, managers, and sales representatives in the computer industry.

## REFERENCES

Achrol, R. D., L. K. Scheer, and L. W. Stern. 1990. Designing Successful Transorganizational Marketing Alliances. Working paper no. 90–118, Marketing Science Institute, Cambridge, Mass.

Anderson, E., and B. Weitz. 1989. Determinants of Continuity in Conventional Industrial Channel Dyads. *Marketing Science* 8 (4): 310–323.

Bucklin, L. P., and S. Sengupta. 1993. Organizing Successful Co-Marketing Alliances. *Journal of Marketing* 57 (April): 32–46.

Gaski, J. F. 1984. The Theory of Power and Conflict in Channels of Distribution. *Journal of Marketing* 48 (Summer): 9–29.

Levine, S., and P. White. 1961. Exchange as a Conceptual Framework for the Study of Interorganizational Relationships. *Administrative Science Quarterly* 5: 583–601.

Liedtka, J. M. 1996. Collaborating Across Lines of Business for Competitive Advantage. *Academy of Management Executive* 10 (2): 20–37.

Morgan, R. M., and S. D. Hunt. 1994. The Commitment–Trust Theory of Relationship Marketing. *Journal of Marketing* 58 (July): 20–38.

Narus, J. A., and J. C. Anderson. 1996. Rethinking Distribution: Adaptive Channels. *Harvard Business Review* 74 (July–August): 112–120.

Sims, D. 1986. Interorganization: Some Problems of Multi-Organizational Teams. *Personnel Review* 15 (4): 27–31.

Smith, J. B. 1997. Selling Alliances: Issues and Insights. *Industrial Marketing Management* 26 (March): 149–161.

Smith, J. B., and D. W. Barclay. 1997. The Effects of Organizational Differences and Trust on the Effectiveness of Selling Partner Relationships. *Journal of Marketing* 61 (January): 3–21.

Varadarajan, P., and D. Rajaratnam. 1986. Symbiotic Marketing Revisited. *Journal of Marketing* 50 (January): 7–17.

Walster, E., W. Walster, and E. Berscheid. 1978. *Equity Theory and Research*. Boston, Mass.: Allyn and Bacon.

# PART III

# From Old to New

# Chapter 7

# CyberSales Management and Direct Selling

Richard C. Bartlett, Sharon Morgan Tahaney,
and Thomas R. Wotruba

## THE PERVASIVENESS OF DIRECT SELLING

Most people have at least one relative, friend, or neighbor (or perhaps themselves) engaged in direct selling now or in the recent past. And most people will have other relatives, friends, and neighbors who have recently bought something from a direct seller. More than 7 million men and women in the United States today are engaged in direct selling (Fact Sheet 1996). Direct salespeople are independent contractors who represent such companies as Mary Kay, Tupperware, Amway, and Shaklee, and who make personal contacts with consumers in their home, their workplace, or at an in-home party hosted by a consumer. Recent studies show that purchases were made from direct sellers in more than one-half of U.S. households over a twelve-month period, and a product or service was purchased from a direct salesperson in nine out of ten households at some point in time (Peterson, Albaum, and Ridgway 1989).

Many factors account for the ubiquity of direct selling in our economy. First, products and services are available in a wide diversity of types, styles, and sizes, with many from companies of long-standing reputation and experience. In turn, this diversity of offerings provides a broad range of selling opportunities for direct salespeople. Second, direct selling firms rarely try to limit the territories or constituencies where their salespeople can seek business. One's customer base is built by making contacts, gaining references, and building relationships with any prospect, rather than being confined (or protected) by geographic boundaries. This, plus the fact that direct selling opportunities are open to persons of every background, demographic, and socioeconomic category, fosters a network of sales effort pervading all segments of society (Bartlett 1994). Further, these independent contractors have the discretion to work as much or as little as they wish, allowing them to fit this endeavor within the demands from other parts of their lives (i.e., other jobs, family responsibilities, or health issues). Many would not pursue direct selling if it required a full-time commitment. Finally, direct selling is attractive to many persons because it satisfies a variety of motivations (Wotruba and Tyagi 1992). While some direct salespeople are primarily concerned about dollar earnings, others give more priority to intrinsic rewards, such as gaining self-assurance and feelings of accomplishment. Still others are likely to be in direct selling because it provides the chance to satisfy social needs such as making friends, gaining recognition, and working on a team. A sizable group simply enjoy being associated with a well-known company and identifying with its highly regarded products. Thus, while every direct salesperson does not earn a large income, not every direct salesperson is seeking a large income as the primary reward from the job experience.

From the customer's perspective, the popularity of purchasing from direct sellers can also be explained by a variety of factors. The breadth of available products and services is one factor since the collective offerings of all direct selling companies provide something for every person, family, and household in the marketplace. Perhaps the primary advantage perceived by buyers is convenience—having the items brought to the customer rather than having to seek out the items in a retail store setting. Coupled with convenience are two other key advantages of buying in this manner. One is the personal attention and service provided by the salesperson, demonstrating the product, determining which ones best fit the buyer's needs, and answering questions about the product's use or functioning (e.g., cosmetics, jewelry, nutritional supplements, or household appliances). The other is the ability of buyers to examine the products, often within the context of their own homes where the items will be used (e.g., housewares, cleaning products, toys, or cookware). Party-plan methods of direct selling also provide a social and entertainment experience, creating new friendships as well as business relationships among the party attendees (Frenzen and Davis 1990).

## DIRECT SELLING AS A BUSINESS STRATEGY

Direct selling is not simply a type of selling, but rather it is the foundation of a distinctive business strategy. While direct selling firms can employ various tactical options (Peterson and Wotruba 1996), the primary character of the direct selling strategy is that it relies on independent contractors to perform its principal marketing activities of promotion and distribution. While other firms use traditional methods of selling consumer goods through retail stores supported by mass advertising, direct selling organizations succeed through the motivated efforts of a multitude of entrepreneurial salespeople whose only cost to their companies involves the commissions paid after sales occur. Though some direct selling organizations do use limited amounts of media advertising, the primary success of this strategy comes from the personal contact between seller and buyer whereby sellers create relationships with their buyers based on convenience and personal attention. In fact, direct selling is the epitome of relationship marketing, initiated when wandering "peddlers" first roamed through towns and rural countryside, bringing intriguing products as well as entertaining advice and stories gleaned from their past travels to welcoming households (Wright 1927).

## REQUIREMENTS FOR SUCCESS IN DIRECT SELLING

For direct-selling businesses to remain viable, they must continually adapt to changing marketplace and competitive conditions. Some research has shown that customer loyalty depends greatly on the desirability of the product itself (Raymond and Tanner 1994). So products in tune with today's market needs and amenable to effective demonstration and personalization must be continually maintained and updated.

But also essential to continued success is the availability of an enthusiastic sales force. Much research has been done on turnover among direct salespeople (Wotruba and Tyagi 1991), providing guidance to company management on ways to reduce turnover and boost job satisfaction. Additionally, compensation must be attractive, since direct-selling firms compete in the labor market for the best-performing direct salespeople.

A third determinant of success is to maintain the proper legal and ethical climate in the relationships between the companies and their independent contractors as well as in the relationships between both those parties and their customers. While legal and ethical challenges have dogged this industry in the past, most major direct-selling firms today (and especially all those who are members of the Direct Selling Association, the industry trade association) have an admirable record for their legal and ethical behavior (Bartlett 1995; Wotruba 1995).

A final significant factor affecting the success of a direct selling strategy is to monitor and adapt to changes within the behavior and lifestyles of their target market groups. For example, lifestyle trends show that consumers are increasingly favoring convenience, experiences that reinforce self-identity, the importance of value from quality and service, flexibility in employment and other demands in their lives, and the desire for more information and communication (Wotruba 1992). Routine patterns in people's lives are changing or disappearing as consumers actively seek ways to flex, diversify, and participate in the new and exciting.

## THE TECHNOLOGY CHALLENGE

One pervasive trend occurring today involves the many manifestations of electronic technology. The use of home computers, cellular phones, fax machines, and other electronic devices is growing substantially each year. Recent estimates by *Advertising Age* state that 27 percent of all adults in the United States have access to the Internet, and Nielsen Media Research reports that 73 percent of Web users spend time online searching for information about a specific product or service (*CyberAtlas* 1997). Familiarity with computers and associated technology will, of course, become routine as today's computer-trained students become tomorrow's average citizens. (More detail on Internet users and their characteristics will follow.)

Electronic technology has the potential of permeating most aspects of our lives, from communications to shopping to education and even leisure time entertainment activities. What will all of this mean for direct selling? For instance, would the adaptation of electronic technology in direct selling help capture the interest of potential recruits and customers alike and better serve the needs of each? Can electronic technology be adapted to assist in providing the convenience, flexibility, and individualized communication that are inherent values in the direct-selling and buying process? Or will electronic technology encroach upon the face-to-face essence of direct selling and eventually replace it? As much as ten years ago, Enis (1986) suggested that direct-selling firms consider providing their salespeople with software and training for use on their personal computers to maintain records and assist in organizing customer information, inquiries, and orders. Much has happened in the intervening ten years to make that suggestion not only reasonable but also somewhat simplistic in light of the potential capabilities of electronic technology today and the promises of tomorrow. If we are not yet on the electronic superhighway, we will soon be left far behind.

## THE INEVITABLE CONNECTION

The question of whether direct selling organizations will tap into emerging information technologies is no longer a question. The answer is an undeniable yes. Sales management is an evolving world, and nowhere are the effects of change more profound than in direct sales. Productivity and value-adding customer services are primary drivers in today's race to stay competitive. With managers, independent contractors, and customers in far flung locations and decision making distributed across a vast number of people, the success of any direct sales organization is how quickly, reliably, and effectively it interacts with people. Emerging technologies, the core of which is networked computing, provide powerful new tools whose importance to direct sales is not techno-prowess, but communication and interaction—the basis for building emotional ties and the essence of success in direct sales.

To borrow from an MCI ad, the interest of direct sales in technology is not about "bits and bytes, bells and whistles." It is about connecting people. Don Tapscott (1996) said it best: "Today, the leader is a collective, networked, virtual force with power flowing from a jointly created and shared vision." In other words, this is the age of a well connected direct sales force.

## A REVOLUTION IN INFORMATION TECHNOLOGIES

In 1937, Richard C. Bartlett's father, Theodore Lester Bartlett, as the first paid employee of the Federal Communications Commission (F.C.C.), stated in a historic brief, "It's inconceivable that more than 25,000 American families would want to sit in a darkened room and watch a flickering picture on an image orthicon tube." Later, in 1947, as an employee of RCA, this same T. L. Bartlett had to argue to the same F.C.C. that "Every American home would want RCA's all electronic color TV." Perceptions change.

Thirty-six years later, in 1983, Steve Jobs dragged a reluctant Richard Bartlett to a computer to prove spreadsheets could indeed be created by manipulating a mouse connected to a little gray box filled with bits and bytes and microchips. Today, this same Bartlett is coauthoring a chapter on the virtues and triumphs of networked computing. Again, perceptions change.

Historically, new technologies have always fallen prey to cautious perceptions. Take, for example, the fax machine. It was invented in 1923, and remained victim of technophobia until the early 1980s. The same was true with the ATM machine—invented in 1965, and not perceived viable by the public until 1985, twenty years later.

The same revolution in perception is now underway for networked computing. It is a revolution measured in decades with its start dating back as far as 1954. That was the year the first commercial computer application was installed in the payroll department of General Electric. The conventional wisdom at that time was that business operations would be dominated by huge, mainframe computers. Decision making would be centralized at the top by those who controlled access to central processing units. At one time, IBM even projected that fifty-five computers could satisfy the data needs of the entire world. A real-life version of George Orwell's *1984* seemed possible with one exception—Big Brother would be replaced by Big Computer.

Reality proved quite different. As it turned out, the real 1984 will not be remembered as a symbol of centralization and mainframe computers, but as the beginning of a democratic and decentralized spread of information. A year earlier, the PC had been named as *Time* magazine's "Man of the Year." In 1984, Apple rolled out its Macintosh. A small company just outside of Seattle was putting the last touches on Windows 1.0. And an obscure military research network, later to be called the Internet, began to expand its presence. The industrial age was being replaced by the information age. The revolution in information technologies had officially begun.

## THE INTERNET IN INFANCY

Nowhere is this democratic and decentralized spread of information more pronounced than on the Internet. Easing access to human knowledge and experience across shared communication space is what the Internet does. As described by Scott Burns (1996), "The Internet isn't slow TV. It isn't electronic newspapers. It isn't home shopping. It isn't a thing at all. It's a process. It's visual. It's auditory. It is interactive." It is the people's medium. Gary Fernandes, Vice Chairman of EDS, underscores the point by saying, "Today, the consumer is driving the shape of the Internet—not producers or technicians."

Millions of consumers are using the Internet as a multimedia playground for data-intensive tasks, such as reading online magazines or downloading images. The number of pages on the Web has catapulted from a few thousand in 1991 to an estimated 54 million in early 1997. Nicholas Negroponte (1997) of the MIT Media Laboratory has predicted more than 1 billion people will be online worldwide by the year 2000.

Initially only academic institutions and the military were linked to the computer network that collectively came to be called the Internet. It all began in the late 1960s when the Defense Department ordered a communications network so dispersed and decentralized that even a nuclear attack would not wipe it out completely. The answer to their demand was created in 1969 when Bolt Beranek & Newman (now BBN Corporation) installed the first "node" at the University of California at Los Angeles. That point was later linked to connections at three other U.S. universities. International links followed, and by 1975, approximately one-hundred nodes had linked together research centers and government facilities worldwide.

The Internet was primarily words and rudimentary graphics. Academic and research users of the Net were tolerant of delays and goofs. Not so today. The Internet has become mission critical to business, and consumers demand instant gratification.

The Internet took its next growth spurt with the introduction and widespread use of "browsers," which are computer programs allowing computer users to view and navigate through electronic "objects" supported on other computers, called "servers." Objects include computer files of text, sound, video, and combinations of these. The process of digitized files zipping around the world among computers at the speed of light was described by *San Francisco Chronicle* columnist Robert Rossnet as "the information sent from one computer to another, broken up into a zillion pieces, scattered across the network, and then reassembled at the other end, just like a transporter on Star Trek."

The Internet grew again and became viable as a new global medium with the formation of the World Wide Web (WWW, or Web). British scientist Tim Berners-Lee invented the World Wide Web in 1991, as a way to help researchers trace references in technical papers. Then to add fuel to the Internet explosion, the University of Illinois's famed supercomputer lab designed Mosaic, point-and-click software for "browsing" the Web. The Web not only brought multimedia capabilities to the Internet, it also brought the hyperlink, the ability to click on a highlighted word and go immediately to another file or location of related information.

## A BASELINE LOOK AT GROWTH

In the case of a revolution like this one, change is inevitable. No one, not even those directly inside the Internet world, knows precisely what the impact of this powerful new communications medium will be. In 1981, there were 213 computers connected to the Internet ("Dateline NBC" 1996). In 1996, there were 50.6 million users of the Internet worldwide (*CyberAtlas* 1997). In 1984, the media mentioned the term "Internet" only seventy-five times. During 1996, the term "Internet" was used by the media over three-hundred thousand times (McGowan 1996).

Numbers and behaviors are changing rapidly as the Internet diffuses into critical mass. How soon this interactive medium will reach the mass population is, at the moment, a guess. Projections vary dramatically—further proof that predicting when the majority will enter the virtual world is mere speculation. However, the key issue is that it is happening, and companies who disregard this medium will do so at their peril. The message is clear—growth is too rapid to ignore. The time for denial is past.

### Numbers and Behaviors

To mark one moment in time in the rapid-fire evolution of networked computing, here is a snapshot of current statistics, behaviors, challenges, and projections:

- The January 1997 Domain Survey uncovered 16.1 million Internet hosts, up from 9.5 million in January 1995 and 4.9 million in January 1994 (*CyberAtlas* 1997).

- Between 1994 and 1995, venture capital investments in Internet companies increased by over 300 percent (*webmarketeer* 1996).

- Men are by far the dominant European users of the Internet, according to a study by International Research Institutes, Brussels. Up to eight times as many men as women surf the Net. The ratio is 8 to 1 in Finland; 4 to 1 in Britain; and 3 to 1 in The Netherlands. In Germany, virtually no women click on at all (Euromen Love the Net 1996).

- Twenty-seven percent of U.S. adults used the Web in past six months (*CyberAtlas* 1997).

- Household PC penetration is up to 39 percent in the United States (*CyberAtlas* 1997).

- The average Internet user spends over five-and-a-half hours a week online (*webmarketeer* 1996).

- Over 65 percent of the 85,000 U.S. public schools have Internet access (*webmarketeer* 1996).
- There is an enormous wave of kids on the Internet—almost all fourteen-year-olds are computer literate (Negroponte 1997).
- In 1991, for the first time ever, U.S. companies spent more on computing and information technologies than in any other capital category (Bosley 1996).
- Rule of thumb for today's technology says: the number of transistors you can put on a single chip doubles every eighteen months (Bosley 1996).
- In 1995, advertisers spent up to $140 million to get their message to users on the Internet and on the big three online services. By the year 2000, this advertising is projected to go as high as $4 billion (McGowan 1996).
- The number of households online has been doubling every twelve months (Massachusetts Institute of Technology 1996b).

## Challenges

- At present, the Internet is nearing gridlock. Netscape Communications Corporation's Chairman Jim Clark replies, "The Internet will get to the breaking point just like the phone system has throughout time . . . and then providers will add capacity to avoid losing customers" (Ziegler 1996).
- "Server" computers that dish out Web pages often are swamped with far more requests than they can handle (Ziegler 1996).
- Routers, the specialized computers that send messages down the correct pipelines scanning a massive address book of about forty thousand area destinations, get overloaded and lose packets. Every day at peak period, the Internet's backbones lose more than 10 percent of the data packets they transmit, says a University of Michigan monitoring group (Ziegler 1996).
- "We're pushing the edge of the interconnect technology," says John Curran, BBN's chief technical officer. "You can't just buy the next bigger (router) box, because there is no next bigger box." Stronger, speedier models are in the works, but Internet growth continues to outstrip the advances (Ziegler 1996).

Vinton Cerf, a senior vice president at MCI and codeveloper of the original Internet, responds to the challenges with, "Every year you have to put in the same amount of capacity as in all the years before. So far this year, MCI has tripled its backbone capacity to 155 megabits per second, and plans to expand to 622 megabits per second by year end. If we're going to sustain this 100% growth rate through the end of the decade, we have some very serious work ahead of us" (Ziegler 1996). Nicholas Negroponte of Massachusetts Institute of Technology thinks the Net is "scaling very well" because of the way it was designed. "I don't think it will come to its knees and crash. I see it as very organic in the way it's capable of living and reproducing itself." A solution to the bandwidth crunch, according to Dr. Andrew Grove, CEO of Intel Corporation, is to bridge the gap between the future when bandwidth will have the necessary capacity to carry the multimedia to the masses and today with "hybrid applications." Hybrids try to stretch technology of today to offer advanced multimedia experiences. Typically they offer ways to download via telephone modems increased amounts of graphics or video off a Website and then store it on a PC's hard drive. The data can then be quickly accessed. Until the big jumps in bandwidth occur, Dr. Grove feels hybrids are one solution to the problem.

### Projections

- EDS Vice Chairman Gary Fernandes estimates that the U.S. Internet services market will be worth $116 billion by the year 2000, and $250 billion worldwide.
- The demand for Web-related developers will grow by a factor of ten over the next three years (*webmarketeer* 1996).
- By the year 2000, Allen Weiner, Director and Principal Analyst for Dataquest, says industry analysts are predicting there will be over 100 million users of the Internet.
- Looking ten years ahead, International Business Machines Corporation predicts in an internal forecast that Internet delays will be among the top issues the industry will face.

### WHO IS ONLINE AND WHY?

Procter & Gamble, the seventeenth largest company on the Fortune 500 list with worldwide sales in 1995 of more than $33 billion, now has more than eighty Internet addresses for development. "We see the Internet as one of the waves of the future in the world of new media," says Elizabeth Moore, company spokeswoman for advertising practices. Why would a company that pioneered newspaper advertising and television advertising, and was the inspiration for naming daytime dramas "soap operas" because of radio sponsorship of their soap products—why would a company this rich in communication history run full speed onto the information superhighway? One reason is that their pioneering spirit has paid off in the past. Another reason could have something to do with who is online with them.

Today, one-half of all Fortune 500 companies have a Website (*CyberAtlas* 1997). Businesses from Wal-Mart to Wall Street are jumping online with a Website and a "we shall see" attitude. AT&T, the company known for delivering technology, has a more deliberate plan in mind. David Robinson, Electronic Marketing District Manager for AT&T, sums it up: "We are turning the World Wide Web into a value-added resource that will enable our clients—and our sales teams as well—to have a resource of information that's up-to-the-minute, twenty-four hours a day, with content they couldn't find anywhere else." Since coming online in November 1995 with 300 home pages, the Global Services portion of the AT&T Website has expanded to more than 1,500 pages with more added literally every day.

Of course, not only are the big guys online. Any business, no matter how small, can be global overnight and look just as successful as the Fortune 500 crowd. Even the Girl Scouts now have a Web store selling cookies online. The Internet levels the playing field. Jim Campbell, President of Anini Beach Vacation Rentals, Hawaii, says: "With a Web page, we can provide a brochure with color photos to people who can be anywhere. Now, we can economically compete with the marketing dollars of the Hiltons of the world."

Consumers are taking to cyberstreets with the same enthusiasm. As of late 1996, Internet users comprised only 11 percent of the total U.S. and Canadian population age sixteen and over; however, 25 percent of that segment had annual incomes of more than $80,000, and almost 64 percent were between twenty-four and forty-nine years of age (Castaneda 1996). According to FIND/SVP's recent American Internet User Survey, baby boomers in their thirties and forties are nearly as likely as younger adults to use the Internet, making up 53 percent of the estimated 50.6 million adult users. Those aged fifty and older account for 35 percent of Internet users and those aged eighteen to twenty-nine represent only 31 percent of the total adult audiences in the United States (Miller 1996).

According to a National Seminars Group executive briefing on the Internet, typical Internet users are as follows:

Average age: 35

32 percent are female (expected to be 51% by the year 2000).

40 percent are self-employed.

55 percent are homeowners.

41 percent are married.

30 percent have children.

73 percent travel frequently.

64 percent have a college degree.

92 percent use the Internet for personal use.

84 percent use the Internet for business use (The Internet: An Executive Briefing 1996).

This is a look at the average Internet user on the outside, but what about the inside—a psychological profile? VALS (Values And Lifestyles) is a system used to segment the population into eight groups based on psychological attributes. VALS-2 has recently been applied to the Internet, and the result of this psychographic analysis, as reported by Rebecca Heath (1996) in *American Demographics*, is that "Half of all Internet users fall into the Actualizers category, the stereotypical upscale, technically oriented academics and professionals who cruise cyberstreets on a variety of institutional subsidies. Three in four are men, and virtually all have gone to college." A Stanford Research

Institute study put the actualizers at 70 percent of Web users (*CyberAtlas* 1997). Just 10 percent of the general population belong to this psychographic segment of actualizers.

As the Internet matures and the online population grows, these patterns will shift, as will the reasons to go online. At the moment, 50 percent of the under-thirty users say they go online to use e-mail daily, whereas 44 percent of the thirty- to forty-year-olds go online for e-mail use. Obviously, the younger users show a higher tendency to socialize online than the boomers. However, both report they use the Internet to learn about news and hobbies, download software, and retrieve product information. Online shopping peaks among the middle-aged (Miller 1996).

According to W. Russell Neuman (Massachusetts Institute of Technology 1996a) in an MIT Series on Technology and the Corporation, among those who go online, 25 percent go online every day and 50 percent go online at least weekly. Their activities consist of the following:

- Keeping in touch with others by sending and receiving e-mail: 53%
- Participating in discussion groups: 23%
- Getting news: 30%
- Getting information about entertainment: 19%
- Getting information about finance or business: 14%
- Playing games: 7%

## OPPOSITES AND PARALLELS OF THE
## DIGITAL–DIRECT CONNECTION

If there is a downside to the Internet, it is the proliferation of low-grade information alongside high-grade information. Filtering out the info-junk to get to information of value will be an important role in the future (Cronin 1996). Annette Tonti (1995) identifies this role as that of an "intelligent agent" who will act as a user's proxy navigating networks, culling information, and bringing only relevant items to a user's attention. In the digital–direct connection, this "intelligent agent" could very well be a direct seller.

This in-person guide to specific Websites brings human "intelligence" to an online shopping experience. Direct sellers link product demonstrations, providing all the tactile, aesthetic, and experiential qualities this implies, with the in-depth information from the Website. The shopping process is simplified and socialized. Direct service and digital communications, although from polar positions, come together for a powerful new kind of business—a new way of being—with the power to attract people from Prague to Paris, Budapest to Boston.

In physics and in business, opposites attract. And in the case of direct sales and digital communications, these opposites do more than attract. A digital–direct connection manages not from the past, but from the future, viewing the world as a single market and using technology to embrace that market. The result? An individual direct seller is empowered and direct service is merged with digital communications to create a new level of customer service excellence.

### Opposites Attract

*High Touch–High Tech*   Direct sales is a personal experience with the relationship between the customer and direct seller, creating value far beyond the price of the product. Technology creates instant access to a world of products created in all points on the globe. Put the two together—the social experience of direct sales and the reach of technology—and you have a shopping experience that is an extraordinary mix of heart and head.

*Local–Global*   Cyberselling can be both global and local. A global product line and a global community of women are presented by a local direct seller, making cyberselling "feel" local while providing worldwide access and a sense of belonging to a global society of women with world-class tastes. The cyberselling consultant becomes the local hero—she is magic, bringing the world to her community, achieving "insider-ization" and a global strategy simultaneously.

*Independent–Interconnected*   A direct sales organization is a business based on self-responsibility. It is the triumph of the individual. The Internet is a worldwide network—the triumph of consolidation. Cyberselling relies on both, linking individual businesses (person-to-person selling) with a worldwide network for product inventory (Web). Personal fulfillment and a sense of belonging to a worldwide community of consumers are both elements of the digital–direct connection.

*Emerging Markets–Twenty-First Century Technology*   Emerging markets are not locked into developed communications infrastructures and old ways of thinking. These countries are accepting electronic networks as readily as developed countries. They have the advantage of going directly to wireless communication without the time and expense of building an infrastructure dependent on cables. Wireless communication evens the playing field. What was once an inaccessible point on the globe can become as close as a computer screen.

*Cultural Specific–World Class Standardization*   "Be responsive to my culture, but give me the best in the world." That is the request of global consumers. How do you do both? Cyberselling's answer is an online communication exchange. Consumers and direct sellers may tap into an online exchange anytime from anywhere to input specific needs and desires representative of the community. A cyberselling company adjusts SKUs according to these specific local preferences while continuing to offer a homogenous core line to achieve global scale economies.

## Parallels Empower

Some aspects of direct sales and the Internet come from opposite sides of the communication equation; others are perfectly parallel. The following are examples of parallel aspects:

- Structurally, both direct sales and the Internet are decentralized and democratic in spirit and appeal. Alan Weiner (1996), Director and Principal Analyst for Dataquest, said it best: "The Internet is a reawakening of the creative spirit." Direct sales is fueled by this same "reawakening" each time a direct seller realizes a goal and then creates a new one.
- The essence of both direct sales and the Internet is to build relationships of substance through communication and interaction. If companies understand the Net, they use it to build stronger emotional ties between them and their customers; direct sellers build similar emotional ties between customers and companies. Combining the two strengthens interaction and relationships.
- Both present one-to-one marketing opportunities, that in essence allow an ongoing focus group between customers and companies.
- Both provide a value-added shopping experience by way of social capital—the kind that connects people in friendship while creating a foundation for personal fulfillment.
- Both eliminate the barriers to personal and corporate success, thereby leveling the playing field.
- Both bring buyers and sellers together.
- Both encourage personal productivity.
- Both unite like-minded people and build communities.
- Both inspire collaboration.

## LAWS IN THE VIRTUAL WORLD

The topic of security on the Internet has been one of great concern to consumers. There are problems both real and perceived. Control over this issue is difficult since no one owns the Internet. There is no centralized control. Laws are being created that impact online practices, but it is far too early in the evolution of the online environment to expect certainty in the courtrooms of cyberspace.

Patrick McGowan (1996), an attorney and author on the legal issues of the Internet, advises businesses venturing online to implement internal policies and procedures governing employees in the use and risks involved on the Internet. McGowan points out that because it is so easy to put marketing and advertising materials online, too often marketing and product claims are being made without having been first reviewed by the company's attorneys. Failure to adequately "police" information disseminated to the public over the Internet can result in the bringing of an FTC enforcement action, a civil suit by a competitor, or a complaint from a state agency alleging false and unfair advertising.

McGowan goes on to advise direct sales companies to closely monitor the Internet activities of their local distributors. "Since a local distributor's Internet activity has national implications," says McGowan, "the misuse of a manufacturer's trademark or false product claim has impact far beyond that which, in the past, has occurred only in regional magazines or local area newspapers. Even if one can show the local distributor's actions were unauthorized, it may be one or more lawsuits and several years in litigation before vindication accrues."

One step in governing those actions is with an "Acceptable Use Policy" (AUP) added to a company's policies and procedures. This AUP is not a law— it is a guideline which forms the first level of regulations for the Internet. It is a contractual way to manage a relationship as a user or provider and to prove a reasonable attempt at guidance if litigation occurs.

With regard to electronic commerce—actually pushing transactions around the Internet—a new encryption standard, called SET (Secure Electronic Transaction), an agreement on the security of Internet credit card transactions, has been reached between Visa, MasterCard, IBM, Netscape, and others. For the first time, there is now a near-universal standard for credit card-based electronic commerce. Digital cash, or E-cash, one way to buy and sell over the Net that does not necessarily involve credit card billing, is now receiving a lot of press. IBM offers the InfoMarket service as a viable means by which people can exchange copyrighted or confidential electronic information on the Internet (Dawson 1996). These solutions along with Cryptolopes and SmartCards are early in their test period—too early to predict success for any one plan.

The point is security on the Internet is being addressed and solutions are being created. Gary Fernandes, Vice Chairman for EDS, considers security concerns more perception than reality. He points out we typically have no concerns about handing our American Express card to a waiter in a restaurant who disappears for ten minutes, but we are paralyzed with fear about entering a credit card number over the Internet. This executive for a company in which security is of vital importance states unequivocally that security will not be an issue limiting electronic marketing in the future. The global banking community moves more than $2 trillion around the world daily without encryption.

Andy Harris of Integralis, a leading security provider, echoes the sentiment: "We don't see security as an issue that will hold companies back. The solutions available now are so good that it's easier for a hacker to steal the staff!" Harris goes on to suggest a company set up a firewall, use the filter tables generated by a couple of routers, and "be as safe from all but the most determined hacker" (Howlett 1996). Nicholas Negroponte says that Internet security is "not a technical problem," and notes that in France it is legal to send, receive, and store encrypted messages.

Other legal issues on the Internet involve copyright concerns, the distribution of trade secrets, the right to privacy relating to e-mail generated on company property, and the protection of trademarks and service marks. Attorney Patrick McGowan advises online businesses to approach all these concerns carefully and deliberately with contracts and written guidelines.

Whether the government will get more involved with new legislation governing cyberspace is yet to be determined. U.S. policy initially limited export of encryption, but that policy is now being relaxed. The debate rages on concerning pending legislation to amend the current Copyright Act, which was last revised in 1976 (Duncan and Pearl 1996). Dan Duncan, Vice President of Government Relations for the Information Industry Association, stands on the side of change. "The pressures," says Duncan, "of the new environment . . . demand that the United States consider a modest update of its copyright laws." He goes on to say, "Congress must act in the very near future, if the chaos of the current Internet environment is to be tamed to a degree that copyright owners feel secure in providing their valuable products and services online."

Marc Pearl, General Counsel and Vice President of Government Affairs for the Information and Technology Association of America, has a different solution. He feels the recommendations to amend the Copyright Act are partially necessary and partially premature and misguided. Pearl sums up his solution with a two-part answer: "One—current copyright law must be enforced and fine-tuned where necessary; and two—content and access providers need to realize that cooperation and self-regulation, particularly focusing on technological tools, will be more productive and protecting than legislation."

The Direct Selling Association formed an Internet Council that first met in March 1997. Its purpose is to provide a forum for sharing information regarding direct sellers' use of the Internet and Intranet as an enhancement of the traditional direct selling channel. The Council will provide specific guidelines for Association members regarding legal, regulatory, and practical issues raised by the use of the Internet.

Concerns raised by the Council include unauthorized use of the Internet, service and trademark confusion, domain name ownership, regulatory concerns, security issues, claims stated by independent sales force members on the Internet, unauthorized Internet usage by employees, marketing through a website, hyperlink issues, and international implications. The Council is very concerned about fraud on the Internet, particularly business opportunity fraud and pyramid schemes. Such schemes are the number one fraud perpetrated on the Internet as reported by the National Consumers League.

## THE ELECTRONIC EXCHANGE

The link between direct sales and virtual networks is embryonic and evolving; however, according to journalists and consultants, it's quite promising. The buzzword in marketing publications is "non-store" retailing, which is one way to describe both direct selling and electronic marketing. Some consultants are predicting that non-store shopping will make up as much as 55 percent of retail sales by 2010 (Prine 1996), a positive sign for a cyber-enhanced direct sales company. Another positive prediction is the estimated 500 percent increase in the number of people expected to work from their homes by the turn of the century (Faletti 1996). Again, a good sign for virtual direct sales ventures. Both direct sales and electronic networks seem bound for greatness. How they achieve this greatness together is yet to be determined. The full range of opportunities has not been tested. However the audiences benefiting from a cybersales approach are well established and obvious. They are the consumer and the direct seller.

### The Consumer

The consumer brings in full focus the Internet's greatest strength and biggest puzzlement—its interactivity. Unlike traditional advertising to the consumer, Internet marketing is a conversation, a dialogue between the company and its customers. According to Eric Marcus (1995) in "Succeeding Online," the Internet is the perfect medium for consumer education and market creation because "people fundamentally enjoy a well-designed, educational, interactive experience." And even better than being enjoyable, it's effective. As Eric Marcus points out, "We remember 20 percent of what we hear, 40 percent of what we read, and 70 percent of what we interact with."

AT&T provides the perfect example of using the interactive advantage of virtual advertising (Kornet 1996). "We ran a recent program," reports David Robinson, District Manager for AT&T Global Services Marketing, "where visitors were able to register for toll-free 800 service online." By making a substantial part of the site interactive, AT&T has been able to keep clients engaged—even entertained—while educating them about the AT&T advantage. "We posted a game-like situation, 'Choose Your Crisis,'" he recalls. "People say it's fun—but it definitely works too."

Other reasons for an electronic exchange with customers are as follows:

- To gain customer comments, questions, and suggestions for product or service enhancements.
- To offer promotions and loyalty programs to targeted customers.
- To integrate customers into product offerings.
- To position a company as leading edge and in synch with a young-minded market.
- To capture consumer information for building a customer database.

### The Direct Seller

A critical audience for any direct selling company—and the primary market for many—is the direct sales force. The case studies included in this chapter will outline specific tactics using cybersales management to motivate, recognize, inform, and automate sales force activities. Direct sales organizations use Internet technologies with their sales force through internal nets, or "intranets," a way to present and share information on demand. Users access intranets through the same Web browsers they use for the public Internet. The improved communications and wider access to information benefiting sales leaders can produce significant productivity gains. Online communication with a sales force has a number of advantages:

- Allows electronic teaching and recognition opportunities.
- Encourages mentoring relationships unrestricted by geographic barriers.
- Provides more frequent communications with e-mail, news groups, electronic newsletters.
- Simplifies and automates the administrative details of the business.
- Creates global relationships by connecting a global community of direct sellers.
- Makes the process of building downlines in other countries simple. The company can compute taxes and currency conversions and provide genealogies by countries online.

Allen Weiner (1996) of Dataquest describes the intranet opportunity as "the community concept brought to the workplace—a way of facilitating collaboration." A key objective in direct sales. This kind of private virtual network is the ideal format for distributing training manuals, product updates, news, multimedia presentations, video catalogs, status reports, and order processing, as well as facilitating discussion groups.

Intranets are a hit with most companies because they go three-for-three on the universal requirements for projects: (1) cheap, (2) easy, and (3) fast. They allow companies to leverage existing hardware, software, vendors, and infrastructure. They allow management to update information to the field and the field to access that information on a twenty-four-hour a day schedule. Intranets typically reduce marketing costs and slash printing expenses.

As for the future of the electronic exchange between companies and direct sellers, the possibilities are endless. Although speaking for AT&T, David Robinson could just have accurately been speaking about electronic communications and direct sales when he said, "This has a big future. It's where communication is going in the 21st century. And where we are today is probably a baby step compared to where we will be in 5 to 10 years."

## THE MARCH INTO MAINSTREAM

Almost all information can now be digitized reliably, securely, and economically. As computing technologies proliferate, costs plummet, and more companies adopt information technologies into strategic parts of their businesses, new opportunities exist for the Internet to hit critical mass. According to Kevin Bosley (1996), Director of Business, Sales and Services for MCI, there were more PCs sold in the United States last year than television sets, more e-mail messages sent than postal messages (95 billion to 85 billion), and more data-traffic than voice-traffic for the first time in history. The march into mainstream has begun.

Several innovations are now quickening its speed. Appliance-like machines with price tags much less than computers are stepping up the pace. Combine that with even lower-priced machines that have remote controls that work with televisions to connect users to an Internet service for browsing the Web and sharing e-mail, and the march into mainstream is now a full run.

Simplicity and price advantages are doing their share. Convenience offered through new innovations is adding to the process. At the Fifth International World Wide Web Conference in July 1996, a new Internet card was introduced (Mohamed 1996). This card promises to eliminate the lugging, plugging in, and logging on that is inherent with computers. Instead, the Internet card is the Internet connection you carry in your wallet. Working much as a photocopier debit card, this card has enough memory onboard to store your e-mail account information, Internet access, and up to fifty Web bookmarks. Slide it into a card reader at a university, cybercafe, or what have you, type in your name, select your service provider, and you are connected instantly to your account without wasting time logging on. Then the Internet Card is charged with access units that decrease as they are used up. Remove your card and your personal information is instantly wiped from the terminal. The cards at present are limited to specific networks where the system is in place. It is another idea whose time will come, and when it does, the masses will be online and cybersmart.

## CASE STUDIES

The greatest contribution of emerging technologies is to improve a company's communications ability. With better communications, direct sales companies are able to develop closer relationships with their salespeople and customers, increase sales force productivity, improve sales force retention, and boost the visibility of their companies in the marketplace. The case studies on the next few pages demonstrate how three direct selling companies are accomplishing this and more with online strategies. These three highly successful direct selling organizations have done more than endure technology. They have embraced it.

### Mary Kay Inc.

Mary Kay Inc., originally a small regional cosmetics firm, is now a fully integrated manufacturer and distributor of personal care products in twenty-five countries worldwide. In 1996, sales totaled more than $2 billion at the retail level, the company's ninth consecutive record year. Mary Kay Inc. has more than 100 National Sales Directors, more than 9,000 Directors, and approximately 500,000 independent Beauty Consultants worldwide selling to nearly 25 million customers. The largest direct seller of skin care products in the United States, Mary Kay is the number-one brand of facial skin care and color cosmetics in the United States (based on the most recently published industry sales data). Mary Kay manufactures and distributes more than two hundred premium products in nine categories: facial skin care, color cosmetics, hair care, body care, nail care, sun protection, fragrances, men's skin care, and nutritional supplements.

In 1963, Mary Kay Ash started Mary Kay Inc. for the purpose of providing a better economic opportunity for women. Today, the first item on the company's purpose statement is to provide "unparalleled opportunity for women." In thirty-five years, the vision has not changed; however, the pursuit of that vision has. Today, an "unparalleled opportunity" requires exploiting technology to add value to a Mary Kay career.

At present, exploiting technology has translated into two online initiatives: (1) Mary Kay *InTouch*, a sales automation system that connects directors to Mary Kay Inc. for reports, communication, backoffice support and order management; and (2) the Mary Kay Website, at present an electronic advertising and image enhancement tool.

*InTouch*    *InTouch* evolved from a trial-and-learn approach, spanning a thirteen-year period. The first rendition of a sales automation system was launched in 1982, and functioned as a back-office piece with two key components—contact management and inventory analysis. The service was expensive for directors, lacked necessary technical support, and offered nothing unique from Mary Kay Inc. to subscribers. In addition, technology at the time was oriented toward technically proficient users (before the point and click era), a time not conducive to general acceptance.

After this less than illustrious start, a 180-degree shift changed an operations perspective into a sales perspective. The goal became to deliver more information, in the right context, to more people, more quickly, and at a lower cost. The result was a new online service entitled *InTouch*, introduced in 1995. The name itself illustrates the point of difference. Directors link to Mary Kay to stay in touch with sales quotas, reports, and publications, taking them beyond mere office management and into motivation and recognition with consultant-specific information. When revenue is based on goals set by independent salespeople, providing standings toward those goals before deadlines expire has a profound effect on performance. Within one year of its launch, twenty-five hundred Mary Kay directors had subscribed to *InTouch*.

With *InTouch*, directors download vital sales information and communications from the CompuServe online service, making consultant-specific motivation a matter of point and go. Before *InTouch*, directors relied on hard copy reports each month or voice response reports. The paper chase system devoured time and consequently opportunities to increase sales before month's end. Voice response eliminated lost time on the front end, but required long phone calls, extensive cross-referencing of numbers with names, and follow-up work in entering, formatting, and pasting data into status letters. *InTouch* solved all these time concerns.

Another major focus for *InTouch* is order management. This application allows the sales force to create orders on computers, saving endless hours erasing and transferring order information onto manual order sheets. With the order manager software, the sales force can perform "what-if analysis" and leverage sample orders provided by the system to make quick, accurate business decisions regarding orders. Sales Automation gives directors a two-pronged sales advantage: (1) They have time to react before sales goals are missed and (2) they have the freedom to exchange paperwork for peoplework.

*Operational Impact*    *InTouch* provides advantages to the company as well. While the focus is, and always will be, on sales support, significant operational gains have accrued as side benefits. For example, the electronic submission of orders saves personnel time traditionally spent collecting, verifying, and entering orders submitted on paper or by phone. In addition to saving time, the electronic order improves accuracy as well, allowing orders to go directly to the picking lines with far fewer errors than orders calculated manually. Also, costs are reduced, specifically postal costs. Weekly and monthly publications are sent directly online to consultants and directors without the postal meter running. In short, *InTouch* Web technology is cost effective—support costs are lower, electronic information is cheaper to distribute than paper information, and the system is inexpensive to create and maintain. Figure 7.1 shows the *InTouch* screen with the services that can be accessed.

*An Attitude Shift*    Historically Mary Kay Inc. viewed the high touch aspects of this business to be in contradiction to high tech. Experience with technology has proven otherwise. Today the focus is still on the high touch aspects of Mary Kay, but with a fundamental shift in attitude. Mary Kay Inc. now recognizes that high tech is a tool to support and enhance high touch. The two are not contradictory. They are complementary.

*The InTouch Vision*    The vision for *InTouch* is to turn the little gray box on a director's desk into a business assistant ready to greet her each morning with a printout of who needs a call that day and why—a business partner empowering directors to provide personalized promotion and recognition for each consultant in her unit.

The five-year vision for the creation of this cyber-assistant involves components in communications, order entry, back office support, and unit development, all as represented in Figure 7.2. The message here is productivity, collaboration rather than duplication, and just-in-time motivation rather than after-the-fact condolences. No other technology supports productivity as well as a wide-area enterprise network such as *InTouch*. In an "Information Age," with the direct sales environment dependent upon motivation and response,

## Figure 7.1
## The Mary Kay Inc. *InTouch*™ Screen

| Mary Kay *InTouch*™ | |
| :---: | :--- |
| **Services Screen Buttons** | |
| **Button** | **Description** |
| Datebook | The sales force can track appointments and significant events, manage address information, maintain a To Do list, and keep a personal journal. |
| Reports Manager | Vital sales information can be viewed, graphed, copied and pasted, printed, or exported to other software packages with only a few clicks of the mouse button. |
| Communications Manager | Communication is facilitated by the ability to send and receive electronic mail as well as electronic documents. |
| Order Manager | The sales force can realize significant time savings and virtually eliminate calculation errors by using blank or company-supplied sample electronic order forms to create product orders on their PC. |
| Setup | The sales force can elect to receive electronic documents in Spanish as well as English. |
| Connect | A single button click initiates the CompuServe connection that downloads electronic mail, electronic documents, and sales information. |
| | A list of the information received on the most recent successful download can be viewed easily. |
| | Important Mary Kay *InTouch* program notes display automatically following a successful information download. |
| News Flash | Time-sensitive or critical Mary Kay business information can be communicated via News Flash messages. |
| Window | CompuServe's online services are accessible from within Mary Kay *InTouch*. |
| Exit | A single button click closes all Mary Kay *InTouch* modules and returns to Windows. |
| Help | Each Mary Kay *InTouch* module provides detailed online help. |
| Hints | The Hints button activates *balloon help*, which provides brief explanations of the areas touched with the mouse pointer. |
| Support | Questions, comments, or program enhancement suggestions can be sent directly to the Mary Kay *InTouch* Support Center via a pre-addressed electronic mail message. |

*Source*: Mary Kay Inc., www.marykay.com. Copyright © Mary Kay Inc. Reprinted by permission.

**Figure 7.2**
**The Mary Kay Inc. *InTouch*™ Vision**

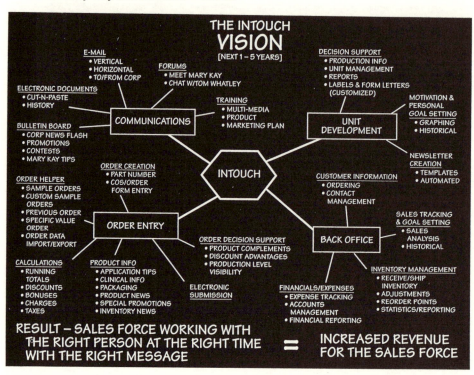

*InTouch* could prove to have a profound effect on sales force efficiency in the twenty-first century.

*The Mary Kay Website*   Retention is another story of great interest in direct selling that technology has the potential to impact. At present, independent consultants and their customers visit the Mary Kay Website to get up-to-the-minute information on everything from the newest products and seasonal makeup looks to facts about the company and the career opportunity. The Website plays a powerful sales support role, and receives thirty thousand "hits" a day.

The key is support—a means to build revenue for direct sellers without increasing their investment of time. One way Mary Kay is enhancing that support is by offering a selection of several Web pages for use within the field. A director may select one site from the set of prepared Web pages and customize it with her name and phone number. This is one way Mary Kay Inc. can open the door to the Web for direct sellers and still maintain control over content. All five hundred thousand Mary Kay consultants will have the opportunity to add their own personal page on the Mary Kay Website.

There are other possibilities of Web support for the Mary Kay sales force. What if a customer, after being taught by a consultant how to use the product and get the most from it, is able to replenish the product online? The reorder goes direct to the pick line, the product direct to the customer, the commission check direct to the consultant. Or, what if Mary Kay's *Preferred Customer Program*, a follow-up mail campaign direct to customers with revenue linked to consultants, could have an online version? Again, the ordering, delivery, and commission process is automatic, and the consultant builds revenue without investing time, a formula certain to discourage termination.

The Web of "today" requires a different strategy. As with any new technology, the potential of the Web has attracted both advocates and naysayers. Its evolution within the Mary Kay organization grew from a defensive strategy. Mary Kay became visible on the Web because competitors were there. Before an offensive strategy will be initiated, the medium must prove to be viable with Mary Kay consultants and customers, and the security and transaction standards of electronic commerce must be above suspicion. As the Web matures, so will its uses. The Mary Kay Website averages thirty thousand hits a day and logged in two hundred fifty thousand hits within five weeks of its introduction. Visit Mary Kay's Website at www.marykay.com. And, according to a 1996 study prepared by Yankelovich Partners Inc. for Mary Kay Inc., women are fast becoming more tech-friendly. In 1985, only 37 percent of women said they "go out of my way to learn about and make use of devices, methods, and products that represent advanced technology." In 1995, 45 percent said they do.

## Amway Corporation

The promise of information-centered networks and technology-driven innovations are creating new ways of making direct sales organizations more responsive and ultimately more productive. Amway Corporation has made such innovations a part of its culture.

Amway is one of the world's largest direct selling companies with more than 400 home care, personal care, nutrition and wellness, home tech, and commercial products and services carrying the Amway name, as well as more than 6,500 other brand name items. In over seventy-five countries worldwide, Amway is marketed by more than 2.5 million independent distributors with recorded sales of $6.3 billion at estimated retail for the fiscal year ending August 31, 1995.

Amway is privately held and was founded in 1959 by Jay Van Andel and Rich DeVos. Steve Van Andel, son of Jay Van Andel, is chairman and Dick DeVos, son of Rich DeVos, is president.

Amway began its digital efforts in the early 1990s with an online computer service called Amway Business Network (ABN), connecting distributors to Amway and to each other electronically. ABN is a partnership with CompuServe, and proprietary for Amway distributors. It provides them with a wealth of general business information and training with online forums; it automatically downloads new pricing, allows them to electronically place orders, and access private data.

*Amway Business Network*    Information and services provided by Amway Business Network include

- *Product.* Search for product information by stock number and key word. Includes prices, usage, demos, contents, literature, features, and benefits.
- *Sales Tax.* Access a database containing current tax rates and tax status by entering your zip code and specific stock numbers.
- *Publications.* Access current and past issues of *New Market News, Newsgram,* and the *AMAGRAM Magazine.*
- *Family Matters.* Get personal updates from members of the DeVos and Van Andel families on what is happening in the world of Amway.
- *Electronic Forms.* Save postage and paperwork by completing forms on your computer and sending them electronically to Amway.
- *Estimated Personal and Group Volume.* Submit your point value (PV)/business volume (BV) volume request and receive an answer electronically within twenty-four hours (except weekends and holidays).
- *What's New This Week.* Read weekly news from Amway, including updates on products, services, events, promotions, and more.
- *For Your Meeting Tonight.* Tap into information and fun facts about product promotions, Amway events, and business information to share with your downline.
- *Free Software and Price Updates.* Keep your price files current by downloading them free from ABN. Also obtain free software upgrades for Instant Order and ABN.
- *Electronic Mail.* Send and receive electronic mail round the clock. Communicate with Amway corporate staff and other ABN members, as well as members of other electronic mail services.

*Instant Order*  Instant Order is a second online communications initiative by Amway and allows distributors to order electronically. The Instant Order software program was developed by Amway exclusively for Amway distributors to save them time and ensure accuracy in order management.

- It processes even large orders in just a few minutes and allows storage of customer and distributor information for frequent drop–ship orders.
- It allows a distributor to check for stock availability.
- It confirms the invoice, checks current personal and group totals, calculates sales tax based on local information, updates current pricing, and prints out orders for uplines.

*CD-ROM*  A third Amway technology innovation is the Amway Product Information CD-ROM. The CD is packed with information in a variety of multimedia formats, such as color photo images, text, audio, and video. Built into the CD is the ability to order products electronically from Amway. Typically, there are more than 1,500 products, samples of support literature, video and audio tapes, label test, uses, markets, prices, demos, and testimonials on the CD-ROM.

*www.amway.com* Another Amway communications breakthrough is its Website, "a great show for customers and prospects." The site is graphic-rich, incorporates audio and video, and functions as an image builder and information supplier. In its first ten months on the Web, the Amway site had over 9 million hits. It contains a wealth of Amway information, an interactive game, tips and helpful hints, answers to national ads, and ways to connect with Amway distributors.

Although Amway's Website now functions solely as an image builder, Amway has more aggressive goals for the future:

- to expand from one Website to dozens of sites representing Amway markets around the world.
- to partner with distributors to help them create their own Websites.
- to actively work with outside providers to find and customize software for full firewall protection allowing a distributor to enter a password and get behind the firewall and have access to Amway Business Network information as well as private information.

*Amway Satellite Network* If computer communication is not sufficient or accessible, you may someday be able to retire to your den and watch Amway's private business channel on television. The Amway Satellite Network channel will potentially bring news and information to Amway distributors several times a week. The goal is to assist distributors in product knowledge and training new distributors or for providing content at group meetings.

Ken McDonald, Vice President of Communications for Amway, expresses Amway's street-smart strategy: "We try to stay on the leading edge of technology and avoid the bleeding edge." In other words, Amway is technology aware and innovative, but cognizant of costs. "We have a fair investment in technology, not a massive one," says McDonald. "We're not buying our own networks."

In the evolution of technology innovations at Amway, Ken McDonald notes an important lesson learned. "We learned we can't do this on our own. We have to work in close partnership with distributors. We have an advisory group, some very active in technology. We work with them and distributor leaders so we don't go in directions that won't have a payback for distributors."

### Shaklee Corporation

Shaklee was founded on the belief that health of the environment is entwined with the health of every person who inhabits it. In 1956, Dr. Forrest C. Shaklee began a family venture manufacturing products he designed to be in harmony with nature. Shaklee Corporation grew rapidly and became a New York Stock Exchange-listed Fortune 500 company. Shaklee now commands a distinct reputation for scientific innovation and quality in its more than two hundred nutritional, personal care, household, and home water treatment products. Attracted by similarity in goals, Yamanouchi Pharmaceutical Co., Ltd., acquired Shaklee Corporation in 1989. Shaklee currently has consolidated sales of more than $750 million and operations in Canada, Mexico, Taiwan, Japan, the Philippines, Malaysia, and Argentina.

*New Era of Customer Service via WWW*   Shaklee went online in August 1995, with a corporate promotional Website including general information on Shaklee Worldwide's multilevel marketing business opportunity, product information, and public relations programs. Visitors to the site are invited to enter a contest for free Shaklee products by filling out a questionnaire concerning their degree of interest in Shaklee. If they request it, their questionnaire information is forwarded via e-mail to a pilot group of Shaklee independent distributors for follow-up.

The number of referrals from these questionnaires has been consistent with similar referral programs for print and billboard advertising. The primary difference has been in the speed of processing the leads. The Website e-mail referrals are processed much faster than the 800 number service, and have been less expensive for Shaklee to set up and maintain. Shaklee distributors involved in this online referral program have been enthusiastic about the process, but have reported little measurable results to date in product sales or recruiting as a result of their follow-up.

Shaklee's business goals for the corporate promotional Website www.shaklee. com were to support the company's North American MLM division, and to enhance Shaklee's global presence with information concerning Shaklee Worldwide companies. Figure 7.3 presents the Website first page. Both these goals have been accomplished, and Shaklee is now planning new online initiatives:

- A proprietary multilevel marketing business management software program on the Windows 95 platform. The program automates product orders and inventory tracking, bonus check payments, as well as contact management and daily planning.
- A business and product reference CD-ROM, including business forms and policies, as well as product reference and research information.
- Sales and marketing presentations are being distributed on floppy disc and CD-ROM.
- The Shaklee Website continues to support corporate sponsorships such as sponsored athletes and teams (both United States and international) at the 1996 Olympics, the International Arctic Project's online environmental education and adventure program for school children, and the professional men and women's cycling Team Shaklee.

## LESSONS LEARNED

Here are some "do's" in creating electronic communication services for the sales force:

**Figure 7.3**
**The Shaklee Website**

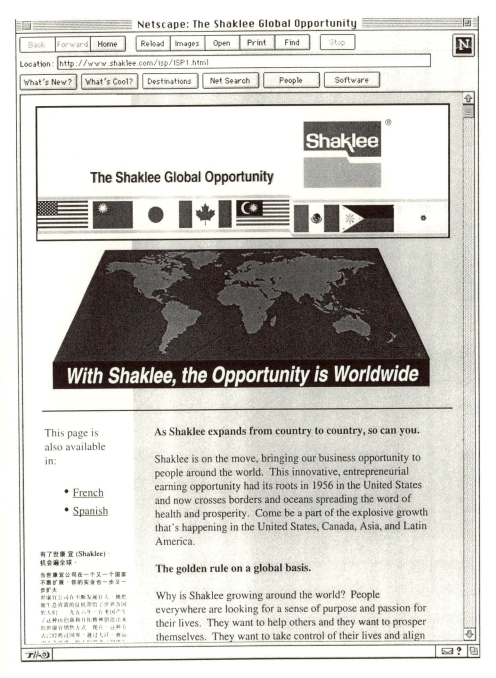

- Do make it so simple that a salesperson need only move a mouse and click.

- Do create an end vision that remains constant, but understand the delivery mechanisms will change dramatically each year with the evolution of technology.

- Do create a stepping stone approach designing initial online reports similar to familiar print versions for easier transition.

- Do consult a representative group from your direct sales force before designing electronic products and services.

- Do have a clear business purpose and clearly identified target user group.

And when building a Website:

- Do understand that interactivity is the greatest strength and biggest puzzlement of Web advertising. Marketing on the Web is a dialogue of information exchange, as opposed to a monologue that only describes regular advertising. Plan to accommodate e-mail communications throughout the organization in an efficient manner.

- Do change your site regularly to entice return visits.

- Do understand the Internet is an information-based culture that implies if marketers want to sell something on the Internet, they would be wise to offer access to information or resources in return (Cronin 1996).

- Do promote your Website. Put something new and exciting in your front window, and place your Web address on all literature and advertising.

- Do revise and revisit your Website continually. To quote Walt Disney on the opening of Disneyland, "As long as there is imagination left in the world, Disneyland will never be completed." Neither will your Website.

- Do remember that 50 percent of the public still have 14.4 modems—keep downloading time to a minimum. Keep major design elements consistent to save time in downloading.

- Do recognize the current limits of technology—online sales and lead generation are still in infancy.

- Do research competitor and similar business sites.

## INTERNET GLOSSARY

**Access Provider** A company that sells Internet connections to people. It typically buys its Internet connection from one of the members of CIX, installs its own news, mail, FTP, and Web servers and distributes the necessary software to its users.

**ASCII** American Standard Code for Information Interchange—a language understood by all computers which encodes numbers and the basic text characters.

**Address** An identification assigned to a computer.

**Archie** An Internet search tool used to locate files available by anonymous FTP.

**Backbone** High speed connections within a network that connects the major Internet computer sites.

**Baud/BPS** Unit of measure of data transmission speed; usually bits per second.

**BBS (Bulletin Board System)** The electronic equivalent of the office pinboard, which typically runs on a single computer with lots of modems hooked up to it. Users dial into it to leave messages and files which can then be read by other people dialing in.

**Bits and bytes** The very stuff of computing. A bit is the smallest piece of information that a computer deals with—either a 0 or a 1. The word bit comes from Binary digIT. Bytes are collection of bits and usually come in the form of seven-bit bytes and eight-bit bytes.

**Browser** A program which allows your computer to download and display documents from the World Wide Web.

**CIX (Commercial Internet Exchange)** The network of the major commercial Internet providers, originally established so that commercial Internet traffic could bypass the NSFnet. It makes up a large part of the Internet's backbone.

**Client** A generic term that refers to those programs that work across networks.

**.com** One of the top-level domains. Stands for commercial.

**Dialup** A connection between machines through a phone line.

**Domain** The part of the Internet name that specifies your computer's location in the world. It is written as a series of names separated by full stops.

**Download** Retrieve files from a computer.

**.edu** One of the top-level domains. Stands for educational.

**E-mail address** This is a unique address within the Internet which lets people send mail to you.

**Ethernet** One of the most popular LAN networking systems, capable of supporting data transfer at ten Mbits per second. Most of the LANs on the Internet are based on Ethernet.

**FAQ (Frequently Asked Questions)** A document often found in newsgroups that answers all the most common questions by newcomers.

**Firewall** A security system designed to restrict access to the computers on a LAN from the outside world, which usually means the Internet.

**Flame** An inflammatory, often offensive message.

**FTP (File Transfer Protocol)** This is the basic way of transferring files across the Internet. (Available as shareware or with most WWW browsers.)

**Gateway** A device that translates data between two different systems on a network.

**Gopher** A search tool that displays information through a system of menus and menu choices.

**.gov** One of the top-level domains. Stands for government.

**Home Page** Technically, an opening page on a World Wide Web site. It is also used as a generic term to refer to a company or an individual's site.

**Host** The computer you contact to get on the Internet.

**HTML (HyperText Mark-up Language)** The language used to create documents on the World Wide Web.

**HTTP (Hypertext Transfer Protocol)** The standard way of transferring HTML-encoded documents between Web servers and clients (browsers).

**Hypertext** A system where documents scattered across many sites are directly linked. Living footnotes. Click on hypertext and it takes you to related information.

**Internet** An interconnected collection of networks. A shortened version of "internetwork."

**Intranet** Bringing Internet technology and Open Standards to your existing business network. Based on five key services: directory services, e-mail, file (including Web services), print, and network management.

**ISP (Internet Service Provider)** A company that hooks you up to the Internet. The same as an access provider.

**ISDN (Integrated Services Digital Network)** Allows you to send digital information at speeds of 128 kb over the normal telephone network.

**LAN (Local Area Network)** A group of computers connected together to form a network. LANs can be very large and spread across a number of buildings.

**.mil** One of the top-level domains. Stands for military.

**Modem** A device that transfers data through telephone lines.

**Mosaic** The first browser, which really started the growth in popularity of the Web.

**.net** One of the top-level domains. Stands for free net.

**Netscape** A second generation Web browser.

**Newbie** A newcomer to the Internet.

**Newsgroup** The Internet's bulletin boards. There are around 14,000 groups covering every subject imaginable.

**Node** Any device connected to the Internet.

**.org** One of the top-level domains. Encompasses nonprofit organizations.

**Packet** A unit of data sent across a packet-switching network.

**Protocol** A set of rules governing communication between computers on the Internet.

**Router** A clever piece of internetworking equipment, routers connect all the networks that comprise the Internet together and exchange packets between them.

**Server** A central computer that makes services and data available.

**Spam** Slang for posting the same message to multiple newsgroups—frowned at.

**URL (Uniform Resource Locator)** A type of address that points to a specific document or site on the World Wide Web.

**Website** A collection of related, linked Web pages.

**World Wide Web** The fastest growing part of the Internet. Made up of HTTP servers. Graphical, multimedia format with a point-and-click interface.

For more Internet terms, try the online glossary of terms on the Web at http://wombat.doc.ic.ac.uk.

## REFERENCES

Bartlett, R. C. 1995. Ethics: Mary Kay's Foundation. *Journal of Business Strategy* 16 (July–August): 16–19.

————. 1994. *The Direct Option*. College Station: Texas A&M University Press.

Bosley, K. 1996. A Revolution in Information Technologies. American Marketing Association Tech Briefing, 10 July.

Burns, S. 1996. Internet Is a Revolution for the '90s. *Dallas Morning News*, 4 August, H1.

Castaneda, L. 1996. New Medium, Old Message. *Dallas Morning News,* 7 January, H1.

Cronin, M. J. 1996. Review of *The Internet Strategy Handbook*, edited by M. J. Cronin. *Executive Book Summaries* 18 (7): part 2: 1–8.

*CyberAtlas*. 1997. www.cyberatlas.com.

"Dateline, NBC." 1996. 21 August.

Dawson, D. 1996. Finally a Way to Sell Information Over the Internet. *NetNews* (2): 18–20.

Duncan, D., and M. Pearl. 1996. Intellectual Property in Cyberspace: Should the Copyright Act be Updated? Direct Selling Education Foundation, *At Home With Consumers* 17 (2): 4–7.

Enis, B. M. 1986. The Direct Selling Industry: A Systematic Appraisal of Future Managerial Issues. Working paper, Direct Selling Education Foundation, Washington, D.C.

Euromen Love the Net. 1996. *Marketing News*, 26 August, 1.

Fact Sheet. 1996. *1996 Direct Selling Industry-Wide Growth & Outlook Survey*. Washington, D.C.: Direct Selling Association.

Faletti, R. 1996. The Ultimate Competitive Advantage in the 21st Century. *Dallas Business Review* (Spring): 43.

Frenzen, J. K., and H. L. Davis. 1990. Purchasing Behavior in Embedded Markets. *Journal of Consumer Research* 17 (June): 1–12.

Heath, R. 1996. The Frontiers of Psychographics. *American Demographics* 18 (July): 38–43.

Howlett, D. 1996. Children of the Revolution. *Internet* 20 (July): 35–38.

The Internet: An Executive Briefing. 1996. A Communications Series Program, National Seminars Group, 27 June.

Kornet, R. S. 1996. Customizing the Web for AT&T's Leading Customer. *DataBriefs* 22: 13–15.

Marcus, E. 1995. Succeeding Online. *Index Review* (4th Quarter): 37–38.

Massachusetts Institute of Technology. 1996a. *Electronic Commerce & Corporate Survival*, Series on Technology and the Corporation. Cambridge Mass.: MIT.

————. 1996b. *Electronic Commerce in the American Home: How Much? How Soon?* Cambridge, Mass.: MIT.

McGowan, P. F. 1996. Legal Issues on the Internet. *Direct Sales: Hot Topics for 1996, An Executive Conference on Direct Selling and Network Marketing*, March.

Miller, T. E. 1996. Segmenting the Internet. *American Demographics* (July): 48–52.

Mohamed, T. 1996. Reviews. *Internet* 20 (July): 49.

Negroponte, N. 1997. EFI Executive Forum (Lecture), 20 February, Orlando, Florida.

Net Results. 1996. *Wall Street Journal*, 25 July, B4, 1.

Peterson, R. A., G. Albaum, and N. M. Ridgway. 1989. Consumers Who Buy From Direct Sales Companies. *Journal of Retailing* 65 (Summer): 273–286.

Peterson, R. A., and T. R. Wotruba. 1996. What Is Direct Selling?—Definition, Perspectives, and Research Agenda. *Journal of Personal Selling and Sales Management* 16 (Fall): 1–16.

Prine, J. 1996. Insider's Guide. *Accessories*, April, 32.

Raymond, M. A., and J. F. Tanner, Jr. 1994. The Role and Importance of the Salesperson in Creating a Competitive Advantage. *Journal of Marketing Theory and Practice* 2 (Summer): 126–138.

Tapscott, D. 1996. *The Digital Economy*. New York: McGraw-Hill.

Tonti, A. 1995. The Power and Promise of Bits. *Index Review* (4th Quarter): 35–36.

*webmarketeer*. 1996. www.webmarketeer.com.

Weiner, A. 1996. Mining the Internet. Dataquest Conference, Dallas Infomart, 22 August.

Wotruba, T. R. 1995. *Moral Suasion: Development of the U.S. Direct Selling Association Industry Code of Ethics*. Washington, D.C.: Direct Selling Education Foundation.

———. 1992. Direct Selling in the Year 2000. In *The Future of U.S. Retailing*, ed. R. A. Peterson. Westport, Conn.: Quorum Books.

Wotruba, T. R., and P. K. Tyagi. 1992. Motivation to Become a Direct Salesperson and Its Relationship with Work Outcomes. *Journal of Marketing Channels* 2 (2): 41–56.

———. 1991. Met Expectations and Turnover in Direct Selling. *Journal of Marketing* 55 (July): 24–35.

Wright, R. 1927. *Hawkers and Walkers in Early America*. Philadelphia: J. B. Lippincott.

Ziegler, B. 1996. Slow Crawl on the Internet. *Wall Street Journal*, 23 August, B1.

# Chapter 8

# Sales Force Performance Management in a Changing Selling Environment

## Greg W. Marshall and Esther J. Ferre

A primary goal of this chapter is to demonstrate that although our knowledge of the dynamics of sales force performance management in general has greatly increased since systematic academic research in the area began in the early 1970s, the trends identified in other chapters of this book suggest many challenges as sales organizations cope with rapid change. One important way to emphasize the need to reassess the role of sales force performance management is to better understand the key changes in the way we sell and the way we manage sales organizations. Fortunately for the reader, much of the current "state of the art," related to changes in sales organizational practices, already has been developed in the prior chapters of this book.

This chapter has the somewhat different mission of examining where the field has been historically in terms of sales force performance management research, and then identifying and discussing contemporary issues based on recent changes in business practice. Framed another way, if the old adage is true that "he who ignores history is condemned to repeat it," we are reluctant to prescribe future directions for sales force performance management until we better understand *where we have been* that has led to current practice as it is.

Our goal certainly is not to present a detailed treatment of every prior academic research project undertaken in sales force performance. Rather, we hope merely to provide a bridge between prior themes in research to potential new applications in sales management practice, given the new organizational and marketplace dynamics of selling, as described in the earlier chapters of this book. Toward this end, we have used as a framework for presenting the historical perspective a modified version of one of the most accepted models, or frameworks, of sales force performance management. Each major topical category within the framework will be represented by a separate section within the chapter. Each of these topical sections contains two distinct parts. First, the historical roots of research and selected exemplar studies will be discussed briefly so that the reader will attain some of the "flavor" of the knowledge base relative to that particular topic. Second, based on key changes in the sales environment and sales organizations identified in prior chapters, a series of questions is posed for the reader's consideration, related to contemporary sales management research and practice. After all the elements of the framework have been covered, a broad discussion is presented on the impact of the move toward relationship and team-based selling on sales organizations' performance management systems. The chapter concludes with some guidelines and questions for thoughtful sales managers and academicians.

Many practicing sales managers and salespeople understand that performance management systems in sales have been notoriously slow to change to accommodate changing organizational realities. Sales professionals regularly experience the resulting "disconnection" between their firm's performance management system and the behavioral factors that sales managers and salespeople *know* are necessary for success. It is paradoxical that the performance management systems that are supposed to *drive* the performance process actually may end up crippling the capability of organizations to take full advantage of such new-age approaches as relationship selling and team selling. In this chapter we consider issues both from historical and future-oriented perspectives. Our hope is this approach will aid sales organizations in "reconnecting" their performance models to sales force best practices.

## A FRAMEWORK FOR STUDYING SALES FORCE PERFORMANCE MANAGEMENT

A framework for studying sales force performance as a separate field of research in marketing was established by Walker, Churchill, and Ford (1977) in the classic article, "Motivation and Performance in Industrial Selling: Present Knowledge and Needed Research." In the article, as well as in a number of subsequent articles and a textbook by the same team, the authors presented an adaptation of the Vroomian expectancy model (Vroom 1964), accompanied by a series of research propositions that have served to drive the majority of scholarly research in sales force performance management for over twenty years. A modified version of the Walker, Churchill, and Ford sales force performance model is presented in Figure 8.1. (Note: Future references to the model in this chapter will refer to the "WCF" model.)

The WCF model is grounded in expectancy theory, which is characterized by the view that behavior by an individual is purposeful, based upon conscious intention, and goal-directed. The theory views behavior as a function

**Figure 8.1**
**A Modified Version of the Walker, Churchill, and Ford (1977) Sales Force Performance Model**

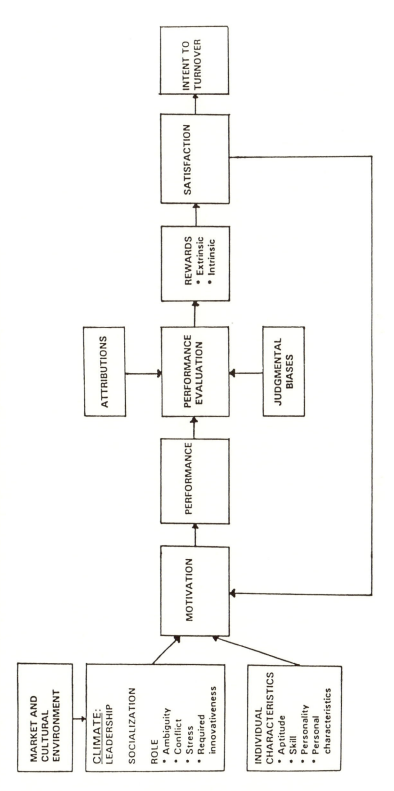

of an individual's anticipations for the future. According to expectancy theory, individuals receive input into their decision making process, the effect of the input on the individual's anticipation of future events is cognitively determined, and motivation is subsequently increased, decreased, or unaffected (Evans, Margheim, and Schlacter 1982).

Putting Vroomian expectancy theory into the terminology of sales force performance, the expectancy process operates as follows: (1) the salesperson's motivation to expend effort on a particular task is impacted by his or her level of expectation that such effort will result in improved performance against some performance dimension; (2) subsequently, this achieved level of performance will lead to increased attainment of a particular reward that is desirable and valuable to the salesperson; (3) the implication is that organizations can train salespeople in key activities that clearly lead to desired outcomes; (4) then, employees are rewarded for such outcomes. The WCF adaptation of the Vroomian expectancy equation is:

$$M_i = \sum E_{ij} \times (\sum I_{jk} \times V_k)$$

where

$M_i =$ motivation: the motivation to expend effort on any task ($i$).

$E_{ij} =$ expectancy: the estimate of the probability that expending a given amount of effort on task ($i$) will lead to an improved level of performance on some performance dimension ($j$).

$I_{jk} =$ instrumentality: the estimate of the probability that achieving an improved level of performance on performance dimension ($j$) will lead to increased attainment of a particular reward ($k$).

$V_k =$ valence for rewards: the perceptions of the desirability of receiving increased amounts of each of a variety of rewards that might be attained as a result of improved performance.

Because the overall paradigm for sales force performance research over the past twenty years has been an expectancy approach utilizing the WCF model, our review of some key research findings across the model will be presented in a format that utilizes the order of the variables in the adapted model presented in Figure 8.1 as a method of organization. It should be noted that to date the WCF model has never been successfully empirically tested as a *whole process* within the sales domain, although various authors have called for such a comprehensive empirical test (c.f., Oliver 1974; Teas 1981). Thus, it seems appropriate to break the individual elements in the model apart for examination of a sampling of the empirical findings related to each element. (Note: Throughout the sections that follow the reader may wish to refer back to Figure 8.1 as needed.)

## MARKET ENVIRONMENT

### Historical Roots

In general, the academic literature has paid little attention to the impact of external environmental factors on sales force performance. Exceptions include the work by Ryans and Weinberg (1979) and LaForge and Cravens (1981), utilizing market response models for sales management decision making. Taking an approach to market response models drawn from marketing strategy (c.f., Abell and Hammond 1979), such models seek to bring order to complex decision processes involving interactive effects of environmental factors (such as control unit attractiveness and business position), organizational factors (such as marketing effort and sales management effort of the firm), and salesperson factors as defined within the WCF model (i.e., aptitude, skill, personality, personal characteristics, and motivation).

The attraction of market response modelling is its ability to depict the general relationships between factors that sales management cannot control and those that generally can be controlled. As the uncontrollable factors change, sales management must respond by adapting the levels of the controllable factors. As such, market response models provide a framework for analyzing these changes and evaluating alternative adaptations. Unfortunately, little work has been done in the last decade to further the knowledge of the use of such models in assessing the impact of environmental variables within the domain of sales force performance.

### Contemporary Issues

1. Can market response models be developed and tested that reflect the increased complexities of relationship-based and team-based selling environments?
2. In particular, because relationship selling involves integrating the client into the full process of long-term account strategy development, can models be developed that effectively incorporate the relevant client-based variables into the decision model?

## CULTURAL ENVIRONMENT

### Historical Roots

As indicated in Figure 8.1, *internal* environmental forces also play a role in sales force performance in the form of organizational culture. Organizational culture may be defined as patterns of shared values and beliefs that provide norms and direct behavior within an organization (Schein 1984; Ouchi 1981). Deshpande and Webster (1989) developed a strong case for the need for a systematic research program on organizational culture issues in marketing organizations. Yet, to date little published work exists in the academic literature addressing the potential impact of organizational culture factors on sales force performance. Williams (1992) developed and tested a scale for organizational culture within a sales context that holds promise for future application. Evidence that organizational culture research has the potential to benefit sales management practice comes from findings in a human resources management study by Posner, Kouzes, and Schmidt (1985) indicating that clarity of company values and strong work group norms significantly lowered worker turnover.

## Contemporary Issues

1. Wholesale organizational cultural change processes have taken place over the past decade, exemplified by organizational re-engineering and quality improvement initiatives such as Total Quality Management (TQM). What has been the impact on sales organizations and the selling function of the initiation of these new organizational approaches and philosophies?

2. Companies are more inclined today to view their sales organization as a *strategic tool*—part of an overall strategy mix designed to build and maintain business and customer relationships. What impact does this corporate view of selling have on sales management practice?

## ORGANIZATIONAL CLIMATE

### Historical Roots

Figure 8.1 depicts the construct of organizational climate as differing from organizational culture. Deshpande and Webster (1989) defined organizational climate as the operationalization of themes that pervade everyday organizational behavior. Climate includes the routines that are rewarded, supported, and expected by the organization. Thus, while culture has traditionally been viewed as an overall "gestalt" of influence within a firm, climate has been operationalized as the "things" that actually take place within firms that impact the workplace and the people in it.

As defined, the impact of climate on sales force performance has been a popular research topic. Disagreement exists, however, as to what specific variables actually comprise the construct of organizational climate. In the organizational behavior literature, Campbell et al. (1970) suggest four factors common to most measures of organizational climate: autonomy, structure of the workplace and position, reward orientation, and the nature of interpersonal relationships. Churchill, Ford, and Walker (1976) adapted the Campbell et al. (1970) framework into the sales domain, recasting the original four climate variables into the following seven: three supervisory variables (closeness of supervision, the amount of influence the salesperson has in determining supervisory standards, and the frequency of communication between the sales manager and salesperson), authority structure, innovativeness demanded of the salesperson, and two interpersonal variables (role conflict and role ambiguity). The Churchill, Ford, and Walker (1976) study represented the first empirical test of the impact of organizational climate on job satisfaction in sales, and found that more than 40 percent of the variation in total job satisfaction among sales personnel was explained by salespersons' perceptions of the seven climate variables (the result was found to be moderated by the amount of time a salesperson held his or her position).

In a subsequent study, Tyagi (1985a) broke organizational climate into the following three components: (1) job characteristics, including challenge, variety, and autonomy; (2) leadership characteristics, or supervisory styles; and (3) the extent of organizational identification (job involvement) by the salesperson. Tyagi studied the impact of these factors not on job satisfaction, but rather on a salesperson's preference for extrinsic versus intrinsic rewards. The major conclusion was that a number of organizational climate dimensions significantly influence salespersons' perceived desirability of extrinsic and intrinsic rewards, with the effect being more significant on the desirability of the extrinsic reward types.

*Leadership*   One subset of studies within the general context of organizational climate has addressed issues of leadership in selling organizations. In a comprehensive review of the leadership literature, Yukl (1989) proposed that the overall approach to leadership research is moving away from trait-based approaches toward a more behavioral-based, integrative view. Such a behavioral approach is consistent with the focus of several studies that have examined the role of leadership in sales force performance. In the first study in this area, Churchill, Ford, and Walker (1976) found that job satisfaction by salespeople was positively impacted by closer supervision by their managers, more frequent communication, and influence by the salesperson in determining performance standards against which he or she ultimately will be evaluated.

Tyagi (1985b) investigated the differential impact of leadership style versus job dimensions on motivation (intrinsic versus extrinsic) of salespeople. Tyagi found that the leadership style of the sales manager was more important for extrinsic motivational value, but that the dimensions of the salesperson's job were more important for intrinsic motivation. This finding has the major impact of implying that when intrinsic motivation is the issue, exhorting sales managers to practice adaptive leadership or any other particular approach to leadership may be of little motivational value—instead, it is the job itself that is key.

Jaworski and Kohli (1991) developed a fourfold typology of supervisor feedback to salespeople based upon locus of feedback (sales outcome versus salesperson's behavior) and valence of feedback (positive versus negative). Results of their study indicate that positive performance feedback focusing on salespeople's behaviors tends to increase salesperson *job satisfaction* to a greater extent than either positive or negative feedback on outcomes. On the other hand, positive feedback on outcomes had a more significant impact on *job performance* (a logical result, since the outcome was positive regardless of whether the behaviors that went into attaining the outcome were favorable or unfavorable).

Though Jaworski and Kohli (1991) did not explicitly examine reasons for the differential impact of the two types of feedback on job satisfaction in their study, salespeople are likely to be more desirous of behavioral feedback in general because it pertains to aspects that they can more readily control (e.g., decision-making, or "process," factors), as opposed to outcomes that may depend upon a number of extraneous factors over which the salesperson has little or no direct control.

*Sales Force Socialization*   A second subset of studies under the umbrella of organizational climate includes work related to sales force socialization. In an organizational behavior context, socialization is defined as a process by which an individual acquires the social knowledge and skills necessary to assume an organizational role (VanMaanan and Schein 1979). Socialization is typically accomplished in sales organizations by such means as training, education, apprenticeship, debasement experiences, and cooperation (Van Maanan 1976).

The general thrust of research on sales force socialization has been in the context of the following quote from Churchill et al.'s meta-analysis on sales force performance (1985, 117): "From a manager's point of view, whom one recruits is important, but probably not as important as what one does with them—and to them—after they have been hired." Dubinsky et al. (1986) drew upon Feldman's (1976) original organizational socialization model to introduce the concept into the sales literature, establishing a goal of facilitating long-term "exchange" relationships among salespeople and managers (as representatives of "the company"). In an empirical test of the Feldman model, the authors' results indicated that sales force socialization significantly impacts performance, job satisfaction, and job commitment.

Taking a somewhat different approach to socialization, Lagace (1990) used a leader–member exchange model (Graen and Schiemann 1978) to study the importance of developing "cadres"—a nucleus of trained people capable of socializing new salespeople, instead of "hired hands"—or individuals whose stakehold in the sales organization is minimal. The development of such cadres is predicated upon importance being placed by the organization on long-term relationships between a salesperson and sales manager, and clearly increases the capability to more effectively transfer the knowledge and skills required for socialization of new organization members.

*Role*   Probably more research has been done examining the impact of various role conditions on sales force performance than any other set of variables in the WCF model. Before discussing the general findings in this area, some definitions are in order:

1. *role ambiguity*: The degree of uncertainty experienced by the individual with regard to relevant dimensions of the job role (Bagozzi 1978).
2. *role conflict*: Expectations or demands of two or more role partners are incompatible and cannot be served effectively at the same time (Walker, Churchill, and Ford 1972).
3. *boundary role person (or, boundary-spanner)*: Organization members who occupy positions in the firm that require them to interact with role partners beyond the formal boundaries of their own organization (Adams 1976, 1193–1199).
4. *role stress*: A potentially deleterious result of the boundary-spanning nature of the sales job. May include role ambiguity and role conflict (Behrman and Perreault 1984).
5. *required innovativeness*: The degree to which the salesperson must produce innovative solutions to nonroutine problems (Churchill, Ford, and Walker 1976).

Most of the early studies by Churchill, Ford, and Walker (i.e., prior to the 1977 WCF synthesis model) were targeted toward determining the impact of the above role variables on sales force performance (c.f., Walker, Churchill, and Ford 1972; 1975; Ford, Walker, and Churchill 1975; 1976; Churchill, Ford, and Walker 1976). The general findings of these early studies are as follows:

1. Perceptions of role conflict tend to have a significant negative impact on a salesperson's satisfaction with role partners (e.g., supervisors and customers), but do not impact satisfaction with the nature of the sales job itself.
2. Perceptions of role ambiguity tend to have a negative impact both on the level of satisfaction with role partners and on satisfaction with the job itself.
3. Ambiguity appears to be relatively more readily actionable by sales management through better communication systems, closer supervision, more accurate job descriptions and goal setting, and other similar methods. Conflict, on the other hand, is much less actionable by management because to a great extent the potential for conflict is between the salesperson and external role partners over which sales management has no control.
4. Increased requirements for innovativeness within the sales role tend to result in feelings by salespeople that they are receiving inadequate support from their companies and supervisors. Consequently, salespeople may experience lowered job satisfaction specific to this lack of support. However, required innovativeness does not appear to significantly negatively impact overall general satisfaction with the sales job.

Regarding role stress as a byproduct of the conflict inherent to the boundary-spanning nature of sales positions, Behrman and Perreault (1984) found a differential effect for conflict on job satisfaction versus job performance. In their study, stress-producing role conflict negatively impacted satisfaction but positively impacted performance, leading the authors to conclude that some aspects of role conflict may be basic to performance of the sales job—even if those aspects potentially reduce the salesperson's job satisfaction in the process. In response to the recognition that previous attempts at understanding the impact of role stress on performance and satisfaction have been conceptually oversimplified, Goolsby (1992) developed a theoretical model for role stress that takes into account a number of other variables beyond boundary role conditions that are hypothesized to impact organizational and personal outcomes. The addition of these other variables, categorized as extrinsic supports (social support and organization strategies) and intrinsic supports (coping skills and individual resources), results in a theory of role stress that is contextually much richer than previous conceptualizations. However, the model has yet to be empirically tested.

### Contemporary Issues

1. Clearly, over the past decade the degree of salesperson and sales manager autonomy, type of work structure, viewpoint on effort versus rewards, and nature of interpersonal relationships all have changed relative to the changes in sales organizations and the selling function. Specifically, what dimensions of sales and sales management jobs have changed and how have they changed?

2. What selling activities are preeminent now, as opposed to ten years ago?

3. How has the nature of change in the requirements for successful selling impacted the criteria for recruiting and hiring new salespeople? That is, are the criteria (e.g., knowledge, skills, and aptitude) for success in selling the same for salespeople today as a decade ago? What specifically are the appropriate current criteria?

4. What should be done about veteran salespeople who were hired into a sales organization under a prior set of success-based criteria, but do not meet the needs of today's selling environment?

5. What are the training and socialization implications of the new organizational forms and new selling approaches?

6. What implications do the new organizational forms and selling approaches hold for effective leadership practices by sales managers?

### INDIVIDUAL CHARACTERISTICS

### Historical Roots

The next major box in Figure 8.1 is labeled "Individual Characteristics." Individual characteristics include aptitude (i.e., inherent ability), skill (i.e., learned proficiency), personality variables, and personal characteristics (e.g., height and weight). Some of the earliest academic research into sales performance effectiveness centered around such characteristics or traits that were hypothesized to be predictive of sales success (c.f., Dunnette and Kirchner 1960; Miner 1962; Mosel 1952; Rich 1966.) Typically, this genre of studies was not theory-driven, and even if hypothesized relationships were prespecified, an explanation of how the salesperson's characteristics affected performance were not considered (Weitz 1979). The explanatory power of differing combinations of characteristics on performance tended to be weak—for example, Ghiselli (1973) demonstrated that even the most commonly used type of selection test for salespeople based upon such criteria typically accounted for only ten percent of variance in performance.

In one well-regarded study, Lamont and Lundstrom (1977) attempted to break down the broad context of salesperson characteristics into related factors in order to better facilitate research. The authors proposed two overall categories of characteristics: personality variables and personal characteristics. Personality variables included dominance, endurance, social recognition, empathy, and ego strength. Personal characteristics assessed were age, height, weight, formal education, outside activities, and civic and professional memberships.

Unlike much of the earlier work in which a few "off-the-shelf" ability variables were related to salesperson satisfaction and performance, Lamont and Lundstrom conducted an analysis of the job in order to identify *a priori* the characteristics underlying sales performance. The authors then searched for theoretical frameworks that included variables defined as potentially having an impact on performance so that existing scales might be employed to measure the desired characteristics in a reliable and valid manner. As a result, in comparison with much of the previous research in sales management involving personality and personal characteristics as predictor variables, the Lamont and Lundstrom models have considerably greater explanatory power—34 percent of variance in overall ratings by managers. A resulting "Profile of the Successful Salesman" emerged that described a person who is (among other traits) tall, exhibits perseverance, has a broad range of interests, and is adaptable and flexible.

Churchill, Ford, and Walker (1979) examined the impact of personal characteristics only (not personality variables) on salespersons' preferences (valences) for different reward types. Lower-order rewards were operationalized as pay and job security; higher-order rewards were recognition, promotion, and liking and respect. Among the findings, older salespeople tended to value higher-order rewards more, salespeople with large families tended to value lower-order rewards more, and overall education level tended to positively impact the valence for higher-order rewards.

*Meta-analysis*    A culmination of the work on individual characteristics was Churchill et al.'s (1985) meta-analysis of the determinants of salesperson performance. A meta-analysis may be thought of as a summarizing analysis of the results of a number of studies focused on some of the same research questions. Churchill and his colleagues reviewed 116 published and unpublished studies yielding 1,653 reported associations between performance and determinants of that performance. Five broad categories of personal, psychological, and situational impactors on salesperson performance were examined: (1) aptitude, (2) skill, (3) motivation, (4) role perception, and (5) personal, organizational, and environmental factors. None of the factors accounted for a great amount of the variance in performance—less than ten percent on average—though the variance explained could have been much higher in any single study. (It should be noted that a particularly troublesome finding was that some of the factors were actually positively related to performance in one context and negatively related to performance in some other context.)

A number of potentially useful implications may be drawn from this meta-analysis:

1. *Enduring* characteristics were less important to performance than characteristics subject to *influence*, thus accentuating the importance of training and performance feedback.

2. Multidimensional models of salesperson performance are superior to unidimensional approaches.

3. Inherent benefits exist in hiring a salesperson who is already trained and familiar with the nature of the sales role.

4. The overall impact of the predictor variables on performance was moderated by the type of product being sold. Therefore, job-specific and company-specific studies on salesperson performance are more apt to yield usable results than global and/or cross-sectional performance studies, despite obvious concerns with generalizability of results generated via more narrowly specified sources of data.

In a follow-up meta-analysis that was more narrowly focused, Ford et al. (1987) included only empirical studies that used biographical or psychological variables to predict or explain variance in performance across sales jobs. As with Churchill et al.'s (1985) meta-analysis, no single set of such factors was found to be a consistently robust predictor of sales performance.

## Contemporary Issues

1. Can any progress be made in the analysis of individual characteristics and sales success, given the substantial prior evidence of problems in incorporating such an approach into a sales force performance management system?

2. Concurrent with the questions raised in the prior section, could a redefined set of individual characteristics be identified that correlate highly and consistently with sales success in the new selling environment?

3. How does adaptive selling operate within relationship and team-based selling approaches? In particular, once an individual salesperson and buyer have forged a true long-term relationship, what is the role of adaptivity on both sides?

## MOTIVATION

### Historical Roots

Figure 8.1 portrays each of the previously mentioned variables as ultimately impacting "motivation." The motivation construct in the WCF model is analogous to the "black box" concept in consumer behavior, in that it is not directly observable. Rather, motivation manifests itself via behaviors (in this case, performance). In Vroomian expectancy theory, the motivation component is defined as the amount of effort expended on a particular task (Walker, Churchill, and Ford 1977). In essence, it represents the criterion variable in the expectancy equation as previously outlined.

A variety of studies have produced empirical support for the Vroomian model with respect to nonselling employees (e.g., Lawler 1968). Also, two studies have been reported in the sales force performance literature that support the robust nature of expectancy theory in predicting sales force motivation (Oliver 1974; Teas 1981). (For a thorough review of expectancy theory in a sales context, see Evans, Margheim, and Schlacter 1982.)

One criticism of the sales force performance literature in general has been its almost exclusive reliance on expectancy as a theoretical base. In the organizational behavior literature, Scholl (1981) has questioned the ability of expectancy theory to consistently explain employee behavior. His skepticism is based on a number of studies demonstrating that many employees whose expectations were not being met still continued to work for their respective organizations (c.f., Vroom and Deci 1971).

Two alternatives to the expectancy paradigm of sales force performance management have been proposed in the academic literature. Scott et al. (1986) presented an organizational behavior modification (OBM) approach that relies on the application of operant conditioning principles to the selling environment, complete with a taxonomy for utilizing the standard feedback strategies of positive and negative reinforcement, punishment, and extinction. A second alternative to expectancy is behavioral self-management (BSM), proposed by Sauers, Hunt, and Bass (1990), who presented a framework for implementing BSM principles. Whereas OBM requires that the behavioral consequences be imposed by others, BSM requires that such consequences by self-imposed. BSM relies heavily on a strong commitment by employees to specified behavioral goals and on empowerment of employees by management to allow freedom of action to achieve the goals. To date, the efficacy of OBM and BSM in sales force management has not been tested empirically.

### Contemporary Issues

1. Is the expectancy paradigm still the proper way to frame the sales force performance management process?

2. How can the efficacy of OBM and BSM approaches to motivation be tested empirically?

3. What other alternative approaches exist from which to approach sales force performance management?

## PERFORMANCE AND SATISFACTION

### Historical Roots

The two most commonly used criterion, or "outcome," variables across the entire body of sales management academic research are *performance* and *satisfaction*. Research in industrial and organizational psychology has focused on the order of the causal relationship of job satisfaction and performance, with mixed results (Locke 1970; Porter and Lawler 1968). Although marketers have not explicitly examined the direction of causality issue, it is clear that there is a relationship between job satisfaction and dimensions of the work itself (Bagozzi 1980). Reflective of traditional Vroomian expectancy theory, the WCF model orders satisfaction *after* performance, but with a feedback loop to motivation. Performance evaluation and rewards are portrayed as mediators (refer to Figure 8.1).

### Contemporary Issues

1. Is the traditional view that satisfaction follows performance still accurate?

2. What new impactors on performance and satisfaction exist based upon the new organizational forms and new selling approaches?

## SALES FORCE PERFORMANCE EVALUATION

### Historical Roots

Hiring and motivating qualified salespeople has always been a high priority in most firms. One potential motivational tool available to the sales manager is the performance appraisal. A performance appraisal executed in a fair and accurate manner provides input for decisions regarding salary and promotions, as well as essential two-way communication between the salesperson and the sales manager for purposes of goal-setting, training, and performance feedback (Dubinsky, Skinner, and Whittler 1989).

*Focus of Recent Appraisal Literature*   Because performance appraisals are so widely used in organizations, an important research goal in the human resources and organizational behavior academic literature has been devising ways to improve the accuracy of ratings (DeNisi, Cafferty, and Meglino 1984). One approach to improving the performance appraisal process has been based upon attempts to eliminate rating errors by analyzing scale construction and administrative techniques. However, as noted by Ilgen and Feldman (1983), future advances resulting from such an approach will probably be very slow and of limited magnitude. Therefore, if performance appraisal is to advance, the total appraisal process must be better understood. To do this, we must focus upon the *appraiser*, the nature of the *appraisal setting* (contextual variables), and the *motives and desires* of those being appraised—that is, the appraisee (Ilgen and Feldman 1983). Thus, much of the recent academic research on performance evaluation has focused on cognitive processes and on integration and application of theories, instead of development of procedures for appraisal administration.

Three distinct areas of research interest are evident within the sales force performance appraisal literature: (1) identification of appropriate evaluative criteria to utilize in making ratings; (2) investigation of the role of causal attributions in sales manager ratings of sales personnel; and (3) the impact of human judgment (especially judgmental biases) on sales force performance ratings. Each of these literatures will briefly be reviewed.

*Determining Evaluative Criteria*   How do you know a salesperson has been successful? In the introduction to a 1956 Conference Board report titled "Measuring Salesmen's Performance," G. Clark Thompson, Director of the Division of Business Practices for the Conference Board, made the following observation:

Sales volume alone is no longer considered a good measure of a salesman's worth. For volume without profit is generally valueless, and volume achieved at the expense of future sales can prove to be a liability. There are so many uncontrollable factors that may affect the amount of sales booked by individual salesmen that the sole use of volume as a measurement of performance may be very misleading. The size and richness of the territory, the distance from the factory, the intensity of the competition in the area, the amount of promotional and supervisional support are just a few of the variables which can greatly alter sales results even when salesmen are evenly matched.

It follows that a good system of measuring sales performance is a prerequisite to an intelligent training program and the key to personal counseling. It is also a safeguard against the loss of salesmen who have a good potential but have not yet realized it. (Umemura 1956, 3)

Fifteen years later, Cotham and Cravens (1969, 79) noted that, "The exclusive use of actual (raw) performance data to measure salesmen's contributions to the firm can be misleading. It should be limited to comparisons of selling under similar circumstances and when a single performance measure is used."

Such early recognition that selecting appropriate performance criteria for sales personnel is critical to the motivational value of the entire performance management system established a research agenda which, though dormant during much of the 1970s, has seen a resurgence of interest over the last fifteen years. An early article of the recent genre was by Behrman and Perreault

(1982). A self-report performance scale was developed and evaluated based on the responses of two hundred salespeople and forty-two managers from five major industrial firms. Factor analysis of the job performance variables revealed five general categories of evaluative criteria for use in salesperson evaluation: sales objectives (e.g., market share, profit, and sales volume), technical knowledge, providing information (e.g., paperwork handling and maintaining company records), controlling expenses, and sales presentations (e.g., overall selling skills).

Jackson, Keith, and Schlacter (1983) took a different approach, asking 213 sales managers from a variety of companies to indicate what performance measures they actually used to evaluate sales personnel. These measures were grouped into output bases (e.g., sales, market share, accounts lost or gained, profit, and orders), input bases (e.g., calls, expenses, and ancillary activities such as reports, training meetings conducted, and letters and calls to prospects), and qualitative bases (e.g., product knowledge, selling skills, planning ability, and judgment). In a follow-up study, Morris et al. (1991) used a similar methodology in which senior sales managers from two hundred industrial product and service companies were asked to rate the importance of a variety of performance measures. In this study, the performance measures were categorized as quantitative and qualitative in nature.

Anderson and Oliver (1987) reviewed and contrasted two sales force control systems: behavior-based and outcome-based. Behavior-based control systems require active managers, backed by a significant management information-gathering staff who vigorously monitor and direct the operations of the sales force. Managers typically have a well-defined idea of what they want salespeople to do and work to ensure the sales force behaves accordingly. Sales results are presumed to follow, often in the long term. On the other hand, outcome-based control approximates a market contracting arrangement wherein salespeople are left alone to achieve results in their own way using their own strategies. Salespeople are held accountable for their results (outcomes) but not for how they achieve the results (the behavior).

Anderson and Oliver recognized that these polar extremes are stereotypical and that most sales force control systems involve a mixture of the two evaluative criteria, albeit tending to lean in one direction to another. However, one finding of the Churchill et al. (1985) meta-analysis previously mentioned was the overwhelming tendency for sales managers (and the performance appraisal systems they use) to emphasize outcomes rather than process, particularly in determining compensation. A major reason is the ready availability of simple, seemingly equitable measures of sales volume or dollars (Anderson and Oliver 1987). As such, a set of outcome criteria may become a surrogate for the process undertaken by the salesperson to achieve the outcome, with a tendency to believe that the end is reflective of the means.

Cravens, Ingram, LaForge, and Young (1993) designed a study to empirically test a wide range of propositions about behavior-based versus outcome-based sales force control systems, as conceptualized by Anderson and Oliver. Their results provided support for the relationship between behavior-based systems and specific sales force characteristics, different sales force performance dimensions, and sales organization effectiveness. In addition, their results implied a limited role for incentive compensation in sales force control systems and suggested the need for a proper blend between field sales management and compensation control.

*Causal Attributions in Salesperson Evaluation*    Attributions are the process by which a person makes judgments as to the causes of his or her, or another person's, behavior. Teas and McElroy (1986) proposed the inclusion of causal attribution research within the domain of sales force performance. These authors used concepts of attribution theory developed by Heider (1958), Kelley (1967), and Weiner (1986) to examine the role of attributions within the expectancy-based formulation of salesperson motivation, with particular emphasis on attribution theory's potential usefulness in explaining some of the linkages among perceptions of sales force performance and expectancy perceptions.

One particular focus of the research on attributions has been the effect of territory difficulty on performance ratings. Territory difficulty is important because in order to administer accurate and fair performance appraisals, sales managers must adjust ratings by taking into account the differences in territory difficulty among the salespeople they supervise. However, a phenomenon known as the "fundamental attribution error" (Ross 1977) predicts just the opposite—that contextual or background information (such as territory difficulty) will be systematically ignored by raters, and instead evaluations will be based on "person" factors such as perceived ability and effort. This area of inquiry has been addressed in four studies by Mowen and his colleagues, utilizing experimental designs. Two earlier studies (Mowen, Brown, and Jackson 1981; Mowen et al. 1985) found support for the fundamental attribution error. Two later studies (Mowen, Fabes, and LaForge 1986; Marshall, Mowen, and Fabes 1992) found that sales managers utilized territory difficulty in making their ratings. The authors suggested that an improved, perhaps more vivid format used for presenting performance information in the later studies (i.e., a spreadsheet format as opposed to a scenario format in the earlier studies) may have contributed to the increased saliency of territory difficulty information in those later studies. An implication for sales managers is the importance of arranging performance information in a highly useable format prior to making ratings.

Two other studies utilizing experimental designs have contributed to the knowledge of the role of attributions in sales force performance evaluation. Using an attributional model of leadership formulated by Green and Mitchell (1979) and Mitchell, Green, and Wood (1981), Dubinsky, Skinner, and Whittler (1989) examined the effects of two different levels of work history (good–poor) and two different levels of task difficulty (high–low) on sales managers' attributions and responses to a salesperson's failure to obtain a sale. The results suggested that both internal information (work history) and external–situational information (task difficulty) about the salesperson affected causal attributions sales managers made concerning a salesperson's performance, thus confirming the findings of the two later studies by Mowen and his colleagues.

McKay et al. (1991) used a scenario format with an experimental design that varied level of salesperson effort and ability in order to examine the relationship between managers' perceptions of salespersons' performance and the types of corrective actions or rewards offered to salespeople. The perceptions of effort and ability were found to differentially impact both corrective actions selected for poor performers and reward actions for good performers.

*Judgmental Biases in Salesperson Evaluation*   For over twenty years, behavioral decision researchers have investigated human judgment and choice, focusing on gaining a better understanding of the factors that cause decisions to be "suboptimal" (Nisbett and Ross 1980). Research findings in behavioral decision theory indicate that managers often take decision-making shortcuts by applying judgmental heuristics, or rules of thumb, that may lead to poor decisions.

The use of judgmental heuristics introduces systematic biases due to a shortcoming in information processing by the manager. Examples of such biases include the following: the fundamental attribution error (Ross 1977), the availability heuristic (Tversky and Kahneman 1974), decision framing (Tversky and Kahneman 1981), the preference–reversal phenomenon (Mowen and Gentry 1980), the hindsight bias (Fischhoff 1975), the outcome bias (Marshall and Mowen 1993), and the order effects bias (Hogarth and Einhorn 1992). Each of these biases has the potential to cause "suboptimal" decisions (for a review of decision heuristics and biases from a marketing perspective, see Gentry, Mowen, and Tasaki 1991; Mowen and Gaeth 1992).

A number of factors may contribute to the susceptibility of sales managers to judgmental biases in the evaluation of sales personnel. First, the day-to-day activities of many practicing salespeople tend to take place apart from the direct observation of the sales manager. Second, most sales positions typically contain a fairly large set of performance dimensions with varying degrees of priority attached. In fact, the relative priority of any given task can change quickly as customer needs, company demands, or perceived rewards dictate. Third, by the very nature of personal selling, a tendency exists for managers to encourage entrepreneurial behavior from their sales personnel. Churchill, Ford, and Walker (1976) described such behavior in terms of the "innovative role" of the salesperson in which he or she is required to produce innovative solutions to nonroutine problems. The expectation is that effective salespeople can make appropriate decisions, independent of the supervisor, that will lead to sales success. To do this, salespeople must be empowered to make these decisions and to follow the courses of action they believe are best. Unfortunately, such choices may be inconsistent with those of the sales manager. The importance of effective decision-making skills by sales personnel has been well documented in literature (c.f., Behrman and Perreault 1984; Churchill, Ford, and Walker 1976; Lamont and Lundstrom 1977; Weitz 1981; and Weitz, Sujan, and Sujan 1986).

A fourth factor that may contribute to biases is the boundary-spanning role held by salespersons between their companies and constituents. As previously mentioned, salespeople are susceptible to a number of well-documented role problems (e.g., conflict or ambiguity). When such role problems occur, loyalties may be compromised and jobs incompletely understood, with specific duties inadequately described or totally unspecified (Feldman 1981). Finally, salespeople are among the first in any organization to be directly impacted by externalities, such as the environment, the economy, competition, and the overall market (Adkins 1979). Such externalities may differentially influence the decision processes of salespeople and their sales managers.

In the context of sales force performance appraisal, the biases introduced when judgmental heuristics are employed by sales managers could negatively impact the accuracy and fairness of ratings. As a result, rewards may be misappropriated. Ultimately, the motivational value of the entire performance appraisal process may break down.

## Contemporary Issues

1. W. Edwards Deming, a leader of the quality improvement movement, has suggested that formal performance appraisals by management are unnecessary when employees are empowered to act for the good of the enterprise. Could the formal appraisal process be discarded in sales organizations?

2. How could the values of a quality improvement initiative be incorporated into the appraisal process in sales organizations? (Note: Cravens, LaForge, Pickett, and Young [1993] have described one approach to this issue.)

3. How could a sales organization best incorporate behavior-based criteria into the appraisal process? What specific criteria should be examined? How should the instrumentation be developed?

4. How are managerial attributions of individual salesperson performance toward effort, ability, territory difficulty, and luck affected when selling is accomplished by a team?

5. Similarly, how does a team selling environment impact the potential for judgmental biases in sales managers' evaluations of sales personnel?

## REWARDS

### Historical Roots

The next-to-last box represented in Figure 8.1 is labeled "rewards." A surprisingly small number of studies have been specifically designed to examine the role of rewards within the domain of sales force performance. One such study by Churchill, Ford, and Walker (1979) was reviewed earlier in this chapter within the context of personal characteristics of salespeople and reward preferences.

Two types of rewards are available, as defined below by Tyagi (1985a):

1. *intrinsic rewards*: Rewards that come directly from the performance itself. The salesperson bestows these upon himself or herself. Examples are feelings of accomplishment, self-worth, and developing one's skills and abilities.
2. *extrinsic rewards*: Rewards that are bestowed upon the salesperson by someone else. Examples are monetary income, promotion, and recognition or respect received from a supervisor.

Two studies conducted within the sales domain examined the relative impact of various organizational climate variables on internal versus external motivation (Tyagi 1982) and internal versus external reward desirability (Tyagi 1985a). These studies produced mixed results, prompting Tyagi to suggest that more work in the area is needed, especially regarding how situation-specific climate dimensions can impact the relative desirability of internal versus external rewards.

## Contemporary Issues

1. A whole new generation of individuals has entered the selling profession over the past decade. How has this generational change in the sales ranks affected the overall importance of intrinsic versus extrinsic rewards?
2. What types of reward structures are appropriate to properly take into account a combined individual and team selling effort?

## INTENT TO TURNOVER

### Historical Roots

The last element in Figure 8.1 is "intent to turnover." Much empirical support has been generated that establishes a linkage between job dissatisfaction and intent to turnover (c.f., Fern, Avila, and Grewal 1989; Futrell and Parasuraman 1984; Lucas et al. 1987). Organizational commitment, a concept that might be considered an antithesis to intent to turnover, also has received attention in the sales management literature (c.f., Chonko 1986; Ingram, Lee, and Skinner 1989; Sager and Johnston 1989).

On a broad level, organizational commitment may be viewed as another alternative to the expectancy paradigm. Scholl (1981) has suggested that organizational commitment is a stabilizing force that acts to maintain a behavioral direction when expectancy conditions are not met and do not operate.

Briefly, an individual internalizes expectations of others concerning his or her behavior. According to commitment theorists, when an individual's behavior is directed by these internal normalized pressures, behavior no longer depends upon relationships with outcomes and rewards (the expectancy viewpoint). Thus, a salesperson who has a strong commitment to the organization is likely to behave according to internalized norms rather than performance–reward relationships (Chonko 1986).

Whereas expectancy theory assumes that work effort is the result of the interaction between the individual and aspects of the work situation (e.g., rewards), an organizational commitment approach suggests that certain individuals may exhibit behavioral tendencies (e.g., commitment) that may vary between individuals but are relatively constant across work situations. Viewed in this way, commitment is a value-based, normative evaluation of alternative behaviors leading to performance. As such, an organizational commitment approach to motivating salespeople addresses the problems of task definition, observability, performance measurement, and role complexity associated with appraising and rewarding sales personnel. High commitment among employees has been found to lead to lower turnover and, thus, to higher organizational performance (Mowday, Steers, and Porter 1979), as well as to higher levels of satisfaction on the job (Hunt, Chonko, and Wood 1985).

### Contemporary Issues

1. How have the new organizational forms and new selling approaches affected organizational commitment?
2. Do the things that impact turnover somehow operate differently in the new selling environment versus traditional sales organizations?
3. How can organizational commitment be strengthened in an era of downsizing, job expansion, and employee outsourcing?

## PERFORMANCE MANAGEMENT IN THE NEW SELLING ENVIRONMENT

So far, we have traced the historical roots of research in sales force performance management, and have noted a number of questions related to contemporary issues that sales managers should consider. In this section, we more specifically address the impact of two of the most pervasive current themes in the new selling environment: relationship selling and team-based selling. In considering these trends, it becomes apparent that the prior expectancy-based approach only partially supports the needed management changes required to align an organization's performance management system with current sales force best practices. What emerges is still a rewards-based process, but one that is modified substantially from prior practice by the very different performance dimensions required for successful relationship and team-based selling.

## From Transactions to Relationships

Changing market conditions have driven the requirement to attain a better balance between relationship and transactional selling strategies. Sales managers need to be more directly involved with their sales representatives to determine the appropriate transactional and relational balance in their jobs, and then to develop the appropriate supporting reward systems. The considerations for achieving this balance should include the nature of the customer base, long-term revenue opportunity from the client base, potential for repeat business, competitiveness of the product offering, and customer expectations. Assuming these criteria are appropriately evaluated, the sales manager can develop performance management systems to support the relational selling strategy.

One of the key considerations in developing a more relational model is that of managing expectations from an organizational, sales force, and customer perspective. The sales manager must understand the company's expectations to effectively lead, motivate, and measure the sales force. Then, the salesperson and the customer both need to understand the objectives and mutual value of the *relationship*, and balance these against the transactional requirements that are inherent in any buyer–seller encounter. Obtaining customer buy-in to a relational selling strategy avoids the pitfall of investing effort on a customer who does not want or value a broader-based relationship with their suppliers.

To ensure that the correct expectations are identified, a sales manager might consider having the salesperson develop a relationship plan for each key customer. Such a plan would identify key strategies necessary for building and developing the customer relationship and the specific objectives on which to measure success. These objectives likely will be a combination of both outcome- and behavior-based criteria, and must provide a good baseline for measurement of performance.

In an environment that demands a higher level of relationship selling and longer term objectives, the manager needs to develop an overall performance management system that supports the new approach. Different sets of measurements must be implemented to motivate the behavior toward these objectives. And these measurements must be consistent within the overall sales strategy, the performance evaluation, and the variable compensation system processes. That is, overall *alignment* of the system is key.

The implementation of a company's sales objectives may vary, but generally the guiding objectives will be consistent throughout the organization. However, the relational selling objectives probably will be vaguely defined at best. This makes a fallback to sales volume objectives and transactional approaches the lower risk approach for sales management, particularly when strong pressure exists to increase sales. Management often will revert to transactional successes for evaluations and rewards in such an environment. Therefore, sales management must understand the degree to which they want to motivate transactional versus relational types of behavior. In the development of a performance and reward system, sales management can continue to have shorter-term sales objectives and customer satisfaction objectives (outcome-based), but they also must include behavioral elements that increase the emphasis on the relational aspect of the selling effort. Another option is to measure a sales-person on the relational sales elements only, through an approach such as management by objectives. For the appraisal instrument, behaviorally anchored rating scales (BARS) may be appropriate (Locander and Staples 1977).

Examples of more relational-oriented reward systems that are still outcome-based might include the recognition of the solutions content of the sale, the strategic importance of the sale to the long-term relationship with the customer, the long-term revenue opportunities created for both parties, and the degree of customer partnership demonstrated in the selling effort. In addition, the more behavioral aspects might be measured through the customer's perceived value of the relationship, the level of executive engagement by the salesperson, the executive-to-executive relationships developed between the companies, and those activities in which a salesperson engages with the customer to develop a more positive relationship.

Although the selling efforts described can be difficult to quantify beyond the revenue value, the sales manager must develop criteria that reflect relational selling success for the particular territory or product area. Often, customer input can be the best source for defining the relational expectations and how the selling effort can be delivered to meet the customer's expectations. Although the transactional performance elements should probably be defined at a headquarters level, the sales manager should have discretion in managing and evaluating the relational elements to provide adequate flexibility in meeting unique territory requirements.

Special recognition can also be given to salespeople that develop long-term relationships with a particular set of customers through higher-level positions and more lucrative sales plans. The sales force must know with certainty that customer relationships are important to the company's management and that the sales force will be rewarded for building these longer-term relationships.

In order for this approach to be effective, management must be committed to the approach at all levels within the company. It can be very difficult for a field sales manager to drive the relational behavior of a sales unit if upper management is focused only on the short term sales objectives. Success in implementing relationship selling requires that the company's marketing and sales objectives support the premise of a more relational sales approach. Certain incentive programs can be implemented at a headquarters level to drive the change to a more relational-based model. Headquarters recognition programs should be expanded beyond the achievement of sales objectives and focus also on the specific behaviors driving the achievement of those objectives.

The specific measurements that best motivate relational selling behavior for a particular company should be consistent across the sales objectives and compensation, the performance evaluation process, and other special rewards and recognition. Particularly, when a company is driving change, a consistent message must permeate the performance management system. To give a salesperson a good performance evaluation for developing relational skills, only to subsequently compensate him or her for tactical sales objectives, will not drive the necessary behavioral change.

The major challenge in moving toward a more relational selling model is that of simultaneously maintaining short-term sales goals. The building of customer relationships takes time, so the sales manager must develop the skills to distinguish when sales volume shortfalls in the near-term reflect legitimate relationship-building efforts versus a true performance deficiency on the part of the salesperson. Often, interim evaluation objectives can provide the sales manager and salesperson with a tool for measuring the progress against a longer-term sales objective. Providing for compensation and performance evaluation for achieving these interim objectives reinforces the relational objectives for the sales force.

At the end of this chapter are some guidelines and criteria for an appropriate performance management system that is more relational based.

### From Individual to Team-Based Selling

The behavioral changes necessitated by the trend toward team-based selling can be just as challenging as the move from transactional to relational selling. Most salespeople have been measured, evaluated, recognized, and compensated on their performance as *individuals*. As such, it is often very difficult to effect change on a salesperson's ingrained viewpoint that selling is an individual effort. The entire scope of academic research presented earlier in the chapter was predicated upon the paradigm "salesperson as entrepreneur." Yet, as companies have continued to downsize and rightsize, an underlying issue continues to be the individual's contribution versus a team effort.

As always, balance becomes a primary issue. To what degree does one drive teamwork to the detriment of individual performance? The sales manager is the organization member who can have the greatest impact in driving the proper balance and still continue to motivate the sales force. Teamwork is an "attitude" that is created, rather than a set of criteria or measurements. The sales manager must look at the organizational dynamics to determine how to create an atmosphere that encourages teaming. Roles need to be clearly defined so that everyone understands the value of each team member in achieving the team objective. The sales manager needs to be particularly sensitive to the degree of teaming required, because teamwork will not be achieved unless the salesperson sees real value in it.

As with relational selling, the teamwork element needs to be implemented in a consistent manner throughout the organization and supported by executive management. The support and practice of teamwork must be modelled by all levels of management such that it becomes the organizational norm of behavior.

Specific measurement elements can be included in the performance management system to encourage teamwork. A teamwork element should be included in the performance and reward systems for both outcome and behavioral elements. Outcome-based criteria might include a sales objective for some level of teaming, such as the sales unit. A sales manager must evaluate the team dynamics to determine what the right level of teaming should be. The more a salesperson can effect the outcome-based team element, the more pertinent the measurement becomes. Depending on the size of the company, the measurement of a salesperson on the success of the company may dilute salesperson's effectiveness if he or she does not feel able to affect the outcome. However, if the salesperson can impact the results of a sales unit or a particular product area, this could be a more effective level of teaming to include in the performance management system.

The behavioral aspects of teaming are more difficult to define. Behavioral criteria might include how the salesperson provides leadership to others on the team through assistance on sales strategy, transfer of skills and knowledge, and assimilation of the new team members. The salesperson's teamwork "attitude" can be measured through the individual's active involvement with the team, the promotion of the team's success before individual success, and the encouragement of all the members of the team.

A sales manager also might want to establish a program where members of the team can provide recognition to each other for effective teamwork. This type of recognition could be implemented in several ways, such as a one-on-one "thank you," or a team announcement. A nominal cash award, gift certificate, or token tends to enhance the value of such a program.

In evaluating the behavior-based team criteria, the sales manager might consider getting input from other team members. Many companies utilize a 360-degree feedback program in their evaluation processes to ensure the team's input is received and considered in the process. The manager must judge his or her particular unit to determine if this additional input is needed in order to fairly evaluate the teamwork behavior.

## GUIDELINES AND QUESTIONS FOR THOUGHTFUL SALES MANAGERS AND ACADEMICIANS

Below are presented some general issues and criteria for consideration in developing a relational and team-based performance management system.

1. Evaluate your company's sales strategy and objectives.
   - What are the primary outcome-based and behavior-based objectives?
   - What is the relational selling component?
   - What is the teamwork-based component?

2. Evaluate your sales unit's sales strategy and objectives.
   - Are they the same as or complementary to the company's?
   - Identify disconnects, if appropriate.
   - What is the degree of relational selling required?
   - What is the degree of teamwork required?
   - Gain input from your sales force.

3. Relational Selling Criteria.
   - Does the salesperson have a documented relationship plan that includes:

     key customer personnel and executives?

     objectives and action plans for each key customer or group?

     customer buy-in to the plan?

     an investment coverage model? That is, what is the return if we invest in the relationship?

     periodic reviews with management on status and progress?
   - Does the salesperson make recommendations to management on the coverage model for his or her territory?
   - Does the salesperson understand the customer organization and have key relationships with:

     executives?

     middle managers?

     purchasing?

     decision makers?
   - Is the salesperson viewed by the customer as:

     a business consultant?

     bringing value to the customer's business?

     a member of the "team"?

     understanding the customer's industry and/or business?

     interested in the long-term relationship versus the short-term revenue?
   - What initiative does the salesperson demonstrate to learn the customer's industry or business?

4. Team-Based Selling Criteria.
   - Is the salesperson a passive or an active member of the team?
   - Does the experienced salesperson provide mentoring to the younger team members?
   - Does the salesperson promote the success of the team rather than his or her individual success?
   - Does the salesperson regularly recognize other team members for a job well done?

- Does the salesperson demonstrate enthusiasm and a positive attitude with all team members?
- Does the salesperson make an effort to get to know the other team members on a personal basis?
- Does the salesperson encourage formal and informal team meetings to facilitate discussion among members of the team?

5. Does the performance management system:
   - Identify all measurement and reward systems (e.g., performance evaluation, sales plan, special recognition, or promotions)?
   - Develop specific relational selling and teamwork criteria and incorporate consistently into all performance and measurement systems?

## REFERENCES

Abell, D. F., and J. S. Hammond. 1979. *Strategic Market Planning: Problems and Analytical Approaches*. Englewood Cliffs, N.J.: Prentice Hall.

Adams, J. S. 1976. The Structure and Dynamics of Behavior in Organizational Boundary Roles. In *Handbook of Organizational Psychology*, ed. Marvin D. Dunnette. Chicago: Rand McNally.

Adkins, R. T. 1979. Evaluating and Comparing Salesmen's Performance. *Industrial Marketing Management* 5 (June): 207–212.

Anderson, E., and R. L. Oliver. 1987. Perspectives on Behavior-Based Versus Outcome-Based Salesforce Control Systems. *Journal of Marketing* 51 (October): 76–88.

Bagozzi, R. P. 1980. Performance and Satisfaction in an Industrial Sales Force: An Examination of Their Antecedents and Simultaneity. *Journal of Marketing* 44 (April): 65–77.

———. 1978. Salesforce Performance and Satisfaction as a Function of Individual Difference, Interpersonal, and Situational Factors. *Journal of Marketing Research* 15 (November): 517–531.

Behrman, D. N., and W. D. Perreault, Jr. 1984. A Role Stress Model of the Performance and Satisfaction of Industrial Salespersons. *Journal of Marketing* 48 (Fall): 9–21.

———. 1982. Measuring the Performance of Industrial Salespersons. *Journal of Business Research* 10 (September): 355–370.

Campbell, J. P., M. D. Dunnette, E. E. Lawler, III, and K. E. Weick, Jr. 1970. *Managerial Behavior: Performance and Effectiveness*. New York: McGraw-Hill.

Chonko, L. B. 1986. Organizational Commitment in the Sales Force. *Journal of Personal Selling and Sales Management* 6 (November): 19–27.

Churchill, G. A., Jr., N. M. Ford, and O. C. Walker, Jr. 1979. Personal Characteristics of Salespeople and the Attractiveness of Alternative Rewards. *Journal of Business Research* 7: 25–50.

———. 1976. Organizational Climate and Job Satisfaction in the Salesforce. *Journal of Marketing Research* 13 (November): 323–332.

Churchill, G. A., Jr., N. M. Ford, S. W. Hartley, and O. C. Walker, Jr. 1985. The Determinants of Salesperson Performance: A Meta-Analysis. *Journal of Marketing Research* 22 (May): 103–118.

Cotham, J. C., III, and D. W. Cravens. 1969. Improving Measurement of Salesman Performance: A Method for Evaluating Multiple Aspects. *Business Horizons* 12 (June): 79–83.

Cravens, D. W., R. W. LaForge, G. W. Pickett, and C. E. Young. 1993. Incorporating a Quality Improvement Perspective into Measures of Salesperson Performance. *Journal of Personal Selling and Sales Management* 13 (Winter): 1–14.

Cravens, D. W., T. N. Ingram, R. W. LaForge, and C. E. Young. 1993. Behavior-Based and Outcome-Based Salesforce Control Systems. *Journal of Marketing* 57 (October): 47–59.

DeNisi, A. S., T. P. Cafferty, and B. M. Meglino. 1984. A Cognitive View of the Performance Appraisal Process: A Model and Research Propositions. *Organizational Behavior and Human Performance* 33 (June): 360–396.

Deshpande, R., and F. E. Webster, Jr. 1989. Organizational Culture and Marketing: Defining the Research Agenda. *Journal of Marketing* 53 (January): 3–15.

Dubinsky, A. J., R. D. Howell, T. N. Ingram, and D. N. Bellenger. 1986. Salesforce Socialization. *Journal of Marketing* 50 (October): 192–207.

Dubinsky, A. J., S. J. Skinner, and T. E. Whittler. 1989. Evaluating Sales Personnel: An Attribution Theory Perspective. *Journal of Personal Selling and Sales Management* 9 (Spring): 9–21.

Dunnette, M. D., and W. K. Kirchner. 1960. Psychological Test Differences Between Industrial Salesmen and Retail Salesmen. *Journal of Applied Psychology* 44 (April): 121–125.

Evans, K. R., L. Margheim, and J. L. Schlacter. 1982. A Review of Expectancy Theory Research in Selling. *Journal of Personal Selling and Sales Management* 2: 33–40.

Feldman, D. C. 1976. A Contingency Theory of Socialization. *Administrative Science Quarterly* 21 (September): 433–450.

Feldman, J. M. 1981. Beyond Attribution Theory: Cognitive Processes in Performance Appraisal. *Journal of Applied Psychology* 66 (April): 127–148.

Fern, E. F., R. A. Avila, and D. Grewal. 1989. Salesforce Turnover: Those Who Left and Those Who Stayed. *Industrial Marketing Management* 18: 1–9.

Fischhoff, B. 1975. Hindsight ≠ Foresight: The Effect of Outcome Knowledge on Judgment Under Uncertainty. *Journal of Experimental Psychology: Human Perception and Performance* 1 (August): 288–299.

Ford, N. M., O. C. Walker, Jr., and G. A. Churchill, Jr. 1976. The Psychological Consequences of Role Conflict and Ambiguity in the Industrial Salesforce. In *Marketing: 1776–1976 and Beyond*, ed. K. L. Bernhardt. Chicago: American Marketing Association.

———. 1975. Expectation-Specific Measures of the Inter-Sender Conflict and Role Ambiguity Experienced by Industrial Salesmen. *Journal of Business Research* 3 (April): 95–112.

Ford, N. M., O. C. Walker, Jr., G. A. Churchill, Jr., and S. W. Hartley. 1987. Selecting Successful Salespeople: A Meta-Analysis of Biographical and Psychological Selection Criteria. In *Review of Marketing*, ed. Michael J. Houston. Chicago: American Marketing Association.

Futrell, C. M., and A. Parasuraman. 1984. The Relationship of Satisfaction and Performance to Salesforce Turnover. *Journal of Marketing* 48 (Fall): 33–40.

Gentry, J. W., J. C. Mowen, and L. Tasaki. 1991. Salesperson Evaluation: A Systematic Structure for Reducing Judgmental Biases. *Journal of Personal Selling and Sales Management* 11 (Spring): 27–38.

Ghiselli, E. E. 1973. The Validity of Aptitude Tests in Personnel Selection. *Personnel Psychology* 26 (Winter): 461–477.

Goolsby, J. R. 1992. A Theory of Role Stress in Boundary Spanning Positions of Marketing Organizations. *Journal of the Academy of Marketing Science* 20 (Spring): 155–164.

Graen, G., and W. Schiemann. 1978. Leader–Member Agreement: A Vertical Dyad Linkage Approach. *Journal of Applied Psychology* 63: 206–212.

Green, S. G., and T. R. Mitchell. 1979. Attributional Processes of Leaders in Leader–Member Interactions. *Organizational Behavior and Human Performance* 23 (June): 429–458.

Heider, F. 1958. *The Psychology of Interpersonal Relations*. New York: John Wiley & Sons.

Hogarth, R., and H. J. Einhorn. 1992. Order Effects in Belief Updating: The Belief Adjustment Model. *Cognitive Psychology* 24: 1–55.

Hunt, S. D., L. B. Chonko, and V. P. Wood. 1985. Organizational Commitment and Marketing. *Journal of Marketing* 49 (Winter): 112–126.

Ilgen, D. R., and J. M. Feldman. 1983. Performance Appraisal: A Process Focus. In *Research in Organizational Behavior*, Vol. 5, ed. B. M. Staw. Greenwich, Conn.: JAI Press.

Ingram, T. N., K. S. Lee, and S. J. Skinner. 1989. An Empirical Assessment of Salesperson Motivation, Commitment, and Job Outcomes. *Journal of Personal Selling and Sales Management* 9 (Fall): 25–33.

Jackson, D. W., J. E. Keith, and J. L. Schlacter. 1983. Evaluation of Sales Performance: A Study of Current Practices. *Journal of Personal Selling and Sales Management* 3 (November): 43–51.

Jaworski, B. J., and A. K. Kohli. 1991. Supervisory Feedback: Alternative Types and Their Impact on Salespeople's Performance and Satisfaction. *Journal of Marketing Research* 28 (May): 190–201.

Kelley, H. E. 1967. Attribution Theory in Social Psychology. In *Nebraska Symposium on Motivation*, ed. D. Levine. Lincoln: University of Nebraska Press.

LaForge, R. W., and D. W. Cravens. 1981. A Market Response Model for Sales Management Decision Making. *Journal of Personal Selling and Sales Management* 2 (Fall–Winter): 10–16.

Lagace, R. R. 1990. Leader–Member Exchange: Antecedents and Consequences of the Cadre and Hired Hand. *Journal of Personal Selling and Sales Management* 10 (February): 11–19.

Lamont, L. M., and W. J. Lundstrom. 1977. Identifying Successful Industrial Salesmen by Personality and Personal Characteristics. *Journal of Marketing Research* 14 (November): 517–529.

Lawler, E. E., III. 1968. A Correlational–Causal Analysis of the Relationship between Expectancy Attitudes and Job Performance. *Journal of Applied Psychology* 52 (December): 462–468.

Locander, W. B., and W. A. Staples. 1977. Evaluating and Motivating Salesmen with the BARS Method. *Industrial Marketing Management* 7 (February): 43–48.

Locke, E. A. 1970. Job Satisfaction and Job Performance: A Theoretical Analysis. *Organizational Behavior and Human Performance* 5: 484–500.

Lucas, G. H., Jr., A. Parasuraman, R. A. Davis, and B. M. Enis. 1987. An Empirical Study of Salesforce Turnover. *Journal of Marketing* 51 (July): 34–59.

Marshall, G. W., J. C. Mowen, and K. J. Fabes. 1992. The Impact of Territory Difficulty and Self Versus Other Ratings on Managerial Evaluations of Sales Personnel. *Journal of Personal Selling and Sales Management* 12 (Fall): 35–47.

Marshall, G. W., and J. C. Mowen. 1993. An Experimental Investigation of the Outcome Bias in Salesperson Performance Evaluations. *Journal of Personal Selling and Sales Management* 13 (Summer): 31–47.

McKay, S., J. F. Hair, Jr., M. W. Johnston, and D. L. Sherrell. 1991. An Exploratory Investigation of Reward and Corrective Responses to Salesperson Performance: An Attributional Approach. *Journal of Personal Selling and Sales Management* 11 (Spring): 39–48.

Miner, J. B. 1962. Personality and Ability Factors in Sales Performance. *Journal of Applied Psychology* 46 (February): 6–13.

Mitchell, T. R., S. G. Green, and R. E. Wood. 1981. An Attributional Model of Leadership and The Poor Performing Subordinate: Development and Validation. In *Research in Organizational Behavior*, ed. L. L. Cummings and B. M. Staw. Greenwich, Conn.: JAI Press.

Morris, M. H., D. L. Davis, J. W. Allen, R. A. Avila, and J. Chapman. 1991. Assessing the Relationships among Performance Measures, Managerial Practices, and Satisfaction When Evaluating the Salesforce: A Replication and Extension. *Journal of Personal Selling and Sales Management* 11 (Summer): 25–35.

Mosel, J. N. 1952. Prediction of Department Store Sales Performance from Personnel Data. *Journal of Applied Psychology* 36: 8–10.

Mowday, R. T., R. M. Steers, and L. W. Porter. 1979. The Measurement of Organizational Commitment. *Journal of Organizational Behavior* 14: 224–247.

Mowen, J. C., and J. W. Gentry. 1980. Investigation of the Preference Reversal Phenomenon in a New Product Introduction Task. *Journal of Applied Psychology* 65: 715–722.

Mowen, J. C., S. W. Brown, and D. W. Jackson, Jr. 1981. Cognitive Biases in Sales Management Evaluations. *Journal of Personal Selling and Sales Management* 1 (Fall–Winter): 83–89.

Mowen, J. C., J. E. Keith, S. W. Brown, and D. W. Jackson, Jr. 1985. Utilizing Effort and Task Difficulty Information in Evaluating Salespeople. *Journal of Marketing Research* 22 (May): 185–191.

Mowen, J. C., K. J. Fabes, and R. W. LaForge. 1986. Effects of Effort, Territory Situation, and Rater on Salesperson Evaluation. *Journal of Personal Selling and Sales Management* 6 (May): 1–8.

Mowen, J. C., and G. J. Gaeth. 1992. The Evaluation Stage in Marketing Decision Making. *Journal of the Academy of Marketing Science* 20 (Spring): 177–187.

Nisbett, R., and L. Ross. 1980. *Human Inference: Strategies and Shortcomings of Social Judgment.* Englewood Cliffs, N.J.: Prentice Hall.

Oliver, R. L. 1974. Expectancy Theory Predictions of Salesmen's Performance. *Journal of Marketing Research* 11 (August): 243–253.

Ouchi, W. G. 1981. *Theory Z.* Reading, Mass.: Addison-Wesley.

Porter, L. W., and E. E. Lawler, III. 1968. *Managerial Attitudes and Performance.* Homewood, Ill.: Richard D. Irwin.

Posner, B. Z., J. M. Kouzes, and W. H. Schmidt. 1985. Shared Values Makes a Difference: An Empirical Test of Corporate Culture. *Human Resource Management* 24 (Fall): 293–309.

Rich, L. 1966. Can Salesmen Be Tested? *Duns Review* 87 (March): 40–41.

Ross, L. 1977. The Intuitive Psychologist and His Shortcomings: Distortions in the Attribution Process. In *Advances in Experimental Social Psychology*, Vol. 10, ed. L. Berkowitz. New York: Academic Press.

Ryans, A. B., and C. B. Weinberg. 1979. Territory Sales Response. *Journal of Marketing Research* 16 (November): 453–465.

Sager, J. K., and M. W. Johnston. 1989. Antecedents and Outcomes of Organizational Commitment: A Study of Salespeople. *Journal of Personal Selling and Sales Management* 9 (Spring): 30–41.

Sauers, D. A, J. B. Hunt, and K. Bass. 1990. Behavioral Self-Management as a Supplement to External Sales Force Controls. *Journal of Personal Selling and Sales Management* 10 (Summer): 17–28.

Schein, E. H. 1984. *Organizational Culture and Leadership*. San Francisco: Jossey-Bass.

Scholl, R. W. 1981. Differentiating Organizational Commitment from Expectancy as a Motivating Force. *Academy of Management Review* 6: 589–599.

Scott, R. A., J. E. Swan, M. E. Wilson, and J. J. Roberts. 1986. Organizational Behavior Modification: A General Motivational Tool for Sales Management. *Journal of Personal Selling and Sales Management* 6 (August): 61–70.

Teas, R. K. 1981. An Empirical Test of Models of Salesperson's Job Expectancy and Instrumentality Perceptions. *Journal of Marketing Research* 18 (May): 209–226.

Teas, R. K., and J. C. McElroy. 1986. Causal Attributions and Expectancy Estimates: A Framework for Understanding the Dynamics of Salesforce Motivation. *Journal of Marketing* 50 (January): 75–86.

Tversky, A., and D. Kahneman. 1981. The Framing of Decisions and the Psychology of Choice. *Science* 211 (January–March): 453–458.

———. 1974. Judgment Under Uncertainty: Heuristics and Biases. *Science* 185 (July–September): 1124–1131.

Tyagi, P. K. 1985a. Organizational Climate, Inequities, and Attractiveness of Salesperson Rewards. *Journal of Personal Selling and Sales Management* 5 (November): 31–37.

———. 1985b. Relative Importance of Key Job Dimensions and Leadership Behaviors in Motivating Salesperson Work Performance. *Journal of Marketing* 49 (Summer): 76–86.

———. 1982. Perceived Organizational Climate and the Process of Salesperson Motivation. *Journal of Marketing Research* 19 (May): 240–254.

Umemura, G. M. 1956. Measuring Salesmen's Performance. In *Conference Board Reports: Studies in Business Policy*, no. 79. New York: National Industrial Conference Board.

VanMaanan, J. 1976. Breaking In: Socialization to Work. In *Handbook of Work, Organization, and Society*, ed. R. Dubin. Chicago: Rand-McNally.

VanMaanan, J., and E. H. Schein. 1979. Toward a Theory of Organizational Socialization. In *Research in Organizational Behavior*, Vol. 1, ed. B. M. Staw. Greenwich, Conn.: JAI Press.

Vroom, V. 1964. *Work and Motivation*. New York: John Wiley & Sons.

Vroom, V., and E. L. Deci. 1971. The Stability of Post Decision Dissonance: A Follow-Up Study of the Job Attitudes of Business School Graduates. *Organizational Behavior and Human Performance* 6: 36–49.

Walker, O. C., Jr., G. A. Churchill, Jr., and N. M. Ford. 1977. Motivation and Performance in Industrial Selling: Present Knowledge and Needed Research. *Journal of Marketing Research* 14 (May): 156–168.

———. 1975. Organizational Determinants of the Industrial Salesman's Role Conflict and Ambiguity. *Journal of Marketing* 39 (January): 32–39.

———. 1972. Reactions to Role Conflict: The Case of the Industrial Salesman. *Journal of Business Administration* 3 (Spring): 25–36.

Weiner, B. 1986. *An Attributional Theory of Motivation*. New York: Springer-Verlag.

Weitz, B. A. 1981. Effectiveness in Sales Interactions: A Contingency Framework. *Journal of Marketing* 45 (Winter): 85–103.

———. 1979. A Critical Review of Personal Selling Research: The Need for a Contingency Approach. In *Critical Issues in Sales Management: State-of-the-Art and Future Research Needs*, ed. G. Albaum and G. Churchill. Eugene: University of Oregon, College of Business Administration.

Weitz, B. A., H. Sujan, and M. Sujan. 1986. Knowledge, Motivation, and Adaptive Behavior: A Framework for Improving Selling Effectiveness. *Journal of Marketing* 50 (October): 174–191.

Williams, M. R. 1992. Organizational Culture as a Predictor of the Level of Salespersons' Customer Oriented Behavior. Ph.D. diss., Oklahoma State University, Stillwater, Oklahoma.

Yukl, G. 1989. Managerial Leadership: A Review of Theory and Research. *Journal of Management* 15: 251–289.

# Chapter 9

# Global Sales Force Management: Comparing German and U.S. Practices

Sönke Albers, Manfred Krafft,
and Wilhelm Bielert

There is widespread agreement that successful sales negotiations depend on the degree of ability to adapt to the other party's manner of thought and communication. This is all the more true when sales negotiations are occurring between parties coming from different cultures (for a literature review see Campbell et al. 1988; Graham 1985). While a growing body of literature exists regarding the culturally dependent practice of selling, the respective area of sales management has remained largely underresearched. Much of what is known about the management of sales forces across cultural lines is anecdotal (Still 1981, 9; Hill and Still 1990, 57). This presents a serious problem for multinational firms in the United States when they are deciding how to manage the sales forces of their subsidiaries in other countries. In the last twenty years, there have been an increasing number of research studies on sales management issues such as the advantages of working with a direct sales force versus independent agents, the hiring and firing of salespeople, procedures for performance measurement, and the type of compensation. The results of these studies may offer us a clear understanding of how a sales force is to be managed effectively, but the great majority of this research published in international journals was carried out on the sales forces of companies in the United States. It is thus uncertain whether the results can be generalized to apply to all countries in the world (Hofstede 1980).

It is very doubtful that good sales management practices in the United States would also be appropriate in other countries. Traditionally, business in the United States is very highly transactional as opposed to being relationship-based. The latter is found much more often in Japan, and to a lesser extent in Europe. Placing the emphasis on relationship marketing means that short-term performance measurement is inadequate. As a consequence, cultures making that emphasis are more likely to work primarily with all-salary compensation plans. In addition, relationships can be built only if the persons involved are not dismissed at the rate that is normal in the United States. Yet another important issue is that the termination of contracts may be evaluated as an unusual business occurrence: for instance, changing agents in Japan more than three or four times in ten years will get your company blacklisted (Keegan 1989, 477). Many countries have specific laws protecting the agent in his relationship to his company. We must therefore try to identify the forces that make sales management practices culturally dependent, in order to be able to offer recommendations on proper sales management techniques for culturally diverse countries. In this chapter, the expression "sales agents" (or "agents") will be used for independent salespersons, while employed salespersons are called "sales representatives" (or "reps"). Although these terms are used interchangeably in the United States, foreign laws make clear distinctions between them.

The chapter is organized as follows. First, we will describe the forces that make sales management culturally dependent. These forces include differing work values, communication styles, and laws. Then the sales management issues that need to be adjusted for country-specific differences are selected. We will go on to analyze the ways in which these issues are affected by variant conditions in foreign countries. We will address the differences between employing direct salespeople versus independent agents, as well as the hiring and firing decision. We will discuss how the setting of objectives and the use of performance measurement systems are dependent upon differing work values. We will examine differences in the ways of compensating salespersons. Although this article does address the major dissimilarities identifiable within the world arena, the focus is on a comparison of sales management practices in the United States and Germany. This will then allow a multinational firm in the United States to adapt its procedures to use in West European countries such as Germany, Switzerland, and Austria. There are also many similarities to Scandinavia, The Netherlands, Belgium, Luxembourg, and France. The comparison helps, moreover, in understanding the consequences of differing work values, communication styles, and laws, as implemented in different sales management practices.

## THE NECESSITY OF ADJUSTING
## FOR COUNTRY-SPECIFIC DIFFERENCES

### Dimensions of Differences

In traveling around the world, one clearly observes differing attitudes toward work. Some cultures are more "doing-oriented," others are more "being-oriented." Obviously, these people adhere to different work values. In addition, the type of communication between people affects management practice. Some of the values shared in a given place might even have been codified as law, thereby further enforcing this behavior in future. In the following, variation in work values, types of communication, and law are described in more detail.

## Work Values

Geert Hofstede was one of the first researchers to question the adaptability of U.S. management theories to other cultural contexts (Hofstede 1980). He undertook an extensive survey spanning more than 100,000 employees of a large multinational company in sixty-six of its national subsidiaries. All categories of personnel were interviewed. The survey was administered in the late sixties and early seventies with one replication in twenty different languages. Sixty out of the 150 questions dealt with the values and beliefs of the respondents on issues related to motivation, hierarchy, leadership, and well-being in the organization. With the aid of factor analysis, Hofstede was able to derive four dimensions on which national cultures exhibit considerable dissimilarities in work values (Hofstede 1991):

1. *Power Distance*  This measure indicates the degree of separation between bosses (exercising their power) and their subordinates (receiving orders from and reporting to the superiors). In cultures with low power distance, members of the organization tend to feel themselves to be fairly equal, whereas in high power distance cultures it is perceived to be difficult to meet and talk to higher ranking people. Here, real power is very much concentrated at the top. Power distance also means that, when evaluating others, emphasis is placed primarily on social class rather than age, gender, or the like.

2. *Uncertainty Avoidance*  This measure expresses the tendency of people to avoid risks and to prefer stable situations. Cultures exhibiting uncertainty avoidance tend to develop uncertainty-reducing rules and risk-free procedures, which are seen as a necessity for efficiency. It is also interesting to note that these cultures are often characterized by a higher level of aggressiveness that creates, among other things, a strong inner urge to work hard.

3. *Individualism–Collectivism*  This measure represents the emphasis a culture places on the well-being of individuals as compared to groups. In collectivist countries, people distinguish between members of their own groups and others, supporting and working for the group in exchange for loyalty. As a consequence, group values are favored (i.e., sense of belonging, or sense of personal sacrifice for the community). In individualistic societies, however, the individual is seen as the basic resource and individual-related values are therefore strongly emphasized (i.e., personal freedom, human rights, and equality between men and women). Basically, people must care for themselves and their immediate families. Any type of exchange takes place only if a return can be or is expected.

4. *Masculinity–Femininity*  This measure indicates the degree to which a society favors assertiveness, earning money, showing off one's possessions and not much looking after others (masculinity), versus nurturing roles, interdependence between people, and caring for others (femininity). This dimension was so named such because, on the average, men tended to score more highly on one extreme and women on the other, regardless of the culture.

Hofstede (1991) reports that the culture of the United States with respect to individualism and power distance can also be found in Great Britain, Canada, Australia, and New Zealand (small power distance, individualist society). Germany, Switzerland, and Austria, as well as the Nordic countries of Norway, Sweden, Finland, and Denmark also exhibit low power distance but are more collectivist. Much greater power distance is found in such countries as France, Spain, Italy, and Belgium. A very different type of culture is presented in the cluster with all of the Asian, African, Arabian, and Latin American countries: These exhibit high power distance as well as a collectivist approach to well-being.

Although the preceding comparison does not indicate any differences between the Nordic and the German-speaking countries, there is indeed a substantial discrepancy. All the Nordic countries are more feminine, meaning that the employees look after one another more: this is not the case for German-speaking countries, as well as the United States, Great Britain, and Australia. In this light, it is no surprise that Scandinavian researchers in particular have developed and advocated the relationship-approach to marketing. This also has implications for team orientation and performance measurement.

A very interesting picture is presented in Figure 9.1, which indicates the countries' positions according to uncertainty avoidance and to individualism–collectivism. Again, the United States, Great Britain, Canada, and Australia are in one cluster maintaining very individualistic behavior and a low uncertainty avoidance. Germany, Austria, and Switzerland are in a distinct cluster scoring higher on uncertainty avoidance, as well as lower on individualism. This allows for greater team orientation but also requires higher salary compensation plans. Quite a different camp is represented by countries like Singapore, Hong Kong, Malaysia, and the Philippines: These are organized in a collectivist manner, yet show a weak tendency toward uncertainty avoidance. In great contrast to the U.S. culture are countries in Latin America, East Asia (like Japan and South Korea, Taiwan and Thailand), Africa, and Arabia. They are collectivist and also have a high tendency to avoid uncertainty.

## Communication

The different meanings of communication styles across the world's cultures has long been recognized as an issue when it comes to sales negotiations (Hall 1960). Cultural differences in communication are also relevant, however, when choosing appropriate sales management practices. In addressing

**Figure 9.1**
**Map of Fifty Countries and Three Regions Ranked in Terms of Uncertainty Avoidance and Individualism–Collectivism Indexes**

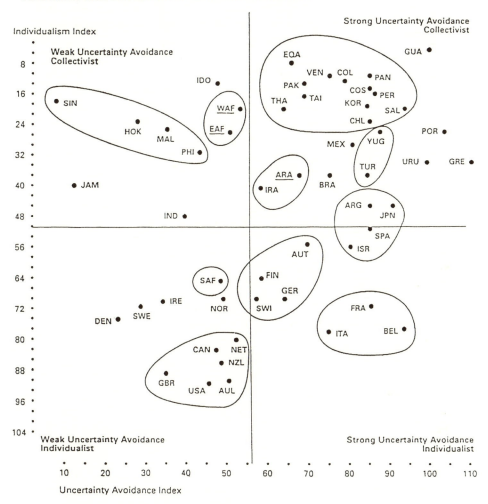

*Source*: Hofstede 1991 (reproduced with permission).

*Key*: ARA = Arab-speaking countries (Egypt, Iraq, Kuwait, Lebanon, Libya, Saudi Arabia, United Arab Emirates); ARG = Argentina; AUL = Australia; AUT = Austria; BEL = Belgium; BRA = Brazil; CAN = Canada; CHL = Chile; COL = Colombia; COS = Costa Rica; DEN = Denmark; EAF = East Africa (Ethiopia, Kenya, Tanzania, Zambia); EQA = Equador; FIN = Finland; FRA = France; GBR = Great Britain; GER = Germany F.R.; GRE = Greece; GUA = Guatemala; HOK = Hong Kong; IDO = Indonesia; IND = India; IRA = Iran; IRE = Ireland (Republic of); ISR = Israel; ITA = Italy; JAM = Jamaica; JPN = Japan; KOR = South Korea; MAL = Malaysia; MEX = Mexico; NET = The Netherlands; NOR = Norway; NZL = New Zealand; PAK = Pakistan; PAN = Panama; PER = Peru; PHI = Philippines; POR = Portugal; SAF = South Africa; SAL = Salvador; SIN = Singapore; SPA = Spain; SWE = Sweden; SWI = Switzerland; TAI = Taiwan; THA = Thailand; TUR = Turkey; URU = Uruguay; USA = United States; VEN = Venezuela; WAF = West Africa (Ghana, Nigeria, Sierra Leone); YUG = Yugoslavia.

the task of setting objectives as well as performance measurement, one is dependent upon explicit versus implicit contextual messages. The American anthropologist Hall has emphasized that communication mechanisms incorporate both verbal and nonverbal parts, that they can integrate feedback mechanisms and are not independent of context. Components of context include location, people involved (i.e., age, gender, dress, or status), and the immediate context of the conversation itself (i.e., work, negotiations, or sales calls). Cultures such as Germany and Switzerland deliver precise and explicit messages with low context; cultures in North America are similar. The advantage in this is that the information is very precise, requiring no interpretation mechanism originating from within the culture for the purpose of explaining that message.

Particularly in Japan, as well as in Arabia and Latin America, one is apt to find high context communication, meaning that the customary instruments of goal setting and performance measurement are not applicable within these countries (see also Still 1981, 9). Figure 9.2 provides a positioning of the abovementioned countries according to the context, and the explicit versus implicit character of messages in various cultures.

**Figure 9.2**
**Messages and Context**

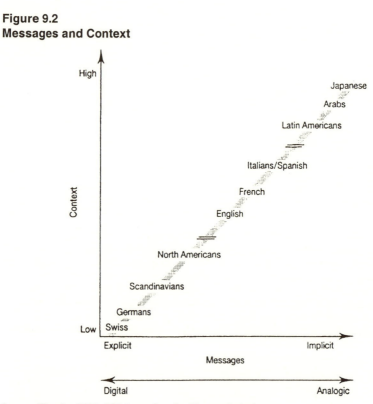

*Source*: Usunier 1993, 103 (reproduced with permission).

### Law

Coming from the free market frame of reference, U.S. law concerning employed sales reps and independent sales agents is straightforward. The company and the salesperson can simply decide upon any contract clauses and make them binding. Sales representatives can easily be fired, such that it is thus unnecessary for management to regard hiring decisions as long-term decisions. Similar ideas are prevalent in the world of British influence, such as Canada, Great Britain, Australia, New Zealand, South Africa, Hong Kong, the Bahamas, and Singapore. On the other hand, there are many countries in which the law gives sales agents and sales reps a stronger position. These laws deal in particular with the termination of contracts and the compensation associated therewith. Keegan (1989, 479) describes some common ground rules regarding these national laws. Of greatest importance for sales managers are the following negative aspects recurring in the laws of many countries:

1. Applicable jurisdiction is national (civil) law, not U.S. (common) law.
2. Local labor laws determine compensation for dismissal.
3. Notice prior to cancellation of contracts is necessary.
4. Indemnity increases with the length of the relationship.
5. Laws granting the agent compensation and similar rights may not be waived by contract.
6. The agent must be compensated for the increased value of the market he has created for the principal.
7. "Just cause" is defined by existing law or the terms of the contract.

We find many differences among the various countries and regions. The most blatant and punitive laws are in the Central American countries. South American countries weigh in with a maze of legislation that Keegan suggests was drawn up as a lawyers' employment act. The Middle Eastern and North African countries are developing a growing number of laws for the protection of agents: compensation is by statute in many countries, and reliance on the Shari'a, or Islamic law, for resolving conflicts is prevalent. The Far Eastern countries are comparatively free of these one-sided laws. Generally, the parties may agree to the terms of the agency contract as they see fit. Europe itself boasts a labyrinth of national protective laws; these are weighted in the agent's or rep's favor, compounded by the fact that Europeans are rather prone to litigate. An overview and some highlights of European countries' laws are as follows:

BELGIUM (often used as a prime example of overprotective European law). Terminal compensation for agents and distributors includes the value of any increase in goodwill, plus expenses incurred in developing the business, plus the amount of compensation claimed by discharged employees who worked on your account. Minimum notice is three months. Definite-term contract may become indefinite-term after two extensions. Only Belgian law is applicable.

DENMARK. Local Chamber of Commerce decides whether termination is just. It is customary to give agent one year's commissions. Minimum notice is three months.

FRANCE (most protective law in Europe for agents). Terminal compensation is usually no more than one year's commission. A special feature of French law is that the agent does not have to prove he has gained any clients for the principal or that there were any clients at all. The fact that the agent has lost the right to represent the principal may entitle him to compensation. If parties agree to a "trial" contract of a specified duration, the principal is not obliged to pay compensation if he does not renew. No laws have been enacted for regulation of distributors.

GERMANY. Terminal compensation of one year's commission is customary. An unusual feature of German law is that the agent may die or decide to retire and still be entitled to terminal compensation. Minimum notice is three weeks for contracts up to three years' duration, otherwise three months. Choice of law is allowed, but agent may not waive his right to compensation.

ITALY. Agents are entitled to damage compensation and social security charges. Principal is liable for "clientele's indemnity" when the agent is terminated without just cause. This amounts to 3 percent of all commissions received by the agent while the contract was in force. No laws have been enacted for regulations of distributors.

THE NETHERLANDS. Whether a just or unjust termination, the agent is entitled to up to one year's commission as goodwill compensation (a full year is usually awarded). Minimum notice is one month if specified, otherwise four months. Choice of law is allowed, but agent may not waive any of his rights. No laws have been enacted for regulations of distributors as yet.

SWITZERLAND. Agents are entitled to a maximum of one year's net profit from new clients gained for the principal. Minimum notice is one month. Only Swiss law is applicable. (Keegan 1989, 481)

Keegan (1989, 479) indicates his belief that the laws often serve to protect only the bad salespeople and actually make no small contribution to inferior performance. On the other hand, one finds that successful countries with high uncertainty avoidance tendencies and the collectivist approach have protective laws that are simply in line with the cultures. Regardless of the laws, termination is considered a serious occurrence that must be explained to customers and also resolved in a positive manner by and for both parties.

## SALES MANAGEMENT ISSUES

The management responsible for selling a company's product line must first make decisions regarding the use of a direct sales force versus independent sales agents. This is, on the whole, a vertical integration decision. It sustains long-term impact on the performance of the selling function. The changing of agents is looked upon with suspicion in many collectivist countries in particular, such that a firm is required to make a well-considered decision. For multinational firms the decision is, in addition, influenced by the degree to which they are familiar with a certain foreign market. The issue of working with independent sales agents as compared to employed reps is further influenced by the rules and laws that control the hiring and firing of salespeople. While in the United States, a salesperson can be fired on short notice; this is not possible in a large number of other countries. If it is hard to fire employed salespeople, working with independent agents becomes a more attractive option—even if the termination of such a contract involves some kind of indemnity. Difficulty in firing salespeople also exerts influence on the setting of objectives and on performance measurement.

Once a direct sales force has been established, management faces the task of controlling its salespeople. This is achieved primarily through the setting of objectives, the allocation of resources to salespeople in order to fulfill the objectives planned, and finally through measurement of performance in the evaluation period. These tasks are clearly the outcome of the management process of analysis, planning, implementation, and control. However, it should be noted that this feedback process might well be unsuitable for generalization for other countries. It hinges upon a very individualistic approach and the understanding that the individual salesperson is able to influence future results. With the importance of extrinsic rewards in the western world, management must also deal with compensation. Rather than offering a fixed salary, it might try to motivate its sales force by means of commissions, bonuses, and sales contest incentives. This approach works well in cases where the salespeople can be extrinsically motivated. In numerous countries evincing a collectivist culture, however, because of the higher degree of uncertainty avoidance and the fact that status is dependent upon the fixed salary, such motivational approaches would be inappropriate (Hofstede 1980; Still 1981, 7–8).

The four issues we have mentioned above are most relevant when addressing the influence of culture on sales force management. We will now discuss how the choice of specific sales management practices is influenced by work values, communication type, and law. The discussion is begun with a general evaluation, and will then be complemented by a detailed comparison of the situation in the United States versus Germany.

## DIFFERENCES IN SALES ORGANIZATION

The choice between employment of a direct sales force or contracting with independent agents is a decision influenced by the work values. Anderson and Coughlan (1987) find support for this argument: U.S. firms prove more likely to integrate the personal selling function in Western Europe than in Japan and Southeast Asia, which are culturally more dissimilar. Working as an independent agent is only possible if the uncertainty avoidance tendency is relatively low. The employment of independent agents follows the transactional way of thinking common in the United States but not as common in more collectivist countries. Clearly, the decision must also be influenced by whether a company's own direct sales force is able to cover the whole area, as opposed to needing to use independent sales agents, who are allowed to sell complementary products from other companies. Some industrial goods companies thus rely on employed sales forces alone, if they can indeed cover multiple markets due to common or similar languages (such as the German-speaking countries or Scandinavia). On the other hand, it is nearly impossible to cover culturally diverse countries like the Philippines or Indonesia. With over two hundred different languages in these regions, such markets are obviously best served via independent sales forces (Hill and Still 1990, 58). In Table 9.1, we can see that the use of independent manufacturer agents is not as common in Germany as in the United States, due to the fact that Germany has a more collectivist and uncertainty avoiding culture.

However, comparison of a study by Anderson (1985) with the results of a study by Krafft (1996) indicates that a large extent of the probabilities of choosing either independent agents or employed reps in the United States and Germany can be explained by variables from Transaction Cost Analysis. Among other findings, employed sales forces can be associated with idiosyncratic (transaction-specific) assets, smaller sales forces, lower travel requirements, lower percentages of time devoted to selling, and difficulty in evaluating a salesperson's performance.

The hiring of salespeople is also influenced by culture. The reputation of sales positions in a country determines whether it is possible to hire the best and most capable persons. In countries where social status largely depends on the amount of money earned—which is the case in the United States—it is relatively easy to motivate the most capable persons to work as salespeople.

**Table 9.1**
**Sales Force Structure in the United States and Germany**

| Aspect | Dartnell USA (1994) | Kienbaum Germany (1995) | Albers/Krafft Germany (1992) |
|---|---|---|---|
| Use of Independent Sales Agents | 30.2 % | 9.3 % | 22.6 % |
| Tenure of Salespersons (in years) | 7.2 | 12.0 | 7.8 |
| Turnover Levels of Salesforces | 15.8 % | | 6.1 % |
| Women in Salesforces | 22.8 % | 3.0 % | 10.8 % |
| Age of Salespersons (in years) | 37.5 | 45.0 | 41.5 |
| Graduate Degree of Salespersons | 5.7 % | 5.0 % | 11.6 % |

*Source*: Heide (1994); Kienbaum Vergütungsberatung (1995); Albers and Krafft (1992).

In countries where status depends on belonging to a certain group, sales positions must be constructed in such a way that they offer a significant amount of intrinsic, status-increasing rewards. This is especially true for cultures with a collectivist approach (see Still 1981, 7).

In a country in which selling is mostly transactional, salespeople tend to be young and may not have a high degree of education. The company simply hires the type of people who are confident enough to succeed in the selling position. If this turns out not to be the case, contracts with these people are terminated. In countries having a more collectivist approach, salespeople are more engaged in offering their product expertise to the customer than in merely selling. In this situation, salespeople tend to have a higher degree of education, are, on the average, older, and will remain with the company longer. A comparison between the United States and Germany as presented in Table 9.1 yields exactly these results. The data in this table are based on annual surveys administered by consulting firms in both countries, as well as on a comprehensive survey we undertook years ago.

In many countries, the firing of employees is restricted to special cases or "just cause," as defined by law or contract. In Germany, for instance, employees can be fired only in the case when the whole company is downsizing. The company is then required to follow certain principles that do not allow the firing of poor performance people only. If downsizing, a company can only fire those employees who will be, socially speaking, the least affected. For example, a person single-handedly supporting a family of four or more people can only be fired after all of the singles have been fired. Another criterion is the tenure of the employees. If a person has been employed for more than ten years, their dismissal would present extreme difficulty. These restrictions in law are accompanied by a behavior of not changing positions with companies too quickly. As a result, salespersons' tenure is much higher in Germany than in the United States, while German sales forces exhibit far less turnover than their U.S. counterparts. In Germany, it is furthermore unclear whether an employee is leaving a company of his own accord or because the firm wished to be rid of him. The reason for this is that in a case of termination by the employee, she or he is excluded from unemployment benefits by the state. Therefore, the company and employee often agree on a termination by the company, although the termination may have been initiated by the employee. Yet even under the restrictive law in Germany, the firing of people does remain possible. In such situations, companies aim to make the position as unattractive to the employee as possible. They also look for legally liable errors a salesperson might have made, such as an incorrect statement of travel expenses.

Finally, it should be noted that the percentage of women in sales forces is very high in the United States, as well as in some Nordic countries and in France. This is due to the fact that these countries offer day-care for children both in school and in kindergarten. Such facilities are not available in Germany, making it rather difficult for women to work in addition to taking care

of the family. This has also been influenced, moreover, by the cultural understanding that women should first take care of the family before pursuing a
career in business. As a result, Germany scores high on masculinity in Hofstede's
approach, whereas France and Scandinavia exhibit a more feminine culture.
Unfortunately, the same argument does not hold for the United States, in
spite of its rather high percentage of women in the labor force. This is because the United States is a competitive culture in which women are encouraged to work and "be tough" rather than "only" caring for others. The more
feminine cultures of France and Scandinavia do not mean that companies in
these cultures strive any less for efficiency than masculine cultures. Sellers
who underperform will simply be entitled to a greater amount of understanding. It is only after the organization has done everything within its power to
help the salesperson increase his or her performance that a final decision is
made (Usunier 1993, 321).

## DIFFERENCES IN GOAL SETTING
## AND PERFORMANCE MEASUREMENT

The setting of objectives is strongly influenced by the preciseness and
contextuality of communication styles across cultures (Hall 1960). Objectives that are very precise, quantified and negotiated in an open manner, cor-
respond to cultures in which people communicate fairly explicitly within a
low context. On the other hand, the greater the tendency to communicate
within a high context, the more a system based solely on numbers will seem
inferior. In high-context societies such as Japan, numbers are considered efficient, but oversimplified. In cultures with a high tendency to avoid uncertainty, salespersons are more frequently employed on an all-salary basis. In
order to motivate such people to act in the best interest of the firm, setting the
proper objectives is of great importance. The power distance is quite often
very high in these countries. As a result, objectives cannot be negotiated but
must be set by the sales managers. There then exists the danger that management will set objectives that are too high. Although all the members of such a
culture are aware that performance level achieved will be low, it will none-
theless be a higher one than if such an ambitious objective had not been set
(Usunier 1993, 318–319).

After setting objectives, the degree to which they have been achieved must
be measured. The accuracy of systems of performance evaluation and incentive calculation is always higher in situations of explicit communication. This
type of orientation rewards individual merit. In high-context cultures combined mostly with an implicit communication style, the evaluation phase does
not necessarily need to be precisely and formally implemented, since the
objective may be significantly higher than that which the salespeople can
realistically attain. There is an unwritten agreement in the organization that
sales objectives are not wholly realistic. In these countries, one rarely finds

any formal and quantified evaluation practices. Even so, it is very often implicitly clear within the company whether a salesperson is a high performer or not (Usunier 1993, 319).

In some countries, a precise measurement of salespeople's performance is impossible because the one being evaluated is put at risk of losing face. This is to be avoided at all costs in a culture adhering to nonconfrontational ethics (such as Southeast Asia).

Many firms these days, even in the United States, are trying to form cross-functional teams in order to serve their customers better than before. In an individualistic country, which places emphasis on individual achievement and competition within the sales force, this is not an easy task. Compensation schemes could help to achieve healthy cooperation among team members— whereby collectivist countries certainly have some advantages in implementing such approaches. In the United States, team compensation still wrestles with the problem of how to split the whole team's bonus according to the individual performances of team members. In collectivist-leaning countries, this is not such an issue and motivation is mostly intrinsically oriented. The following chapter on differences in compensation will show how the use of performance-based incentives (such as commissions) is related to specific work values.

## DIFFERENCES IN COMPENSATION

Given the dissimilar work values of various cultures, it is clear that the type of compensation will be heavily influenced by these values, or as Gestetner (1974, 104) points out, "The psychological and social traditions of one country can necessitate different salary structures . . . from those in the home country." Countries with a high tendency to avoid uncertainty will exhibit more frequent use of all-salary compensation plans. This is also true to a lesser degree for cultures with a high power distance, since that means that sales reps are to a much greater extent subordinates who must obey their superiors' commands. When a country's approach is more collectivist rather than individualistic, one may also find a reluctance to make too much use of variable incentives. This is due to people being much more group oriented, making performance measurement and the calculation of incentives for individual performance significantly more complicated. One could also speculate that a salary is the favored form of compensation in countries that are more feminine than masculine. As discussed above, a feminine approach means that an organization takes much better care of its weak members, this being possible only if such weakness is not punished by decreased incomes due to low variable incentives. Consequentially, it is in the United States that one finds the least use of all-salary plans and the highest proportion of variable incentives where combination plans are concerned. In European countries having a more collectivist approach and a higher tendency of avoiding uncertainty (such as the German-speaking countries), or in the more feminine countries like France or the Scandinavian nations, we can expect greater use of all-salary compensation plans and a lower share of variable incentives. In Latin America and East Asia (such as Japan), all having an even stronger tendency to avoid uncertainty and exhibiting very collectivist behavior, the percentage of all-salary plans is yet higher, and the amount of variable incentive use yet lower.

Indication that the above hypothesis is true is found in Table 9.2, which shows the use of types of compensation plans for different sales positions in the United States as compared to Germany. We see that the use of all-salary compensation plans is almost three times higher in Germany than in the United States. This is true for both account reps and sales managers. A special problem arises from the fact that "all incentives plans" are allowed in the United States, whereas in Germany such plans are only permitted in contracts with independent sales agents. A company working with a direct sales force must pay some kind of salary; otherwise, these people would be considered independent sales agents, thus making it possible for them to obtain a terminal compensation of one year's commission if their contract is terminated.

Table 9.3, showing the variable proportion of compensation for different sales positions does not yield as clear a picture as that which was hypothesized. While at first glance we find a higher variable proportion in Germany than in the United States, this is due to the different definitions used in both surveys. Dartnell reports that the average percentage of total compensation allotted to incentives for all companies is 39.4 percent. In Table 9.3, this split

**Table 9.2**
**Use of Types of Compensation Plans for Different Sales Positions**

| Sales position | Dartnell, USA (1994) | | | Kienbaum, GERMANY (1995) | |
|---|---|---|---|---|---|
| | All Salary | Combination Plans | All Incentive | All Salary | Combination Plans |
| Entry Level Sales Reps | 5.3 % | 87.5 % | 7.2 % | 30.0 % | 70.0 % |
| Intermediate Sales Reps | 5.6 % | 80.9 % | 13.5 % | 14.0 % | 86.0 % |
| Senior Sales Reps | 5.5 % | 81.7 % | 12.8 % | 10.0 % | 90.0 % |
| Major Account Reps | 9.1 % | 85.5 % | 5.4 % | } 12.0 % | } 88.0 % |
| National Account Reps | 4.0 % | 96.0 % | 0.0 % | | |
| National Account Manager | 8.3 % | 91.0 % | 0.7 % | | |
| District Sales Manager | 15.2 % | 84.1 % | 0.7 % | 17.0 % | 83.0 % |
| Regional Sales Manager | 9.2 % | 89.7 % | 1.1 % | 28.0 % | 72.0 % |
| Top Sales Executive | 8.0 % | 89.8 % | 2.2 % | 23.0 % | 77.0 % |

*Source*: Heide (1994); Kienbaum Vergütungsberatung (1995).

**Table 9.3**
**Compensation Pay Levels and Variable Proportion for Different Sales Positions (In U.S. Dollars, 1US$ = 1.50DM)**

| Sales position | Compensation Pay Level | | Variable Proportion | |
|---|---|---|---|---|
| | Dartnell, USA (1994) | Kienbaum, Germany (1995) | Dartnell, USA (1994) | Kienbaum, Germany (1995) |
| Entry Level Sales Reps | 30,200 | 49,500 | 24.1 % | 30.0 % |
| Intermediate Sales Reps | 40,000 | 63,400 | 26.6 % | 32.0 % |
| Senior Sales Reps | 55,600 | 72,600 | 30.3 % | 35.0 % |
| Major Account Reps | 53,100 | ⎫ | 18.8 % | ⎫ |
| National Account Reps | 63,300 | ⎬ 82,500 | 18.7 % | ⎬ 24.0 % |
| National Account Manager | 69,900 | ⎭ | 24.3 % | ⎭ |
| District Sales Manager | 60,900 | 87,800 | 28.7 % | 24.0 % |
| Regional Sales Manager | 64,400 | 102,300 | 24.3 % | 26.0 % |
| Top Sales Executive | 81,000 | 129,400 | 24.7 % | 21.0 % |

*Source*: Heide (1994); Kienbaum Vergütungsberatung (1995).

between incentives and salary is only made for those companies making use of a salary. We have already learned, however, that a substantial number of companies employ all-incentive plans, which explains the discrepancy between the two figures. The variable proportion in Germany is well beneath 39.4 percent. Longer tenure and the difficulties in firing salespeople—resulting in a rather low turnover rate in Germany—further explain the higher use of all-salary plans, as well as the lower percentage of variable incentives. In Germany, salary itself is often used as a special kind of incentive; that is, the salary may be adjusted according to one's past performance. In the United States, annual increases in salary are not seen as very important, because the salesperson loses all claim to high future salaries in the event that he or she is fired.

It is interesting to discover from Table 9.4 that pay levels in Germany for the various sales positions are much higher than in the United States. This is partly due to higher levels of education, longer tenure, and higher costs of living. It may also be attributed to the more frequent use of salespeople in professional situations in which the salespersons must command a high level of product knowledge. Regarding the United States, the larger number of women represented and the more transactional approach may further explain some of the discrepancies evinced in Table 9.4.

Finally, it should be noted that the risk premium for being paid according to a combination plan as opposed to an all-salary plan is somewhat higher in Germany than in the United States. This can be attributed to the higher uncertainty avoidance behavior typically found in Germany. It is, in addition, worth noting that dissimilarities in the utilization of all-salary plans are much greater

**Table 9.4**
**Compensation Pay Levels by Sales Positions (In U.S. Dollars, 1US$ = 1.50DM)**

| Sales position | Dartnell, USA (1994) | | | Kienbaum, GERMANY (1995) | |
|---|---|---|---|---|---|
| | All Salary | Combination Plans | All Incentive | All Salary | Combination Plans |
| Entry Level Sales Reps | 28,900 | 31,900 | 27,700 | 48,200 | 50,200 |
| Intermediate Sales Reps | 37,200 | 41,300 | 40,700 | 54,800 | 64,700 |
| Senior Sales Reps | 50,000 | 56,500 | 64,000 | 58,700 | 74,600 |
| Major Account Reps | 48,000 | 52,600 | 105,900 | ⎫ | ⎫ |
| National Account Reps | 57,200 | 62,000 | 98,300 | ⎬ 85,100 | ⎬ 82,500 |
| National Account Manager | 58,600 | 75,800 | 45,500 | ⎭ | ⎭ |
| District Sales Manager | 53,000 | 68,600 | 85,800 | 88,400 | 87,800 |
| Regional Sales Manager | 60,500 | 68,200 | 80,700 | 90,400 | 106,900 |
| Top Sales Executive | 74,500 | 86,500 | 75,000 | 125,400 | 130,700 |

*Source*: Heide (1994); Kienbaum Vergütungsberatung (1995).

across industries than across cultures (Hill and Still 1990). In general, we find that companies selling industrial or pharmaceutical goods pay comparatively high percentages in terms of salary, whereas the realm of financial services can be characterized by greater variable incentives (Krafft 1995, 246).

## CONCLUSION

This chapter has demonstrated that the recommendations of textbooks and journal articles on sales force management in the United States are not easily to be generalized to other cultures. The reason for this is that different cultures uphold different work values, apply different types of communication, and operate under different kinds of law. Particularly useful for understanding the application of different sales management practices is a study on work values by Hofstede. He found that cultures differ with respect to power distance, uncertainty avoidance, masculinity versus femininity, and individualism versus collectivism. The contextuality, as pointed out by Hall (1960), plays an important role regarding communication. In contrast to the United States, where all aspects of a contract between a firm and its salespersons are negotiable, the law in most of other countries awards the sales agent or the employed salesperson the stronger position in the event of a termination. Except for those in the United States, independent sales agents are often paid for building relationships for the firm, while employed salespeople can be fired only in special cases, such as a downsizing of the company. This has a measurable impact on such sales management issues as vertical integration, hiring and firing, the setting of objectives, performance measurement, and compensation. Due to somewhat more collectivist behavior and a higher tendency to avoid uncertainty, one finds less use of independent agents and more stable relationships between companies and salespeople in other countries. This also enforces the idea of relationship marketing, as opposed to the transactional marketing common in the United States. In countries characterized by individualistic behavior and a low power distance, objectives are set for the salespeople, rather than measuring their actual performance and then deciding what actions should be taken to improve that performance or even to dismiss him or her. Because of the importance of objectives in the achievement of the salesperson, these are frequently negotiated between salespeople and management. Such an approach is not workable in countries with a high power distance; in such cases, it is expected that superiors will determine the goals without engaging in a discussion thereof with their subordinates. In many countries exhibiting collectivist behavior and a higher uncertainty avoidance, precise performance measurement may be impossible because the individual's contribution cannot be perfectly assessed. The situation is even more extreme in countries with a high-context communication style; in the Far East, for example, it is important that a person never lose face, implying that precise performance management cannot be applied. In terms of compensation, the frequent use of all-incentive plans in the United States is not transferable to countries showing a higher tendency to avoid uncertainty or more collectivist behavior. In such countries, we can expect more frequent occurrence of all-salary plans, and a higher percentage of salary on the average in the total compensation.

In this chapter we have also compared in greater detail the dissimilar situations in the United States and Germany. Germany may be characterized by a higher tendency to avoid uncertainty, and rather collectivist behavior. One consequently finds a more frequent use of all-salary plans as well as a lower proportion of variable incentives. As it is more difficult to fire salespeople in Germany, tenure is longer and the turnover rate is lower, making it possible to follow a more relationship-oriented approach than the transactional approach as is common in the United States. It is to be noted that the total level of pay is much higher in Germany than in the United States. This may be explained by the higher education level, higher average age, longer tenure, and by the fact that there are far fewer women employed in selling in Germany. Selling is more an issue of providing good product knowledge to one's customers than employing efficient selling skills.

This chapter emphasizes that Hofstede's argument for the "cultural relativity of management theories" applies to global sales management. In other words, one may conclude that simply adopting recommendations found in

U.S. textbooks and journal articles regarding sales management practices, and trying to apply those ideas in countries around the world is most inadvisable. One ought to incorporate the respective cultural differences before arriving at recommendations on sales management practices in specific countries. Moreover, it would be prudent for U.S. multinational companies to adjust their sales management procedures according to the culture in which they are to be applied.

## NOTE

The list of country laws on pp. 199–200 is reprinted from W. J. Keegan, *Global Marketing Management*, 4th ed. (Englewood Cliffs, N.J.: Prentice Hall, 1989), 481. Reprinted by permission of Simon & Schuster.

## REFERENCES

Albers, S., and M. Krafft. 1992. Steuerungssysteme für den Verkaufsaußendienst (Sales Force Control Systems). Manuskripte aus den Instituten für Betriebswirtschaftslehre der Universität Kiel nr. 306, University of Kiel.

Anderson, E. 1985. The Salesperson As Outside Agent or Employee: A Transaction Cost Analysis. *Marketing Science* 4: 234–254.

Anderson, E., and A. T. Coughlan. 1987. International Market Entry and Expansion via Independent or Integrated Channels of Distribution. *Journal of Marketing* 51 (January): 71–82.

Campbell, N. C. G., J. L. Graham, A. Jolibert, and H. G. Meissner. 1988. Marketing Negotiations in France, Germany, the United Kingdom, and the United States. *Journal of Marketing* 52 (April): 49–62.

Gestetner, D. 1974. Strategy in managing international sales. *Harvard Business Review* 52 (September–October): 103–108.

Graham, J. L. 1985. Cross-Cultural Marketing Negotiations: A Laboratory Experiment. *Marketing Science* 4: 130–146.

Hall, E. T. 1960. The Silent Language in Overseas Business. *Harvard Business Review* 38 (May–June): 87–96.

Heide, C. P. 1994. *Dartnell's 28th Sales Force Compensation Survey 1994–1995*. Chicago: Dartnell Press.

Hill, J. S., and R. R. Still. 1990. Organizing the Overseas Sales Force: How Multinationals Do It. *Journal of Personal Selling and Sales Management* 10 (Spring): 57–66.

Hofstede, G. 1991. *Culture and Organizations: Software of the Mind*. London: McGraw-Hill.

———. 1980. Motivation, Leadership and Organization: Do American Theories Apply Abroad? *Organizational Dynamics* (Summer): 42–63.

Keegan, W. J. 1989. *Global Marketing Management*. 4th ed. Englewood Cliffs, N.J.: Prentice Hall.

Kienbaum Vergütungsberatung GmbH, ed. 1995. *Vergütung 1995. Führungs- und Fachkräfte im Außendienst* (Compensation 1995. Managers and Reps in Personal Selling). Gummersbach: Kienbaum Personalberatung.

Krafft, M. 1996. Neue Einsichten in ein klassisches Wahlproblem? - Eine Überprüfung von Hypothesen der Neuen Institutionenlehre zur Frage «Handelsvertreter oder Reisende» (New Insights into a Classic Choice Problem? An Investigation of Hypotheses of the New Institutional Economics Regarding the Choice between Outside Agents or Employed Reps). *Die Betriebswirtschaft* 56: 759–776.

———. 1995. Ein empirischer Test von Hypothesen der Prinzipal–Agenten–Theorie und der Transaktionskostenanalyse zum Festgehaltsanteil von Reisenden (An Empirical Test of Hypotheses of Principal–Agent–Theory and Transaction Cost Analysis Regarding the Proportion of Salary). *Zeitschrift für betriebswirtschaftliche Forschung*, Sonderheft 35: 245–267.

Still, R. R. 1981. Sales Management: Some Cross-Cultural Aspects. *Journal of Personal Selling and Sales Management* 1 (Spring–Summer): 6–9.

Usunier, J.-C. 1993. *International Marketing: A Cultural Approach.* New York: Prentice Hall.

# PART IV

# The Future

## Chapter 10

# Selling in the Future:
# Synthesis and Suggestions

### Robert C. Conti and William L. Cron

- The health care industry changes from "fee for service" to managed care, from single physician to group practices, from individual physicians having almost complete decision-making authority to formularies. In reaction to these changes, Allegiance completely reorganizes its sales force, changes compensation systems, and invests in substitutes for a face-to-face sales force.

- The grocery industry rapidly consolidates with new forms of retailers such as membership warehouse clubs taking sales away from traditional supermarkets. Retailers are no longer interested in hearing what your promotion can do for sales of your products through their stores, but what the promotion will do for category or department sales. Procter & Gamble (P&G) attempts to develop a new kind of relationship with its key grocery chains involving sharing of critical information. As a result, P&G's salespeople are designing customer specific sales promotions that must be sold back at P&G's headquarters. Almost everything about P&G's sales force program is changed.

- As regulatory constraints are relaxed, many financial services companies become conglomerate-like organizations of loosely joined, often acquired, businesses. In Canada, the Royal Bank Financial Group encompasses commercial banking (Royal Bank of Canada), personal banking (Royal Bank of Canada), a brokerage house (Dominion Securities), a discount broker (Action Direct), and a trust company (Royal Trust). In order to service those high-value clients who are most profitable, advice is needed across a broad range of products and services. To establish coordinated customer servicing across these different businesses, the Royal Bank Financial Group changed its compensation program, established client referral programs, instituted coordinated marketing planning meetings, trained its people in making joint sales calls, and set up omnibus trade fairs.

Allegiance, Procter & Gamble, and the Royal Bank Financial Group are just three examples of companies described in earlier chapters of this book that have initiated sweeping changes to their sales programs as a result of significant developments in their competitive environments. These developments include changing competitors, customer markets, government regulations, and technology. You may be facing exactly the same or similar challenges in your business today—customer consolidation, coordinated customer solutions, maturing markets, or global competition. Close examination of the earlier chapters in this book and their descriptions of what individual companies have done to address these challenges may be of particular value.

The purpose of this chapter is to synthesize the individual company experiences presented in earlier chapters by articulating a set of eight challenges facing sales force managers. The perspective we adopt in this chapter is that there are a set of sales force issues that, to be successful, most companies must at the very least begin to think about, and in some cases fully address.[1] They are as follows:

1. Developing a vision of the sales force's role in your marketing program.
2. Growing the professional intellect of the sales force.
3. Designing true collaboration between sales marketing and service.
4. Defining a disciplined customer relationship selection process.
5. Meeting sales growth targets through global sales opportunities.
6. Nurturing a broader skill set for managers.
7. Identifying a stronger set of performance metrics.
8. Clarifying the role of technology as an enabler.

To a degree, these issues are "old wine packaged in new skins," in that they have been on the minds of top sales executives for ten, even twenty years. But the illusion of business as usual may be part of the problem. Very fundamental changes in how these issues are resolved are required in today's competitive reality. This is not intended as a comprehensive list, but it is our observation that these issues are fairly pervasive. The following discussion elaborates on the nature of these changes and describe approaches to taking advantage of the opportunities that are presented.

## DEVELOPING A VISION OF THE SALES FORCE'S ROLE IN YOUR ORGANIZATION

In successful sales forces, there is something more going on than simply selling and meeting quotas. There is something that drives the most successful sales forces towards maximum impact and ensures that they meet their targets. We are talking about vision.

Vision has gotten some bad press in recent years, and for good reason. In too many cases, it has become a catchall phrase for dreaming big dreams. While a vision should point towards an overall target, in successful sales forces, vision exists as a tangible guidance mechanism. A clearly articulated vision provides direction to salespeople and management. It is quite easy for some of your salespeople to head a little bit in one direction, while others go in another direction. After a time, you are too far apart to communicate, and the whole effort starts to fall apart. Vision should operate as a map that guides you forward, and lets you know if you are still together.

The notions of identifying a target and constructing a road map to help an organization reach a target is not in and of itself new to today's sales forces. What is different is that sales forces are being asked to focus not only on the top line in terms of revenue, but are increasingly held responsible for bottom-line profitability. This development requires an expanded vision of the role of the sales force in your organizations. If you carefully read the job descriptions of the innovative sales forces described earlier in this book, these sales forces are no longer simply "box pushers." A complete description of their responsibilities would include their roles as field product portfolio managers, company resource coordinators, account relationship managers, and in some organizations, account promotion managers. They are still required to produce top-line results, but what is changing and becoming a bigger part of the job are their other responsibilities. Not only do these developments require an expanded vision of the sales force's role, but the vision itself is fundamentally different.

One approach, which has come to be known as open-book management, is particularly useful, given the sales force's expanded role.[2] Open-book management rests on the simple but potent idea that companies do better when people care about the success of the business. Quite simply, employees should actively concern themselves with a company's business objectives. If the sales force is to act with the organization's business objectives in mind, senior management must see that three conditions exist:

- Information previously shared only among those in charge must be seen—and understood—by everyone in the organization. That means all relevant information—not just sales and shipments, for instance, but also financial goals, asset commitment levels, income statements, and forecasts.

- Salespeople must be held responsible and accountable for making their unit's budget or profit goals. Recognizing that performance reflects many elements, salespeople and managers must learn to identify and watch key drivers of performance and to forecast and reforecast these drivers in their business analysis.

- In addition to paying for sales, the compensation system must reward salespeople for the success of the business. That frequently involves creating a sizable bonus plan, often supplemented by stock ownership.

The net effect of successful open-book management is to help the sales force understand why they should care about achieving particular results. In other words, it helps to bring the heart as well as the mind into the process.

A particularly powerful example of open-book management is Physician Sales & Service, Inc. (PSSI), a distributor of supplies to doctors' offices. PSSI has climbed from start-up to industry leader with revenues approaching $1 billion in only fourteen years. Chief Executive Patrick Kelly believes that a big part of PSSI's success is due to open-book management. Salespeople are paid a combination of commissions, bonus and stock ownership, all of which are tied to profitability measures, not just sales volume. Employees own a sizable portion of PSSI's stock, and the income levels of most veteran salespeople are almost twice the industry's average.

## GROWING THE PROFESSIONAL INTELLECT OF THE SALES FORCE

Companies are increasingly coming to realize that selling success lies in the intellectual capabilities of the sales force rather than in its size. The capacity to manage the professional intellect of the sales force—and convert it into customer problem-solving capabilities—is fast becoming the *critical* sales force skill of the time.

Consider the changes in the sales position initiated at P&G and discussed earlier in this book. Instead of simply knowing how to present a promotion developed by the brand management team, P&G salespeople today must know how to develop an account specific promotion for which they will be held accountable both by P&G and the customer. This requires a level of knowledge about consumer behavior, retail grocer strategy, and marketing not heretofore required or utilized. The strategic consequences of developing and exploiting this intellect are profound. Once a company gains a knowledge-based competitive edge, it becomes ever easier for it to maintain its lead and ever harder for its competitors to catch up through imitation.

What is professional intellect? According to James Quinn and his colleagues, the professional intellect of an organization operates on four levels, presented in order of increasing importance:

*Cognitive knowledge* (or know-what) is the essential knowledge that is achieved through training and certification. In sales, this would include basic product knowledge, selling techniques, territory management processes, and account management steps.

*Advanced skills* (know-how) apply the cognitive knowledge to complex real-world problems. This level of professional intellect creates value for the organization. An example of advanced skills discussed earlier in the book is when Coca-Cola fountain division salespeople recommend new products and ways to merchandise these offerings.

*Systems understanding* (know-why) is the understanding of cause-and-effect relationships underlying a discipline. This understanding permits professionals to solve larger and more complex problems. Intuition is perhaps the ultimate expression of systems understanding. This level of intellect is needed for salespeople to be adaptive and to address the strategic customer issues that are the focus of relationship marketing at its highest level. We are talking about the difference between P&G salespeople pushing monthly product promotions versus their continuous inventory replenishment program. As was mentioned earlier, 80 percent of the time spent selling the replenishment program is spent on identifying customer needs, codeveloping joint business plans, and providing support.

*Self-motivated creativity* (care-why) consists of will motivation and adaptability for success. Self-motivated creativity promotes enhancement of knowledge advantages and aggressive adaptation to changing external conditions.[3]

Professor Quinn and his associates have conducted extensive field studies of professional organizations and have concluded that the best practices for managing intellect include the following: (1) recruiting the best people; (2) forcing intensive early development through on-the-job training, mentoring, and peer pressure; (3) providing substantial rewards and performance incentives; (4) increasing professional challenges; (5) continuous evaluation; and (6) weeding out less successful people. Successful sales forces have focused on improvements in these areas for some time. These practices continue to be fundamental to winning organizations. However, the times call for additional and new approaches to leveraging professional intellect. Economic conditions require that sales forces become more productive as companies must operate within ever-tighter margins. At the same time, the customer problems that system sellers face are more complex and require the application of a breadth and depth of knowledge not often heretofore brought to customer problems. New and effective methods for developing and updating the professional intellect of the sales force are needed.

One means by which to boost sales force problem-solving abilities is by capturing and distributing knowledge in systems and software. Consider Merrill Lynch's retail brokerage business where roughly 18,000 brokers operate out of more than 500 geographically dispersed offices to create custom investment solutions for clients. Electronic systems and proprietary software quickly enable less-trained people to achieve the performance levels of much more experienced brokers. In addition, information technology permits large brokerages to be both efficient and flexible, serving millions of clients worldwide with sophisticated investment advice, and detailed, up-to-date information on thousands of complex financial instruments.

One of the biggest hurdles facing professional sales forces today is overcoming salespeople's reluctance to share account and territory information. Information sharing is critical because intellectual assets, unlike physical assets, increase in value with use. Because client knowledge is their true power base, strong inducements are necessary.

To facilitate sharing, Andersen Worldwide developed an electronic system known as ANet, linking its 82,000 people operating in seventy-six countries with data, voice, and video interlinks. By posting problems on electronic bulletin boards followed up by visual and data contacts, Andersen is able to self-organize instantly around a customer's problem anywhere in the world.

ANet cost large sums of money to be spent on hardware, travel, and professional training, to encourage people to utilize ANet. The results were initially disappointing, despite the technological elegance of ANet. Utilization picked up, however, once changes in incentives and cultures were initiated to make the system work. Most important, participation in ANet began to be considered in all promotion and compensation reviews. In addition, senior partners began using ANet to communicate with associates. Thus, senior management at Andersen communicated to associates their support for the ANet initiative.

## DESIGNING TRUE COLLABORATION BETWEEN SALES, MARKETING, AND SERVICE

Has anything like the following situations occurred in your company or others of which you aware?

• A new product, originally scheduled for introduction in the first quarter of the next fiscal year, is ready to go now, and so product management introduces the new product in the fourth quarter. Worldwide sales plans are revised, but the order-fulfillment process could not properly handle the new line. Besides, sales is working hard to make their annual numbers and earn this year's trip for top performers. Training classes for the new product are lightly attended and judgments as to the marketability of the product are quickly made.

• Sales has targeted a global account for a major network upgrade and has contacted most of the key decision makers at the account. Through their local reps, however, service has contacted all decision makers and, unaware of the upgrade efforts, has been promoting their success at routine maintenance of the existing network system. Their success apparently helped to undermine their own company's upgrade proposal.

Coordination between sales, marketing, and service has probably always been an important issue for organizations. There are a number of significant developments making collaboration between these three even more important today. First, markets are becoming increasingly fragmented, so value and profits reside in more and more tightly defined niches. Product variety often expands significantly as a result. This places increased coordination pressures on both product and sales. Second, shorter product life cycles are placing increased burdens on all three functional areas. The number of products assigned to product managers, for instance, is reported to have increased by 50 percent or more during the past decade.[4] Shorter product life cycles also decrease the time available to establish and assimilate relevant coordination mechanisms, leading to a tendency to focus on short-term fixes that may not address core coordination issues.

A third reason for increased coordination pressures is the buyer's shift in focus from minimizing nominal supply price to focusing on the total supply chain, with its emphasis on optimizing the total cost-in-use of doing business with a vendor. Cost-in-use components fall into three categories, as shown in Table 10.1. Supply chain initiatives seek to lower these costs, while sustaining value-based pricing policies that reflect the total benefits for the customer. The upshot is the development of strategies emphasizing customized product offerings, as well as adapting delivery, handling, and other order-delivery activities to the customer's operating characteristics. For all these reasons, closer coordination between sales, marketing, and service is required.

After interviewing managers in a variety of industries about coordination problems, Frank Cespedes has arrived at some intriguing suggestions for successful collaboration between sales, marketing, and service.[5] It is interesting to note that he feels teamwork, perhaps a somewhat overemphasized selling approach, is not sufficient for true collaboration. Rather, Cespedes recommends changes in organizational structure, in market information systems, and in career development paths.

*Organizational Structures* Coordination issues are particularly difficult when product technology is complex and fast changing. In this case, some firms have established formal liaison units, staffed by sales as well as product personnel. These liaison units provide a decision-making mechanism where important tradeoffs and marketing information reside at the interfaces between product, sales, and service groups, rather than within each area. For instance, there is a natural tendency for the product group to emphasize state-

**Table 10.1**
**Cost-in-Use Components**

| Acquisition Costs | + | Possession Costs | + | Usage Costs | = | Total Cost-in-Use |
|---|---|---|---|---|---|---|
| Price | | Interest cost | | Field defects | | |
| Paperwork cost | | Storage cost | | Training cost | | |
| Shopping time | | Quality control | | User labor cost | | |
| Expediting cost | | Taxes and | | Product longevity | | |
| Cost of mistakes in order | | insurance | | Replacement costs | | |
| Prepurchase product evaluation costs | | Shrinkage and obsolescence | | Disposal costs | | |
| | | General internal handling costs | | | | |

of-the-art technology products that end up being too costly for the sales force to sell. On the other hand, the sales force has a tendency to emphasize quick-selling products. The results, however, may be a failure to erect switching barriers, resulting in high customer churn.

Establishing liaison units, permanent or ad hoc, poses significant challenges. A liaison unit represents another layer of management; as a result, such units require a critical mass of products and customers to be economically feasible. Further, liaison units usually face a challenge from line managers in the other functional areas who are likely to see such units as interlopers. Due to their organizational position, liaison units are often the focus of many contentious negotiations. As a result, staffing of these units is of critical importance.

*Market Information Systems*   As markets fragment, the demands made on information systems are compounded. An appropriate information infrastructure is to prevent collaboration meetings from degenerating into finger-pointing rather than joint problem-solving sessions. Traditionally, marketing research has reported to product management, while account information resided with the sales force. For true collaboration to take place, there must often be an overhaul of marketing information systems so that marketing research and information systems are more closely aligned. The American Express Card Division, for instance, found it necessary to combine information from twenty-two separate sources of account data to produce one database, or "Knowledge Highway" as the firm calls it.

Another case example of effective market information system development is *InTouch* designed by Mary Kay Inc. to improve communications with its far flung sales representatives. As discussed in Chapter 7, the goal of the 1995 redesigned *InTouch* is to deliver more information in the right context to more people, more quickly, and at a lower cost. Directors can now download vital sales information and company communications, while the sales force can place orders on-line, saving time preparing manual order sheets.

*Career Development Paths*   Organizational restructuring and shared information databases will help achieve greater coordination, but for true collaboration to take place, Cespedes believes that the individuals involved must have a better understanding of and commitment to the big picture. This perspective is particularly difficult, given differences in the traditional career paths for sales, product, and service, and the different labor markets from which these people are typically drawn. Traditional career profiles for each functional group are quite divergent. Almost all product management hires are developmental, and subject to an up-or-out promotion philosophy involving frequent rotation among product groups. Personal interaction between sales and product management people is largely limited to the obligatory stint in the district sales office by new brand assistants. Meanwhile, approximately eight of every ten salespeople historically are expected to become career salespeople. Success depends on building long-term account relationships in a territory. Only 20 percent are hired for developmental purposes to be targeted for promotion into sales management and beyond. Customer service is somewhat like sales in lacking an up-or-out mentality, but even more so. The expectation of service personnel is to be kept in the same territory on a more or less permanent basis in order to maintain account relationship continuity. Given these disparities, it is no wonder there is animosity between the different groups and little commonality in perspective on marketing and customer issues.

A variety of approaches are available to achieve better coordination and cross-fertilization of people. Some companies have created new positions that are really a blend between sales and product marketing. In creating these positions, companies are attempting to move up within the organization the local knowledge that is unavailable at headquarters, while ensuring that field activities are consistent with and support company-wide operating and marketing objectives. Campbell Soup established "brand sales managers" in twenty-two regions to localize many decisions previously handled at headquarters' product management, such as trade spending. Frito-Lay has acted similarly in creating the "zone marketing manager" position. In high-tech areas, Hewlett-Packard and IBM have created the positions of "Field Marketing Specialist" and "Area Product Manager" respectively. Notice in each of these cases that the title is a mixture of terms normally associated with marketing and sales.

In addition to job movement between the two areas, many companies are looking to their training and reward programs to achieve closer alignment between sales and service. Sales and service people are provided joint training programs, and account-based bonuses are shared between the two areas. One telecommunications firm takes the additional step of having sales and service people that are assigned to the same account evaluate each other's performance in such areas as "quick response" and "contribution to customer satisfaction." Regardless of the approach, the focal objective is to create a consistent and shared customer contact perspective.

## DEFINING A DISCIPLINED CUSTOMER RELATIONSHIP SELECTION PROCESS

The current business and academic press would leave one with the impression that collaborative supplier–customer partnerships are the only way to do business today. As businesses gain experience attempting to institute partnering relationships, they are discovering that a partnering relationship is not always appropriate, and very difficult to implement in practice. Actually, it was never the intention of many of the proponents of partnering for companies to establish strategic partnering relationships with all customers.

Any companies that do business together have some sort of relationship. Barbara Jackson was one of the first to discuss a continuum of working relationships that characterize different industries.[6] Purely *transactional relation-*

*ships* are ones in which customers are looking for a good basic product, delivered in a timely fashion along with accepted standards of service and support, and sold at highly competitive prices. The other end of the continuum is anchored by *collaborative partnering relationships* in which the intent is to achieve mutual benefits by significantly lowering total costs and/or increasing value through a process of extensive social, economic, service, and technical ties established over time. Between these two extremes business may be established a variety of relationships incorporating some of the characteristics of each type of relationship.

Early discussion of customer relationships focused on how different industries tended to be more transactional or more collaborative in nature. Rather than occupying a single point on the continuum, however, industries are better characterized as a range of relationships, referred to as the industry relationship bandwidth. The bandwidth of an individual firm in an industry reflects the explicit or implicit relationship strategy of the firm.

In the past, salespeople individually and collectively had a great deal of freedom in choosing the type of relationship they wished to establish. Individual salespeople chose their prospects, established very close personal relationships with certain accounts, selected from their firm's product lines the offerings they would spend time against, and in some cases determined the price that individual customers would pay. Firms attempted to control and direct the behavior of the salespeople through performance evaluation, compensation, and direct supervision. What is different today is that the mix of customer relationships is now considered by many companies to be a source of strategic competitive advantage. The level of resource commitments to individual customer relationships is greater, which heightens the importance of successful relationship execution. The arms-length control mechanisms of the past are no longer appropriate, and a more disciplined approach is needed.

Anderson and Narus note that one of the keys to this is to incorporate the customer relationship decision within the context of a firm's overall segmentation and marketing planning.[7] They propose a six-step approach:

1. Segment the market by product application and customer capabilities.
2. Assess the value of the product offering to customers in each segment.
3. Target segments, and customer firms within segments, for various kinds of relationships.
4. Develop and implement relationship-specific product offerings.
5. Evaluate relationship outcomes and reassign accounts.
6. Periodically update the value of the relationship offering.

The field sales force is intimately involved in each step of the targeting process, but particularly with respect to targeting individual customers, implementing relationship-specific product offerings, and evaluating relationship outcomes. It is with respect to these three steps that the discipline of a planning framework is needed to guide and coordinate the traditional control mechanisms listed earlier.

One of the most important aspects of this framework is developing a clear notion of the criteria for determining an appropriate customer relationship. That is, what are the customer firm and marketplace characteristics on which such a decision should be based?[8] One way of categorizing these characteristics is according to the customer's philosophy of doing business, the relative dependence of the two firms on the relationship, and the leadership edge contributed by a customer firm.

*Business Philosophy*   Most fundamentally, a customer must have a total cost, rather than simply a list price, philosophy towards supplier relationships in order to establish a more collaborative type of business relationship. The signals and nuances of this new customer–supplier philosophy vary by industry and even perhaps between competitors within a single industry. For P&G, the critical signal is the customers willingness to share critical data on inventory levels. More generally, customer business philosophies about supplier relationship may vary along each of the following five dimensions:

- *Planning* Sharing existing plans versus joint planning at an early point of development.
- *Joint Operating Controls* Predetermined performance measures versus joint development of shared goals and targets.
- *Communications* Limited communications with independent electronic communications versus planned, multilevel communications with joint customized electronic communications.
- *Risk–Reward Sharing* Very limited tolerance for loss with "fairness" evaluated each transaction versus high tolerance for short-term loss and a lifetime perspective of "fairness."
- *Trust and Commitment* Trust is limited to the belief that each partner will perform honestly and ethically versus eliminating organizational boundaries and thinking as one entity.

*Relative Dependence*   Experience suggests that collaborative relationships prosper best when the supplier and customer firms have approximately equivalent significance to and dependence on the relationship. Such a situation fosters a mutual interest in resolving conflicts and cooperating to find ways of adding value, reducing costs, and sharing relationship benefits equitably. Switching costs and planning time horizons are two dependence criteria that should be evaluated by customer contact personnel.

*Leadership Edge*   Some firms should be targeted for more collaborative type relationships because they are *lead users* with respect to technology or are *leap-frog* accounts that have the potential to bypass current technology leaders in a segment. This requires forecasting growth of all the key firms in a segment, and evaluating these firms on their use of technology relative to

what is forecasted for the industry. The sales force and management within
Allegiance Inc. are continuously evaluating hospitals to identify lead-users
and leap-froggers. In the U.S. health care environment, leap-frog hospitals
are defined by Allegiance as those (1) committed to managed care, (2) sophisticated in integrated health care systems, (3) understanding strategic
partnering with suppliers, and (4) focusing on total cost versus purchase price.
Obviously, this requires a depth of account understanding not typical of most
sales forces. Is your sales force equipped to do this type of planning? Are
your competitors developing this capability?

## MEETING SALES GROWTH TARGETS THROUGH
## GLOBAL SALES OPPORTUNITIES

Senior sales managers today are looking well beyond their backyard for
growth opportunities. More and more companies believe their major growth
opportunities are outside of North America. Many of the classic "American"
companies such as IBM and Coca-Cola have over half of their revenues generated outside of the United States, and most of their growth goals are targeted for regions outside of the United States as well. Most technology
companies today see their greatest opportunities in Europe and Asia–Pacific.

Managing global sales organizations requires significantly greater skills
and competencies due to the increased complexity of international operations. Some of these increased complexities include understanding cultural
norms, local laws, differing social values, different standards of performance,
language barriers, and geographic distances. Simple tasks, such as assem-
bling your staff for a meeting, become a major challenge. If you want to
conduct a video conference, what time should you conduct the meeting? If
you choose a meeting time at 11 A.M. in your office in New York, your western region manager in California can be on at 8 A.M., your European manager
will begin at 4 P.M., and it will be 3 A.M. for your manager in New Zealand.
There will not be any easy answers some one will be inconvenienced. The
question is, who should it be?

Managing a global sales organization is not the same as managing a large
sales organization in North America. One of the most significant differences
is the use of different sales channels in different areas of the world. In order
to make effective resource allocation decisions, managers must have a comprehensive understanding of the effectiveness and impact of different sales
channels across the world. For example, a telesales channel may be quite
effective when covering the smallest accounts in Europe, but may not be as
effective in South America due to technical and cultural differences.

Other sales management practices will also need to be reviewed, such as
how should sales personnel be compensated? Should there be a single solution for all sales personnel across the globe, or should compensation plans be
developed for each country individually? In the earlier chapter, Global Sales

Force Management, cultural and legal issues associated with compensation in different countries, are described. In Germany, for instance, paying sales agents by commissions only is not allowed. Many leading companies today are beginning to undertake this challenge by developing a universal sales compensation strategy that can be adapted to the unique characteristics of individual countries. Companies such as IBM and Motorola have developed a truly international approach to developing sales compensation solutions. How should you motivate your personnel? Should you focus on individual performance or should you focus on team performance? Managers find different cultures respond differently to these challenges.

One subset of the global sales opportunities is in the management of global accounts. Managing accounts on a global basis is critical to the long-term success of a company. One industry that has faced this challenge for several years was the semiconductor industry. Many of their accounts are truly global accounts. Raw materials are sourced from all parts of the globe, and product is manufactured in multiple countries, then sold to an account in one country for delivery in several countries. These customer needs pose a new range of challenges for the sales executive. What resources are needed where? Should personnel be stationed in the local country, or should they be located back at the corporate headquarters? How should these choices be determined? Some companies that have created leading edge global account programs include Motorola Semiconductor Products, Sea Land Services, Levi Strauss, and IBM. Pushing the knowledge edge of global account programs is enabling a sustainable competitive advantage for these companies.

## NURTURING A BROADER SKILL SET FOR MANAGERS

The old view that the sales executive is simply an experienced sales professional that knows how to bring in new customers is waning. The sales executive of today must not only have the contact and understanding of the customers, they must also have the seasoned management expertise to manage and direct diverse internal company resources while balancing market needs. The distinction between the skills of a highly effective CEO and that of a leading sales executive are narrowing. Many of the most respected CEOs seem to emulate the skills of the best sales executives. Lou Gerstner at IBM has stated that much of his time must be devoted to meeting with customers. In fact, it is not uncommon for internal meetings to be delayed or canceled due to customer meetings exceeding initial time expectations.

One illustration of the evolving jobs that require new skills is the strategic account manager. Many companies have identified select customers to provide the highest level of service and support. These strategic accounts are generally the largest, most important, and most demanding customers. In fact, these customers are viewed as "corporate assets." To meet the needs of these customers, companies have assembled cross-functional teams dedicated to supporting their needs. Strategic account teams extend well beyond the classic sales, service, and support functions. In many cases the strategic account teams include full-time membership from sales, marketing, customer service, finance, product development, manufacturing, and distribution. To effectively manage and deploy these diverse resources, greater management skills are required than simply sales functional responsibility. Interestingly, these skills have their corollaries in the set of skills described in Chapter 3, including developing trust, the emotional bank account, win–win developments, and listening to understand.

The challenge for the future is to identify and develop the individuals that have the potential to excel in this new environment. Many companies have found that this new position of a cross-functional strategic account manager prepares individuals for other general management responsibilities. Some companies has developed a structured management development program that rotates high-potential senior managers to various management positions and assesses their skill set in the process.

Despite the need for skill development, sales management training continues to be an activity in which companies underinvest. A recent study found that 75 percent of all sales managers surveyed were offered no formal training upon promotion to their first management position.[9] Another 57 percent reported never receiving any formal management training, while an additional 15 percent received training only when promoted to a more senior management position.

## DEVELOP A COMPREHENSIVE SET OF PERFORMANCE METRICS

Historically, sales performance metrics were simple—increase revenue over last year. Managers today are faced with many complex tradeoff decisions. Few sales organizations use a single channel of distribution. Most organizations and all large companies use multiple channels of distribution. The addition of these channels has added a significant amount of complexity in effectively managing the business. It is not simply how to grow the top line of the business, but how to "profitably grow the business." Managers must constantly make resource allocation decisions across a range of variables. Illustrations of the decisions that must be made include the following:

- Should we increase the size of our direct sales organization or should we focus on our indirect sales channels?
- What is the appropriate mix of sales and field engineering support personnel?
- What is the optimum mix between sales resources and customer service resources, and how does this balance differ by types of customers?
- Should we grow our geographic sales group or our telesales group?

- Should we allocate more resources on our "strategic accounts" or should we focus on our mid-size accounts?
- What is the role of our catalog group and our new call center?

In order to make the right decisions, better sales performance data must be assembled for the sales managers. Many leading companies today are beginning to undertake this challenge. Companies such as BFI, Anheuser Busch, and Office Depot have incorporated many of these new measurements into their sales management process. Illustrations of the type of data that must be assembled include market data to assess how well the company has penetrated its targeted market segments, and market data that will evaluate new high-potential market opportunities. Sales performance data must be available at the company, region, district, territory, customer, and product level, and must include not only what is sold, but the actual level of resources put up against the sales effort, as well as profitability of the sales. Assessing the profitability of the sales can be quite complex. Companies must take into account these issues:

- The cost of the resource selling the product.
- The amount of time it takes to sell the customer.
- The gross margins associated with the product sales.
- The level of price discounting.
- The amount of advertising support.
- The promotions required.
- The amount of post-sales support.
- The level of ongoing services required.
- The impact on future product sales.

This effort will require a new way of viewing sales. Companies must take an end to end approach when looking at their customers to determine the appropriate level of sales and service support. To accomplish this task, new information technology (IT) systems must be implemented that are designed to meet the needs of the new marketing and sales professional. One of the outcomes of this effort is a better understanding of which customers are profitable customers and which customers are not. The challenge is to determine what to do with the nonprofitable customers. Generally the answer is *not* to eliminate the customer, but to determine how to best serve the customer in order to make them a profitable customer. In some cases, it is as straight forward as moving the account from a geographic sales account to a telesales account. In other cases, it requires a new view on how to service the account that will include the types of product offered and how the products will be bundled to meet the unique customer needs.

## USING TECHNOLOGY TO ENABLE SELLING

Sales organizations are beginning to use technology to aid in the customer relationship and management process. By automating many of the repetitive tasks generally completed by the sales force, managers find that a significant amount of time is freed up for the sales professionals to spend it where they add the greatest value in the selling equation—in the area of customer persuasion. Generally the sales job can be divided in to three distinct functions: (1) customer access, (2) customer persuasion, and (3) customer fulfillment. Technology has the greatest impact in the first and third functions. New data-mining techniques will enable companies to better determine which customers offer the greatest potential and what sales resources should be positioned to interact with the customer. Companies such as IBM and Dun & Bradstreet (D&B) have pioneered these efforts. D&B has been able to leverage their unique customer numbering system to match up internal company data sources with market data sources to help companies assess their position within the market. IBM has been able to bring their programming and computing competencies to develop advanced statistical models that help companies size the market and determine where the greatest growth opportunities exist.

Historically, sales professionals have been tasked with the lead role in finding, selling, and servicing their customers. In many situations, the function of servicing the customers once they have purchased the product took up the greatest amount of time. Companies are learning how to best use technology to free up the time of the sales representative so they can focus their efforts on the persuasion element of their job. Companies like Xerox have automated much of the ongoing maintenance of their copy machines by linking the machines to the central office via telephone lines and conducting regular maintenance before problems occur. This use of technology accomplishes multiple objectives. First, the customer satisfaction is increased due to fewer maintenance problems. Second, the most appropriate resources are put up against the maintenance tasks. Finally, the sales organization is freed up to do what they do best—that is, to work with existing and new customers to sell more products.

## A GROWING URGENCY

Increasingly, the basis of competition is shifting from products and offerings to customers. There is less real product and service differentiation than in the past, and a shorter window of opportunity to exhibit real differentiation. Intense competition for each piece of business is the norm, while the purchasing decision becomes more complex. There is much more complex systems selling or the selling of products and services into larger systems. In the face of these developments, many companies are finding it difficult to meet the needs of more demanding customers in an increasingly competitive world. In such a world, sales force decisions are increasingly becoming important, strategic, boardroom level discussions.

In this chapter, we have attempted to organize the discussion of the earlier chapters into a manageable set of eight issues that most companies must resolve. There are undoubtedly additional issues that any individual company will face, but our experience, as well as that reported in this book, suggests that these issues are fairly pervasive. Though we have attempted to provide some perspective on the nature of these issues and their resolution, the issues are neither easily grasped nor easily resolved. A combination of changes in organization structure, processes, and resources are required. The effects of changes suggested in this and earlier chapters are not likely to be felt in the short term. This is precisely why more and more companies need to begin addressing these issues so that the solution foundation can begin to be constructed. Not taking action today increases the likelihood that time pressures will encourage the use of band-aid type solutions to fundamental selling and sales force issues.

## NOTES

1. There have recently been a number of excellent discussions of new sales force management and selling developments. These include R. Anderson, "Personal Selling and Sales Management in the New Millennium," *Journal of Personal Selling and Sales Management* 16 (4, 1996): 17–32; D. Cravens, "The Changing Role of the Sales Force," *Marketing Management* 4 (2, 1995): 48–57; and A. Magrath, "A Comment on 'Personal Selling and Sales Management in the New Millennium,'" *Journal of Personal Selling and Sales Management* 17 (1, 1997): 45–47.

2. J. Case, "Opening the Books." *Harvard Business Review* 75 (March–April 1997): 118–127.

3. J. Quinn, J. P. Anderson, and S. Finkelstein, "Making the Most of the Best." *Harvard Business Review* 74 (March–April 1996): 71–80.

4. For more information on product variety, see S. Wheelwright and K. Clark, *Revolutionizing Product Development* (New York: Free Press, 1992), Chap. 1.

5. For more information on Frank Cespedes's research findings, see "Once More: How Do You Improve Customer Service?" *Business Horizons* (March–April 1992); "Industrial Marketing: Managing New Requirements," *Sloan Management Review* 35 (3, 1994): 45–60; and *Managing Marketing Linkages* (New York: Prentice Hall, 1996).

6. B. Jackson. *Winning and Keeping Industrial Customers: The Dynamics of Customer Relationships* (Lexington, Mass: Lexington Books, 1985).

7. J. Anderson and J. Narus, "Partnering as a Focused Marketing Strategy," *California Management Review* (Spring 1991): 95–112.

8. For a good discussion of relationship selection criteria see D. Lambert, M. Emmelhainz, and J. Gardner, "So You Think You Want a Partner?" *Marketing Management* 5 (2, 1996); and N. Rackham, L. Friedman, and R. Ruff, *Getting Partnering Right* (New York: McGraw-Hill, 1996).

9. R. Anderson, R. Mehta, and J. Strong, "An Empirical Investigation of Sales Management Training Programs for Sales Managers," *Journal of Personal Selling and Sales Management* 17 (3, 1997): 53–66.

# Suggested Readings

Anderson, R. 1996. Personal Selling and Sales Management in the New Millenium. *Journal of Personal Selling and Sales Management* 16 (Fall): 17–32.

Cespedes, F. V. 1995. *Concurrent Marketing: Integrating Product, Sales, and Service*. Boston, Mass.: Harvard Business School Press.

Colletti, J. A., and L. B. Chonko. 1997. Change Management Initiatives: Moving Sales Organizations from Obsolescence to High Performance. *Journal of Personal Selling and Sales Management* 17 (Spring): 1–30.

Corcoran, K., L. K. Petersen, D. B. Baitch, and M. F. Barrett. 1995. *High Performance Sales Organizations: Creating Competitive Advantage in the Global Marketplace*. Stamford, Conn.: Learning International.

Cravens, D. W. 1995. The Changing Role of the Sales Force. *Marketing Management* 4 (Fall): 49–57.

Dalrymple, D. J., and W. L. Cron. 1998. *Sales Management: Concepts and Cases*, 6th ed. New York: John Wiley & Sons.

Ingram, T. N. 1996. Relationship Selling: Moving from Rhetoric to Reality. *Mid-American Journal of Business* 11 (1): 1–13.

Ingram, T. N., R. W. LaForge, and C. H. Schwepker, Jr. 1997. *Sales Management: Analysis and Decision Making*, 3rd ed. Fort Worth, Tex.: The Dryden Press.

Lewin, J. E., and W. J. Johnson. 1997. International Salesforce Management: A Relationship Perspective. *Journal of Business and Industrial Marketing* 12 (3–4): 248–258.

Moon, M. A., and S. F. Gupta. 1997. Examining the Function of Selling Centers: A Conceptual Framework. *Journal of Personal Selling and Sales Management* 17 (Spring): 31–42.

Peterson, R. A., S. Balasubramanian, and B. J. Bronnenberg. 1997. Exploring the Implications of the Internet for Consumer Marketing. *Journal of the Academy of Marketing Science* 25 (Fall): 329–346.

Reichheld, F. F. 1996. *The Loyalty Effect: The Hidden Force behind Growth, Profits, and Lasting Value.* Boston, Mass.: Harvard Business School Press.

Strahle, W., R. Spiro, and F. Acito. 1996. Marketing and Sales Strategic Alignment and Functional Implementation. *Journal of Personal Selling and Sales Management* 16 (Winter): 1–20.

Weitz, B. A., S. B. Castleberry, and J. F. Tanner, Jr. 1998. *Selling: Building Partnerships*, 3rd ed. Burr Ridge, Ill.: Irwin/McGraw-Hill.

Wilson, D. T. 1995. An Integrated Model of Buyer–Seller Relationships. *Journal of the Academy of Marketing Science* 23 (Fall): 335–345.

# Index

# About the Editors
# and Contributors

SÖNKE ALBERS is Professor of Marketing and Management Science at the Christian-Albrechts-University of Kiel (Germany). He studied business administration and operations research at the University of Hamburg and received his Ph.D. there in 1977 with a dissertation on airline crew scheduling. He served then as an Assistant Professor of Management at the University of Kiel (1977–1984). Before joining the University of Kiel again in 1990, he held positions as Professor of Marketing and Management Science at Koblenz School of Corporate Management (1984–1986) and the University of Luneburg (1986–1990). In 1980–1981, he was a Visiting Scholar at Stanford University, and in 1989 a Visiting Professor at INSEAD. His research interests include sales force management, marketing planning and controlling, and new product management, as well as electronic commerce.

DONALD W. BARCLAY is George and Mary Turnbull Professor and Associate Professor of Marketing at the Richard Ivey School of Business, University of Western Ontario, London, Canada. He is also Marketing Area Group Coordinator and Director of the Marketing Management Executive Program. Recent publications include "Effects of Organizational Differences and Trust on the Effectiveness of Selling Partner Relationships," *Journal of Marketing* 61 (1, 1997) with J. Brock Smith; "Microsegmentation in Business Markets: Incorporating Buyer Characteristics and Decision-Oriented Determinants," *Journal of Business-to-Business Marketing* 3 (2, 1996) with Michael J. Ryan; and "Business Strategic Orientation, Information Systems Strategic Orientation, and Strategic Orientation," *Information Systems Research* 8 (2, 1997) with Yolande E. Chan, Sid L. Huff, and Duncan G. Copeland. Professor Barclay is on the editorial review boards of the *Journal of Marketing, Journal of Personal Selling and Sales Management, Journal of Business-to-Business Marketing, Journal of Business & Industrial Marketing,* and *Marketing Education Review.*

RICHARD C. BARTLETT has a direct marketing management career that spans more than thirty-five years. He is currently Vice Chairman of Mary Kay Holding Corporation, and Chairman of The Richmont Group. The Richmont Group comprises companies engaged in financial services, Asian trade, apparel, sporting goods, fixed-base executive jet operators, and food retailing. Previously, he directed the global growth of Mary Kay Inc. as President and Chief Operating Officer. He began his career at Tupperware, where he pioneered the company's European operations. He serves on the boards of Armor Holdings, Inc., the United States Direct Selling Association (DSA), and the United States Direct Selling Education Foundation (DSEF). He currently serves as Chairman Ex-Officio of The Nature Conservancy of Texas, and a member of the Board of the Dallas Museum of Natural History. He is also a member of the World Economic Forum, The Conference Board, and the Academy of Marketing Science. In addition, he serves on the board of the Better Business Bureau of Metropolitan Dallas, and advisory boards of the Positive Employee Practices Institute, the Center for Retailing at Texas A&M University, the Center for Retailing Education and Research of the College of Business Administration at the University of Florida, the Advisory Council of the University of Texas Press, and the Global Board of Advisors for The Economist Group's *Crossborder Monitor.* He has received numerous professional awards, including Southwestern Marketing Association's 1991 Outstanding Marketer of the Year, International Television Association's 1992 Executive of the Year, DSA's 1994 Hall of Fame, DSEF's 1995 Circle of Honor, Academy of Marketing Science's 1995 Distinguished Marketer of the Year, and Pi Kappa Phi's 1996 Hall of Fame. He is the author of three books: *The Direct Option, The Sportsman's Guide to Texas*, and *Saving the Best of Texas: A Partnership Approach to Conservation.*

GERALD J. BAUER is a Sales Competency Leader and Field Marketing Manager for DuPont. He also leads the DuPont Sales Network and the Channel Partner Network, two intracompany networks in DuPont. In his thirty years with DuPont, he has held a variety of positions including sales, sales management, product management, industry management, customer service management, purchasing management, and sales training. He has served as a conference and seminar speaker in the United States, Canada, Mexico, Latin America, Europe, and Asia. He is also a member of the Management Education Alliance, a collaborate effort between industry and academia. He earned his BBA and MBA in Marketing from the University of Toledo.

MARK S. BAUNCHALK holds a Bachelors of Mechanical Engineering (1979) and an MBA (1996) from the University of Delaware. His DuPont experience spans seventeen years and a broad range of assignments, such as operations, engineering, field sales, sales management, product–business management, strategic planning, and marketing. During the past eleven years, he has had the opportunity to work in sales and marketing roles within multiple polymers business at DuPont. Most recently, he has served as a U.S. Marketing Manager, Teflon Fluoropolymers; National Sales and Marketing Manager, Viton Fluoroelastmers; and North American Sales and Marketing Manager, Tedlar PVF Films. Prior to joining DuPont's refrigerants business as National Sales and Marketing Manager, he was in DuPont's corporate planning group, supporting fluoroproducts and other DuPont business units with their strategic planning efforts. In this role, he also had the opportunity to work on the development of a corporate Sales Enhancement Process used by DuPont business units to design world-class customer interface capabilities.

WILHELM BIELERT is General Manager of FTH Fördertechnik Hamburg GmbH (Germany). He received his Ph.D. at the University of Kiel in 1994. His dissertation dealt with the use of Geographic Information Systems with respect to their application in corporate planning. He then joined an industrial group in Germany. Starting as a Marketing Manager of the group, he was appointed Group Sales Manager and was responsible for the design and restructure of the distribution channel of that group. After finishing that assignment, his interest shifted more toward general management problems. He acquired FTH, his first company. Led by him, FTH is currently in the process of a complete business transformation. His current interest is business transformation, strategic planning, and management accounting.

HERBERT F. BURNAP is the Vice President of Sales and Marketing for Printing Arts/Litho Tech, Inc., one of Chicago's premier commercial printers based in Cicero, Illinois. Prior to his position with PA/LTI, he held a variety of sales, marketing, and management positions at the field, divisional, and corporate levels during a long career with Moore Business Forms. He began a long-term involvement with national and key account marketing in 1982 when he accepted the post of Marketing Manager for Moore's national account program targeted toward the petroleum industry. In 1987, he was entrusted with leadership of Moore's corporate program for national accounts and market sectors. In that capacity, his role encompassed development of the Corporate Account Manager Program. In 1993, he accepted the position of Corporate Enterprise Manager with the responsibility of creating and managing a worldwide program for two of Moore's largest growth partnerships. Following the implementation of a comprehensive print management agreement between Emerson Electric Co. and Moore, he took early retirement in December 1996 after more than thirty years of service. During the past eleven years, he has also served as a board member, chapter chairman, and program director for two annual conferences, Executive Vice President, and finally, as the twenty-eighth President of the National Account Management Association. In his capacity as a practitioner of national and key account marketing, he has served as a conference and seminar speaker across the United States, Canada, Europe, and Australia. In addition, he serves as a member and current President on an advisory board for the Center for Professional Selling at Baylor University's Hankamer School of Business.

LAWRENCE B. CHONKO is a Holloway Professor of Marketing. He received his Ph.D. in 1978 from the University of Houston. He came to Baylor in 1985 after having spent seven years at Texas Tech University. Among his first tasks at Baylor was to found the Center for Professional Selling and Sales Management in which he still plays an active role. He is author and coauthor of five books: *Directing Marketing; Direct Selling and the Mature Customer; Professional Selling; Managing Salespeople, Business, the Economy and World Affairs;* and *Ethics and Marketing Decision Making.* He also has served as editor of the *Journal of Personal Selling and Sales Management.* Author of over one hundred papers, his articles have appeared in leading journals, including the *Journal of Marketing, Journal of Marketing Research,* and *Academy of Management Journal.* Throughout his career, he has served as a consultant to industrial products, consumer products, service, and nonprofit organizations. He has received several teaching awards and continues to work in the areas of professional selling, sales management, and ethics.

KEITH A. CHRZANOWSKI is a graduate of Western Illinois University. He has worked within the human resource function within the United States and Canada for the past thirteen years. Previous employers include Beecham PLC and Schlumberger Ltd. He has guest lectured at Clemson University and at the University of Georgia. Currently, he is Director of Human Resources with Allegiance Healthcare (formerly a division of Baxter International).

ROBERT C. CONTI is Senior Vice President with The Alexander Group, Inc., a marketing and sales management consulting company. The firm works with clients to effectively implement marketing strategies and deploy sales resources to achieve business results. He is responsible for directing the firm's consulting services in the western region and directs the firm's wholesale distribution practice. He has managed projects in a variety of industries including high technology, telecommunications, and wholesale distribution. His areas of expertise include organizational design, sales coverage, quota setting, sales compensation design, sales force communications, sales training, and territory performance. Prior to joining The Alexander Group, he was a consultant with an international compensation and benefits consulting organization where he specialized in sales compensation design and implementation.

WILLIAM L. CRON is Professor of Marketing at the Edwin L. Cox School of Business, Southern Methodist University in Dallas, Texas. He has published over forty articles in leading marketing journals on a variety of marketing topics including distribution, marketing strategy, computerization, organizational performance, and various sales management issues. He serves on the editorial review boards of the *Journal of Marketing, Academy of Marketing Science*, and *Journal of Personal Selling and Sales Management*. He was recently recognized as one of the top ten sales and sales management researchers in the United States. He has coauthored one of the leading sales management texts, *Sales Management: Concepts and Cases*.

KENNETH R. EVANS is Professor of Marketing and Associate Dean of the College of Business and Public Administration, with a BA from the University of California in 1972; an MBA from California State University, Sacramento in 1977; and a Ph.D. from the University of Colorado in 1980. He is a member of the American Marketing Association, Beta Gamma Sigma, Mu Kappa Tau, and Pi Sigma Epsilon. He currently serves on the editorial review board, or as an ad hoc reviewer, for the *Journal of Personal Selling and Sales Management, Journal of Marketing, Journal of Marketing Research*, and *Journal of Retailing*, among others. His research interests include interpersonal influence, sales management, and marketing management and theory. He has published articles in the *Journal of Marketing, Journal of the Academy of Marketing Science, Journal of Personal Selling and Sales Management, Journal of Advertising, Industrial Marketing Management*, and in *Distinguished Essays in Marketing Theory*.

ESTHER J. FERRE has over twenty years in sales and marketing experience with an information technology company, as well as fourteen years in sales management. Currently, she serves as a client executive for a large global customer where she is responsible for overall customer relationships and marketing strategy. In addition, she provides management direction and guidance for a global sales team and is responsible for over $350 million in revenue.

DAVID J. GOOD is currently an Associate Professor of Marketing at Central Missouri State University in Warrensburg, Missouri. He received his Ph.D. from the University of Arkansas. His professional experience at AT&T, Sprint, and a small entrepreneurial firm includes sales, sales management, strategic planning, and marketing management. His research interests are focused on the management of information in the marketing organization, and selling and entrepreneurial strategies. In addition to winning multiple awards for teaching excellence, he has published numerous research works in the *Journal of Personal Selling and Sales Management, Journal of Business Research, Psychology and Marketing, Industrial Marketing Management, Journal of Business Ethics, Journal of Marketing Theory & Practice*, and many national and regional proceedings.

JUDITH M. S. HATLEY is Senior Vice President, Sales, Personal Financial Services at the Royal Bank of Canada in Toronto, Canada. Her responsibilities include providing leadership and direction to improve the revenue generation capabilities of the Personal Financial Services sales force. She holds an undergraduate degree from the University of Western Ontario, and an MBA from York University. Since joining the bank in 1971, she has held a number of positions in retail banking, human resources, and corporate banking. One of her more challenging assignments was as Vice President, Segmentation and Profitability, Personal Banking. In this position, she led a strategic project to accelerate the implementation of market segmentation, market management, and sales management in Royal Bank branches.

THEODORE W. HELLMAN has been with Procter & Gamble in Cincinnati, Ohio since 1972. He is St. Louis Market Manager and Campus Relations Director for Procter & Gamble at the University of Missouri. He was a 1974 member of the Dallas Tornado Professional Soccer Team. He is a 1966 graduate of St. Louis University High. He holds both BS and MBA degrees from the University of Missouri. His interests include Bradley University College of Business, National Council of Advisors, St. Louis Cash for Kids Advisory Board, and Phi Kappa Theta Fraternity Alumni Board of Directors. Other areas of interest are the Theodore Hellman Education Foundation and the Mizzou Quarterback Club of St. Louis.

THOMAS N. INGRAM is a Department Chair and Professor of Marketing at Colorado State University, where he teaches principles of marketing, marketing management, and sales management courses. He previously served on the faculties of the University of Memphis and the University of Kentucky. Before commencing his academic career, he worked in sales, product management, and sales management with Exxon and Mobil. He has received numerous teaching and research awards, including being named the Marketing Educator of the Year by Sales and Marketing Executives International (SMEI). In 1994, he was honored as the first recipient of the Mu Kappa Tau National Marketing Honor Society Recognition Award for Outstanding Scholarly Contributions to the Sales Discipline. He served as the editor of the *Journal of Personal Selling and Sales Management*, Chairman of the SMEI Accreditation Institute, and as a member of the SMEI Board of Directors. He has published extensively in professional journals, including the *Journal of Marketing Research, Journal of the Academy of Marketing Science*, and *Journal of Personal Selling and Sales Management*. He is coauthor of *Sales Management: Analysis and Decision Making*, and *The Professional Selling Skills Workbook*.

MANFRED KRAFFT is an Assistant Professor of Marketing at the University of Kiel (Germany). He studied business administration at the University of Luneburg (Germany) and Oslo (Norway). He received his Ph.D. at the

University of Kiel in 1994. His dissertation dealt with problems of vertical integration of the personal selling function and design of compensation schemes for salespeople. His current research interests are sales force control systems, sales contests, and team selling, as well as customer lifetime value, customer equity, and the impact of interdependencies among products, customers, and regions on marketing planning and control. His most recent project is the development of a sales management panel. This panel is thought of as a database for benchmarks and best practices. Though the panel is restricted to German industrial sales forces at the beginning, Krafft is already working on extending this panel to European and American companies.

RAYMOND W. LaFORGE is the Brown-Forman Professor of Marketing at the University of Louisville. He is the founding editor of the *Marketing Education Review* and has coauthored *Marketing: Principles and Perspectives; Sales Management: Analysis and Decision Making*; and *The Professional Selling Skills Workbook*. His research is published in many journals, including the *Journal of Marketing, Journal of Marketing Research, Journal of the Academy of Marketing Science*, and *Journal of Personal Selling and Sales Management*. He currently serves on the Direct Selling Education Foundation Board of Directors, DuPont Corporate Marketing Faculty Advisory Team for the Sales Enhancement Process, Family Business Center Advisory Board, Board of Trustees of the Sales and Marketing Executives International Accreditation Institute, is Vice President of Marketing for the American Marketing Association Academic Council, and is Associate Editor, Sales Education and Training Section of the *Journal of Personal Selling and Sales Management*.

THOMAS W. LEIGH is Professor and Director of the Coca-Cola Center for Marketing Studies at the University of Georgia. His DBA is from Indiana University and his MBA and BS (Economics) are from Southern Illinois University. He served as Assistant Professor at Penn State, including roles as Faculty Director for the Penn State Executive Management Program and Visiting Professor at Ogilvy and Mather Advertising (New York). He received an MBA teaching award at Penn State in 1987. Long active in the American Marketing Association, he is currently serving as President-elect for the AMA's Academic Council. His research has been published in many journals, including the *Journal of Marketing Research, Journal of Marketing*, and *Journal of Consumer Research*. He serves on the editorial boards of the *Journal of Marketing, Journal of Advertising, Marketing Education Review, Journal of Personal Selling and Sales Management*, and on the DuPont Faculty Advisory Board. His current research emphasizes salesperson knowledge and performance, customer relationship strategy, competitive advantage through sales force strategy, and the impact of marketing and sales interface quality on organizational performance. His executive education experience includes teaching roles at Penn State and Northwestern, as well as such corporate clients as Beatrice Foods, Marriott, Reichhold Chemicals, Siam Cement (Bangkok), Moore Business Forms, Inchcape/Caleb Brett, Armstrong World, CISCO Systems, and CIGNA Insurance.

GREG D. LINK is Vice President of the Franklin Covey Company, a 4,000-member international firm committed to empowering people and organizations to significantly increase their performance capability by applying principle-centered leadership to worthwhile purposes. He orchestrated the sales and marketing strategy that helped propel Stephen R. Covey's book, *The 7 Habits of Highly Effective People*, to record-setting sales worldwide and to the position of the number-one selling book in America in 1991. As a sales professional, he spent his career selling high-end products to executives and other professionals. He set or broke sales records on every sales team he worked with, and was consistently a top salesperson by a wide margin. As a sales manager, his teams set performance records.

GREG W. MARSHALL is Assistant Professor of Marketing at the University of South Florida, Tampa. He received his Ph.D. in Business Administration from Oklahoma State University, with a major in Marketing and a minor in Management. He received his BSBA in Marketing Management and MBA from the University of Tulsa. Dr. Marshall has thirteen years of industry experience in personal selling and sales management, product management, and retailing with companies such as Warner Lambert, Mennen, and Target stores. Dr. Marshall's current research interests include the following: sales force selection, performance, and evaluation; sales force diversity; customers—intraorganizational aspects of service delivery; and marketing management decision making. His articles have appeared in the *Journal of Personal Selling and Sales Management, Psychology & Marketing, Industrial Marketing Management, Journal of Business & Industrial Marketing, Journal of Marketing Theory and Practice, Journal of Marketing Education*, and elsewhere.

J. BROCK SMITH is Associate Professor of Marketing at the Faculty of Business, University of Victoria in Victoria, Canada, where he teaches and conducts research in the areas of relationship marketing, sales management, and marketing strategy. Prior to attaining his Ph.D. at the Ivey Business School, he held a variety of sales and marketing positions with IBM Canada. Recent publications include "Selling Alliances: Issues and Insights," *Industrial Marketing Management* 26 (1997); "Effects of Organizational Differences and Trust on the Effectiveness of Selling Partner Relationships," *Journal of Marketing* 61 (1, 1997) with Donald W. Barclay; and "Team Selling Effectiveness: A Small Group Perspective," *Journal of Business-to-Business Marketing* 1 (2, 1993) with Donald W. Barclay.

MICHAEL J. SWENSON is Associate Professor of Marketing at the Marriott School of Management, Brigham Young University. He received his Ph.D. from the University of Oregon in 1989 and joined the BYU faculty that same year. Formerly an account manager with Xerox and Digital Equipment Corporation, he is a consultant and researcher for The Professional Selling Research Group associated with the Marriott School of Management. He has worked with numerous companies in the United States and Europe, and is an active researcher. His research interests include sales force effectiveness and marketing strategy. He has published articles in the *Journal of the Academy of Marketing Science, Journal of Business Research, European Journal of Marketing, Journal of Personal Selling and Sales Management, Review of Marketing, Journal of Business Forecasting, Journal of Marketing Education*, and other journals and various conference proceedings. He serves as associate editor for the *Journal of Personal Selling and Sales Management*. He is a member of the American Marketing Association and the Academy of Marketing Science.

SHARON MORGAN TAHANEY is President of CreativeWork, and has almost two decades of experiences answering the creative needs of direct sales organizations across the country—ten of those years specifically on Mary Kay projects. She has a Master's degree and a practical understanding of sales force motivation resulting from literally a lifetime connected to direct sales. She spent her childhood in a direct sales family and her adulthood promoting the growth of direct sales organizations through strategic planning and the creation of sales promotions, marketing communications, and stage presentations. Her client list ranges from start-up direct sales organizations to multimillion dollar operations.

THOMAS R. WOTRUBA is Professor of Marketing for San Diego State University. He completed his Ph.D. at the University of Wisconsin in Madison, and has authored numerous textbooks, professional journal articles, monographs, and other publications. He serves on the editorial boards of the *Journal of Marketing, Journal of the Academy of Marketing Science, Journal of Business & Industrial Marketing*, and *Journal of Personal Selling and Sales Management*, and is past editor of the latter journal. His business experience extends from ownership positions in manufacturing, retailing, and agriculture enterprises as well as consulting relationships with numerous business and government organizations in California and across the United States. His work related to the direct selling industry involves membership on the Board of Directors of the Direct Selling Education Foundation as well as the completion of an extensive research study on turnover among direct salespeople. He has served as a consultant and expert witness for a number of direct selling firms.

ISBN 1-56720-036-2

EAN

9 781567 200362

90000>

HARDCOVER BAR CODE